ADVANCES IN
CLINICAL PSYCHOANALYSIS

John E. Gedo, M.D.

INTERNATIONAL UNIVERSITIES PRESS, INC.
New York

Library of Congress Cataloging in Publication Data

Gedo, John E.
Advances in clinical psychoanalysis.

Bibliography: p.
Includes index.
I. Psychoanalysis. I. Title. [DNLM: 1. Psychoanalytic therapy. WM 460.6 G296a]
RC504.G37 616.89'17 81-6572
ISBN 0-8236-0125-0 AACR2

Manufactured in the United States of America

To Paul, who follows the path I would take
if life could be lived again—and better,
Andrew, who replaced a beloved father,
and Nicholas, whose name is victory.

Contents

Acknowledgments

Previous versions of Chapters 4, 5, and 8 were published in the *Journal of the American Psychoanalytic Association,* and an earlier version of Chapter 10 appeared in *The Dream in Clinical Practice,* edited by Joseph Natterson and published by Jason Aronson, New York, 1980. The Chicago Psychoanalytic Society, ever a receptive forum for the creative efforts of its members, has permitted me to assay Chapters 6, 9, 11, and 13 at its scientific meetings. Chapter 12 was presented as the twenty-third Sándor Radó Lecture of the Columbia University Psychoanalytic Clinic for Research and Training, and Chapter 3 formed part of the Distinguished Lecture Series of the Department of Psychiatry of Northwestern University. I am also indebted to the American Psychoanalytic Association (Panel on Current Concepts of Object Relations Theory), the Houston-Galveston Psychoanalytic Society, the Westchester Division of the Department of Psychiatry of Cornell University, the Illinois Psychiatric Society, and the Society for Adolescent Psychiatry for opportunities to present various portions of the material to their membership.

Introduction

In this volume, I plan to consider three topics I regard as inextricably interrelated: psychopathology, psychoanalytic technique, and analyzability. Whichever of these topics we choose as the primary focus of study, the conclusions we reach will depend on the positions we have taken with regard to the others. Because of the complexities involved in a reasoned approach to these matters, the psychoanalytic community has been appropriately conservative in altering Freud's clinical legacy. Scientific progress in psychoanalysis has generally begun at the level of theoretical abstractions comfortably distant from the clinician's pragmatic concerns. At the same time, a spirit of adventure and experimentation has led many psychoanalysts to relax the stringent criteria of analyzability, to introduce unacknowledged variations into their therapeutic technique, and, implicitly, to alter their conceptions of psychopathology. These opposing tendencies in the field have, in recent years, created numerous controversies and a great deal of confusion.

This ferment in the clinical arena has paralleled a

revolution on the theoretical front that has all but swept away the assumptions on which the general framework of psychoanalysis rested in the past. Our traditional metapsychology was based on the axioms of nineteenth-century science about the nature of things. Freud's choice of a conceptual schema based on the unifying construct of energy was extremely progressive for the time, a decisive advance beyond Descartes's rigidly mechanistic system (cf. Toulmin, 1978). A new consensus is about to be forged once again in natural philosophy, one that will replace the concept of energy as a central construct with the concept of information. The contemporary dissatisfaction with Freud's metapsychology can be seen as part of this broad intellectual shift.

In the clinical sphere, the practical consequences of this philosophical change have been immediate and profound. As long as psychoanalysts adhered to the theory of psychic energy (in this country, mostly in the version elaborated by Hartmann [1939, 1964; Hartmann, Kris, and Loewenstein, 1964]), the aim of analytic treatment could only remain—to use Freud's well-known aphorism—"Where id was, there ego shall be," i.e., to tame the unneutralized energies of the repressed unconscious and to establish the reality principle as the primary regulator of behavior. This theoretical model is applicable to the neuroses, conditions in which transferences take place across the repression barrier. Many analysts rigorously followed the logic of this point of view, accepting only those individuals for analysis whose psychopathology was thought to represent derivatives of an infantile neurosis. Others were not content to turn away as "unanalyzable" the vast majority of people seeking psychological assistance. The growing tension of the past quarter-century between legitimate therapeutic ambitions and traditional theoretical convictions probably led to the widespread tendency wrongly to subsume a wide array of pathology under the rubric of the transference neuroses. Predictably, the use of the standard technique of psychoanalysis in a broader spectrum of personalities led to less than happy results (see Erle, 1979).

Abandonment of the traditional metapsychological framework has permitted the elaboration of theories of therapy much more complex than that Freud set forth in 1923 in *The Ego and the Id* (e.g., Loewald, 1960). My own work in this area began with the construction of a hierarchical, epigenetic model of personality organization in *Models of the Mind* (Gedo and Goldberg, 1973). This developmental concept incorporated not only the psychoanalytic model of mental functioning characteristic of the neuroses but models of psychic organization typifying both less differentiated conditions and expectable adult ones as well. This complex model of the mind suggested the possibility of attempting psychoanalytic treatment of the full gamut of nonpsychotic disturbances, provided the technique of analysis was suitably adapted when nonneurotic conditions were dealt with. In other words, this view called for a differentiated set of therapeutic modalities to be used in every psychoanalytic treatment, with each modality differentially suited to deal with the specific psychological issues left unresolved in particular phases of early development.

The hierarchical model Goldberg and I developed in 1973 comprised five subphases and five therapeutic modalities. Each modality was tailored to deal with the principal problem characterizing a different subphase: introspection for the difficulties expectable in adult life, interpretation for the intrapsychic conflicts derived from infantile neuroses, "optimal disillusionment" for archaic idealizations of others or self-aggrandizement, "unification" for any failure to integrate one coherent set of personal goals, and "pacification" for traumatic states. Systematic classification of the analyst's interventions in this manner revealed that every patient brought problems from each subphase within the hierarchy into treatment —in varying proportions, depending on the exact nature of the configuration of the personality. Accordingly, we concluded that successful analyses had always depended on the appropriate use of multiple therapeutic modalities (although, in their official accounts, analysts tended to disavow those interventions they had trouble classifying as "interpretations").

The skeletal theory of psychoanalytic technique presented in *Models of the Mind* justified a very broad conception of analyzability and has led me, in the past decade, to undertake the treatment of the full gamut of patients with archaic personality problems. These clinical ventures, in turn, have convinced me that traditional psychoanalytic concepts have only marginal relevance for the understanding of primitive mental functioning: the observational data I obtained demanded the construction of a revised theory for psychoanalysis. I attempted to describe my complex technical procedures and the clinical observations they have produced in *Beyond Interpretation* (1979a). In that book, my principal goal was the development of a unified clinical theory that could encompass the entire range of psychoanalytic observational data and, at the same time, conform to the requirements of contemporary epistemology (cf. Polanyi, 1974; Polanyi and Prosch, 1975).

My concept of mental functioning as an epigenetic hierarchy of personal aims will serve as the theoretical framework for this volume. For a detailed exposition of the rationale and significance of this concept, however, the interested reader must still consult *Beyond Interpretation*. Here, I wish to pursue a different path—to produce a companion volume that will amplify and illuminate those aspects of my previous work which relate to psychoanalysis as a pragmatic clinical discipline. In order to highlight those issues which are currently in the forefront of common interest and concern, I shall contrast my views with alternative viewpoints, some traditional, others more recent and less widely accepted. In particular, I shall present extensive critiques of two schools of thought which have of late gained some prominence: "self psychology," so-called, and the "object relations" approach.

Lest I be misunderstood only as a conservative revolutionary within psychoanalysis, I shall also try to substantiate my credentials as a radical traditionalist by beginning my exposition with a section once more justifying a maximal expansion of the scope of psychoanalysis as a clinical method. And I shall conclude with a discussion of the art of psychoanalysis from the viewpoint of the theory of knowledge.

SECTION I

THE SCOPE OF CLINICAL PSYCHOANALYSIS

From the point of view of clinical practice, a broadened conception of the criteria of analyzability has promoted new optimism, and undoubtedly constitutes the most important advance in psychoanalysis in the recent past. At the twilight of his career, it should be remembered, Freud (1937) expressed considerable skepticism about the therapeutic potential of the procedure he had devised for the illumination of man's inner life. The psychoanalytic mainstream, following Freud's example, continued to advocate adherence to the standard psychoanalytic technique, unadulterated by noninterpretive compromises; the price of such technical orthodoxy was renunciation of therapeutic ambitions with regard to psychopathological conditions more severe than the neuroses proper. As long as the post-World War II popularity of psychoanalysis continued, it remained feasible to select patients for analysis who met these stringent criteria, although many analysts showed a strong preference for broadening the therapeutic scope of their technique (Panel, 1954).

Twenty-five years ago, the consensus position still excluded from analysis most people who sought psychological assistance, and this policy provided the most powerful impetus for the development of alternative psychotherapeutic methods, frequently based on psychoanalytic insight into mental life (e.g., Fromm-Reichmann, 1950; Alexander, 1956). A whole generation of psychoanalysts in America underwent preliminary training in dynamic psychiatry, a discipline that, for better or for worse, required them to provide ad hoc psychotherapeutic measures to all comers.

Many of us of that generation rebelled against the seeming paradox of a professional orientation that compelled us to direct our most intensive and penetrating treatment efforts to the least impaired of our patients. In the privacy of our consulting rooms, we conducted endless technical experiments, alloying the "gold of analysis" —as Freud (1919) had put it—with the baser metals of our psychiatric armamentarium. The nature of these innovations in technique revolved around efforts to bridge the gap between the available treatment methods from two separate directions. On the one hand, we returned to the ambitions of our predecessors of the heroic age of early psychoanalysis to alter characterological disturbances of various kinds through psychoanalysis proper —i.e., we tended to relax our criteria of analyzability in selecting our patients. (I personally decided before 1960 to attempt analysis with anyone interested in introspective self-inquiry who could safely be treated on an outpatient basis.) On the other side of the gap, our therapeutic work with "sicker" patients, often seen only once or twice a week in face-to-face treatment, was often pushed into a quasi-analytic mold entailing free association, transference interpretations, etc.

The results of these therapeutic hybrids were always fascinating, sometimes helpful, and often interminable —though interminable without dire consequences. As I describe in Chapter 1, I eventually reached the conclusion that better results were, predictably enough, obtained with individuals who were in fact "analyzable" by the usual criteria but had settled for less intensive help for a variety of adventitious reasons. Sicker patients, with unresolved difficulties referable to relatively earlier phases of development, seemed to develop poorly understood, uninterpretable transference bonds which became unmanageable in such therapeutic settings.

At the same time, when we faced a variety of treatment problems unaided *and* unencumbered by the guidelines of Freud's procedure, the very need to improvise taught us about the effectiveness in specific circumstances of a number of diverse interventions. In Chapter 2, I discuss some of these lessons of psychotherapeutic experience and the applicability of these lessons to the attempted analyses of patients whose psychopathology ranges outside the neuroses and related conditions. At any rate, it had become clear to everyone who tried to expand the scope of psychoanalysis that patients whose personality development had been skewed before the oedipal crisis did not have the resources necessary to profit from Freud's model technique. This conclusion was formulated most cogently by Eissler (1953), who called for planful modifications of analytic technique to patch over these deficits.

The systematization of the empirical findings of our psychotherapeutic efforts had to await the introduction of a developmental viewpoint into psychoanalytic discourse. To be sure, this was begun as early as 1905, when Freud applied it to the concept of libido development. It did not form an invariable component of our conceptual approach until the 1960s, however, when it was explicitly endorsed by Anna Freud (1965) in a monograph on childhood psychopathology. Her research group at Hampstead began to write about "arrests in development" as a form of psychopathology (Nagera, 1964, 1966), an idea that could be fruitfully extended to the study of personality disorders in adults. (In Chapter 13, I elaborate the concept of such developmental pathology from the standpoint of my own theoretical proposals.)

But to return to the question of analyzability: the systematic use of the developmental viewpoint has opened the door to elaborate technical interventions tailored to the specific mode of mental organization prevalent at each phase of childhood and in the adult conditions that correspond to those phases. I have proposed an inclusive schema classifying the variety of interventions required by the full gamut of developmental disturbances in *Models of the Mind*, prepared in collaboration with Arnold Goldberg in 1973.

In principle, the therapeutic modalities we conceptualized in that work permit an analytic approach with every patient, regardless of the nature of the personality organization. In practice, as I discuss in Chapter 3, our clinical range is limited by the possibility of regressions into states of helplessness and disorganization that would necessitate hospitalization. In my judgment, such an eventuality is the only contraindication for analysis conducted in accord with the complex theory of technique I advocate. Accordingly, I believe that psychoanalysis is now the treatment of choice not only for the neuroses, but for the whole array of characterological problems, however archaic their genesis. (Many of the issues involved in dealing with archaic transferences will be examined in Section II.) Analytic failures will inevitably occur, of course, but they will be caused by specific dynamic constellations that interfere with the analytic process. In Chapter 3, one such pattern I have found to be intractable is described.

CHAPTER ONE

Indications for Psychoanalysis or Intensive Psychotherapy

The status of psychoanalytic psychotherapy has undergone a process of gradual change in the past 20 years, the extent of which has not yet been generally acknowledged. In the decade following World War II, therapy aimed at personality change through insight was attempted across the entire spectrum of psychopathological disturbances (e.g., Alexander and French, 1946; Deutsch, 1949; Fromm-Reichmann, 1950; Alexander, 1956). In some quarters, such insight therapy was claimed to be superior to the classical technique of psychoanalysis even within the range of optimal effectiveness of Freud's procedure, that of the neuroses proper. By the early 1960s, such exaggerated claims began to be tempered (e.g., Grinker et al., 1961; Tarachow, 1963) while the application of the classical technique was progressively extended to a broadening range of disturbances of character (see Panel, 1954).

At first, traditionalists insisted on distinguishing the purely interpretive techniques they believed to be characteristic of psychoanalysis from the "parameters" that had to be imposed when persons with so-called ego deviations tried to experience the psychoanalytic process (Eissler, 1953). Recent theoretical proposals (e.g., Gedo and Goldberg, 1973) have led to a more complex view of the manifold operations involved in every psychoanalytic procedure, and I have recently given a detailed exposition of my own views about the modalities of treatment involved in psychoanalysis in *Beyond Interpretation* (Gedo, 1979a). Here, I will only repeat my conclusion that psychoanalysis conducted in accord with the changing requirements of the different modalities is currently the treatment of choice for all chronic personality disturbances, provided disorganization requiring hospital care does not constitute a serious risk. A corollary of this viewpoint is that psychoanalytic psychotherapy is now *indicated* only in situational crises or as a supportive measure for persons threatened with disorganizing experiences.

In this chapter, I would like to look back to the clinical procedures I followed in the 1950s with patients whom I would unhesitatingly urge to undertake a psychoanalysis today.[1] In accord with the criteria of analyzability accepted 25 years ago, these individuals were considered to be unsuitable for the classical procedure for a variety of reasons (some of which may be illustrated through the clinical examples I shall provide here).

[1] I have described elsewhere several successfully terminated analyses with persons very similar in their psychic organization to the individuals I am about to discuss here (Gedo, 1979a, 1979c).

Nonetheless, it was clear that these patients required something beyond the support provided by a therapeutic relationship, and each psychotherapist attempted to supply whatever this unknown requirement was through improvisations supposedly based on the psychoanalytic understanding of mental functioning. The following case report is intended to demonstrate the virtues and limitations of our work at that time.

Case 1

A professional man of 30, who had been in intensive psychotherapy with a woman for about a year, was admitted to a hospital and referred to my care because of a suicide attempt. He had been completely unable to reveal his intense hostility to his therapist, although he had experienced her as abrasive and lacking insight. This impression was largely confirmed by her conclusion that he was a schizophrenic, a diagnosis ruled out in the course of a thorough work-up in the hospital. As soon as we agreed to collaborate on his continued therapy, the patient regained his poise and was ready for discharge. He felt he needed help to cope with his disturbed wife, who was also in psychotherapy. He was in his third marriage and was understandably eager to preserve it, especially for the sake of a three-year-old daughter. These family circumstances were probably connected with his suicide gesture, as his "father" had died when the patient was three years old.

Actually, as he had finally found out upon the birth

of his daughter, his family of origin had perpetrated a massive deception on him. The couple he had known as his parents were actually his maternal grandparents; he was an illegitimate child, and his biological mother had pretended to be his oldest sister. But he recollected that the decisive influence in the household resided in an aunt who was full of malice toward him and bullied everyone else into treating him with maximal severity and unrealistic expectations of perfection. He had apparently responded with successful performance, especially in school (and later at work). In his field of expertise, he was already recognized as one of the outstanding contributors. In addition to a job entailing great responsibilities, he was currently engaged in earning a doctorate at a local university.

Outpatient therapy was begun with three sessions a week, a frequency amply justified by the patient's anxiety level when he was thrust back into his stormy marital situation. He felt unbearably guilty about his wish to escape from his wife and about his longings for other women, and his regressive avoidance of these issues through drinking bouts or orgies of self-pity filled him with shame. He thought of himself as an infantile personality who was full of rage about frustrated dependency wishes, but it became fairly evident in a short time that, in actuality, it was his wife who had such needs while he was trying to still his objections to her parasitism by pretending to be no better himself. Even in childhood, the patient's seeming inadequacies had served to justify the contempt with which members of his family had treated him, despite his sense of being intellectually superior to them all. He was well aware of his lifelong search for a paternal figure he could emulate in order to make effective use of such intellectual potentials. The first interruption of our regular schedule already revealed that he had unconsciously placed me in that role.

The establishment of a silent idealizing transference (cf. Gedo, 1975a) permitted the patient to face the fact that his marriage re-created his childhood situation: once again, he was tied to inadequate people. In this context, he was able to recall that his grandmother had actually been affectionate toward him most of the time; his adult behavior was organized around the effort to avoid gratifying his wishes to re-create a relationship that would have the same qualities as the one with her. This insight enabled him to deal better with his wife's masochistic provocations, instead of accepting the part of the sadistic exploiter. He also realized that his frustration in the marriage did not have to do with dependency needs but with despair about his wife's effect on his productivity: he needed someone for whose sake he would be inspired to exercise his capacities to their utmost. One indication that I was beginning to occupy such a place in his emotional life was his increasing self-assertion, not only with his wife but with his employers and professors as well.

Furthermore, he began to test out whether he could safely express his dissatisfactions with me within the treatment, in spite of the fact that he was terrified about the possible consequences of this behavior. Thus he also became aware of his profound need for empathic understanding from me, and he recaptured memories of his childhood despair, loneliness, and chill whenever he felt cut off from his grandmother. He felt full of tearful gratitude about our relationship, although he tried to restrain these feelings, in part by provoking difficulties between us through a series of unreasonable maneuvers involving our schedule, specific guidance about practical dilemmas, etc. He was most appreciative of the fact that he could communicate with me at his own intellectual level, and he recalled that this had also been possible in childhood with his grandmother. Yet he had been full of guilt even then about enjoying her, because he was imbued with the feeling that his very existence constituted a constant threat to his family. Insofar as I was now an advocate of his "right to a life" (Modell, 1965), the patient had to attack me or the treatment, in identification with his detractors.

This promising start led, toward the end of the first year of treatment, to the emergence of a negative transference, vigorously warded off by the patient's insistence on the realities of my adequate performance on his behalf. After an impasse of several weeks, I attempted to circumvent this resistance by instituting the use of the couch and instructing the patient to associate freely. By approximating a quasi-analytic technique, it became possible gradually to demonstrate that his ambivalence to his childhood caretakers was currently being repeated with me. His compromise solution was simultaneously to express his dissatisfaction and to punish himself by missing many appointments in whole or in part. We came to see that his hostility was not simply a reaction to frustrated wishes and needs; it had a competitive aspect as well. He felt humiliated by my therapeutic activities on his behalf and was overcome with remorse whenever he thought he had triumphed over me. The second year of treatment was ushered in by a serious crisis, as the patient tried to avoid these conflicts by provoking a situation at work that led to his forced resignation. Not only did this jeopardize therapy from the financial viewpoint; it also entailed the risk of his having to leave the Chicago area to find suitable employment.

As it turned out, he was able to settle in the region, but his new location made it impossible to maintain our former schedule; the frequency of visits had to be reduced to no more than two per week. At first this did not interfere too drastically with further progress, and he was able to face the fact that he dreaded abandonment or some other retaliation if he dared to make full use of his capacities. He felt that he had destroyed the relationship with his caretakers in this manner as a child. At the same time, he justified his negativism by pretending that I was withholding my magical power to make him feel better, and he denied the fact that his irregular attendance was aimed at me as a form of harassment. Eventually he realized that, in addition to his other reasons for missing appointments, he wished to interfere with my therapeutic effectiveness. It was not possible to determine the precise childhood roots of this motive at the time; in retrospect, it was probably a consequence of a desperate fear of loss of autonomy.

By the end of the second year of treatment, the patient realized that his acute *conflict* about his impulses to attack me stemmed from the fear that he might find an actual deficiency in my performance, as he had with his previous therapist. He understood that he needed to believe in my perfection; his faith in a magical cure was part of this idealization. A corollary of this insight was a marked diminution in his self-abasement—his severely self-damaging behaviors had served to make it easier to idealize the imperfect people around him by making himself inferior to them. When he stopped this pattern of acting out, his wife's psychopathology became unbearable for him. In the therapy, he now felt greatly satisfied by the unprecedented opportunity to have a relationship with a man he could respect. His acceptance of the need for a paternal surrogate led to marked improvements in his day-to-day functioning; we then realized that presenting himself as maximally ill and needful had been the sole way to reach out to the only man of the family in childhood, an uncle by marriage who served as their physician. Significantly, the patient had eventually assumed this uncle's family name.

The development of these positive bonds within the therapeutic relationship rendered the patient quite vulnerable to interruptions of the treatment. In this context, he also reexperienced one of the major crises of his childhood: the interruption of a period of peace and satisfaction, when he and his grandmother had lived apart from the rest of the family. My commitments to other people now filled him with the kind of rage he had experienced on their return to the family home. He was even able to recapture within the transference the childhood conflict about his erotic attachment to the grandmother. His profound sense of guilt was now understandable in terms of the actual preference his grandmother had shown him: she was clearly prejudiced against females, so that her daughters were provoked into severe jealousy of the patient. He always felt undeserving of the fruits of his abilities, whether in the intellectual realm or with reference to his masculinity. After a period of turbulent work on this conflict, these insights permitted him to obtain his wife's consent to an amicable separation.

By the end of the third year of treatment, it seemed that enough progress had been made in understanding the patient's emotional life to permit consideration of an eventual termination. At that point, however, the therapeutic process proved to be unmanageable by means of the procedures at our disposal. The patient never brought up the issue of bringing our work to a close; instead, the matter came up indirectly, and in a most unexpected way: through his skillful provocativeness, he suddenly contrived to be fired from his job. He was then "forced" to cut back to one weekly appointment, and he began to defend himself against the emotions connected with our predictable separation through fantasies that I was now his adversary. He began to stay away altogether shortly before my summer vacation, and he did not contact me upon my return. I encountered him on the street a few weeks later, and he reported that he was still looking for work. I never heard from him again.

To recapitulate, this "intensive psychotherapy" was gratifyingly successful in effecting a number of important adaptive changes in the course of three years, and it was surprisingly productive of significant insights into the dynamics and genetics of the patient's personality. These gains were achieved in the context of a therapeutic relationship, the nature of which never came into sufficiently sharp focus to permit interpretive resolution. Consequently, the archaic transference bonds that arose during treatment persisted and prevented any satisfactory parting of the ways. This patient cut his Gordian knot by unconsciously arranging obstacles that forced a seemingly adventitious termination, one allowing him to avoid confronting the nature of his needs for the therapy. Although we lack convincing evidence on this score, I assume that such a solution entails the acceptance of those continuing maladaptations related to the most primitive aspects of the personality. Thus, we are confronted with something of a paradox: psychotherapy has more power to alter the conflicts generally thought to be best handled through the psychoanalytic method than to deal with those preoedipal issues that were once seen as obstacles to analyzability.

As I stated before, I now manage problems of this kind by attempting the psychoanalytic procedure. In my recent experience (see Gedo, 1975a, 1977a, 1979a), archaic transferences have posed no insuperable problems for analyzability, and their interpretation (once the reasons for such primitive needs have emerged with clarity within the analytic relationship) generally permits us to carry such cases to a successful termination. Nonetheless, I am convinced that we were perfectly correct in selecting the nonanalytic therapies we employed with these patients a generation ago, because the standard analytic technique of that era would have been utterly ineffective and unbearable for them. The man I have just described could not have tolerated a treatment technique aimed exclusively at elucidating his intrapsychic conflicts; he needed a variety of active interventions in other therapeutic modalities (cf. Gedo and Goldberg, 1973, Chapter 11). Such interventions would have included confrontations with the actualities he disavowed through his illusions, encouragement to make consistent choices among mutually exclusive alternative goals, and guidance about maladaptive tension-regulating devices. It is precisely the planful inclusion of these and similar therapeutic activities within the psychoanalytic armamentarium that has permitted the dramatic expansion of the scope of analytic work in the past decade. In other words, the results of "intensive psychotherapy" as I have just summarized them involve no real paradox: whatever insights it can achieve (and however helpful these prove to be), the whole enterprise is contingent on the exploitation of a silent idealizing transference (Kohut, 1971; Gedo, 1975a). In order to underscore this point, I shall briefly present another relevant case, for which I have more information about the eventual outcome of the therapy.

Case 2

An attractive 18-year-old girl of upper-class background was referred to me when she became illegitimately pregnant upon leaving her family for the first time to attend college. Although she seemed depressed and chaotic, she was able to follow advice to obtain an abortion in another country, and she returned for continued psychotherapy in a better state of organization. About two years earlier, she had been hospitalized briefly for a depressive illness, and she was still apathetic on the surface. She behaved like a submissive preadolescent, entirely dependent on her brittle and narcissistic, divorced mother. Her father had remarried shortly after the divorce and then died when the patient was four. She was the youngest and most troubled of four children; she had been very close to a sister who had recently made a brilliant marriage and was currently pregnant for the first time.

We began on a schedule of two sessions a week, while she enrolled in art school and went to live in a girls' club. She was frightened, lonely, and ashamed about never having lived up to her mother's expectations. Yet she also knew that the family's shallow standards enraged her; it was her need to inhibit this anger that made her seem apathetic and immobile. My acceptance of these affects made her feel better than she had in years. I gave her active encouragement to pursue her own aims in order to reinforce this favorable trend and made myself available via telephone whenever she felt threatened by her loneliness. In this context, she became enthusiastic about her various projects for the first time. Yet she remained quite careful to curb her propensity to demand more than any therapeutic situation could offer.

After a few months, she was able to reveal both the secret rebelliousness hidden behind her sweet and submissive demeanor and the erotic fantasies interwoven with her need for quasi-parental care. Her sexual impulses filled her with guilt, which she tried to expiate through self-punitive behaviors. Yet she could not forego sexual contacts with boys, for these warded off her more threatening homosexual longings. In fantasy, she preferred terrifying sadomasochistic struggles; her actual relationships were more gentle, but she found them essentially unexciting. She realized that her fantasies had projected her own violent impulses onto men—she had been full of vengefulness since early childhood, and seeing herself as a victim was one way of reducing her guilt about this. Slowly, she began to experience her competitiveness with other women in the setting of the frustration of her feminine ambitions within the therapeutic relationship. She tried to master these feelings through reversals, e.g., by provoking several boys to compete for her favor. She felt humiliated by her unreciprocated love for me. Although this love was largely erotized, I interpreted it as the emergence of a mother transference. She was then able to express her hostility toward me in a direct manner; the fact that I took these feelings *seriously* made her feel both authentic and significant for the first time.

Toward the end of the first year of treatment, she began to reexperience her lifelong disavowed longings for her father; she was deeply embarrassed by the sexual aspects of these feelings. She remembered her jealousy of her father's second wife, as well as her mother's insistence that the child share the latter's bitterness and contempt for the deserter. She recalled her great fear when, following the father's death, her mother had to go out to work, so that she was suddenly left with strangers. Somewhat later she had attached herself to her brother and found comfort in the sexual games they had played together. These activities were guiltlessly performed at the time. After the brother got married, however, she felt acutely guilty about her conscious murderous fantasies toward her new sister-in-law. Moreover, her intense attachment to her brother, now repeated in the transference, was complicated by her envy of his masculinity. Despite the appearance of this kind of oedipal transference material, any interruption of our regular schedule threw her back into an archaic mother transference in which she was uncontrollably angry about her lack of power over me. My physical absence was the present equivalent of her mother's self-absorption and lack of empathy during her childhood. She pleaded for an opportunity to articulate her ambivalence with appropriate affectivity, and we had a series of moving sessions in which she poured out these feelings. She was explicitly aware that her demand involved a fantasied fusion between us.

In the middle of the second year of our work, she

once again focused on her envy of men, her need to be on top in sexual relations, her desire to remain cool while the man became excited, etc. She enacted these fantasies by working as a model for hosiery ads, an achievement that filled her with exhibitionistic excitement. Thus it became clear to both of us that heterosexual relations were contaminated by her continuing archaic needs—short of an actual symbiosis, she had to be the exclusive center of attention, a veritable goddess of love. In this context, however, she gradually mastered her anxiety about her infantile sexual fantasies (i.e., the anal degradation of the sexual sphere), and her self-restriction in the area of competitiveness with women (mostly her mother) now really diminished. She became aware of wishes to be married and to have children.

In connection with my second summer vacation, she began to relive her reaction to the loss of her father, and we uncovered her denial of the reality of his death. Unconsciously, she was convinced that he watched over her as a guardian spirit, and in the transference she reenacted her fantasy that, in order to retain this "protection," she had to remain entirely faithful to her paternal guardian. Conversely, interpretation indicated, and the patient subsequently acknowledged consciously, a desire to arouse my jealousy by finding a man of her own. Her fear that her chronic anger might destroy me began to emerge. When she found an interesting job, she developed the wish to solve this dilemma by emancipating herself from therapy, but she was afraid that (like her parents, each in a different way) I would abandon her prematurely in retaliation. As part of this attempt, she reduced the frequency of her appointments (eventually to one per week), and I agreed to institute this "weaning" process.

The third year of treatment began with continuing progress: she realized that part of her low self-esteem stemmed from never having experienced the love of a respected father—a void she had filled with highly unrealistic romantic fantasies about movie idols. She had an episode of acute appendicitis at this time, an event she elaborated into a fantasied pregnancy. On my insistence, she got adequate surgical care. Several months of inner struggle followed concerning her uncompromising demand for a loving relationship from me. My summer vacation brought into focus once again the issues of the remarriage of her father, his move to another city, and his death shortly thereafter. This material, in turn, led to the elucidation of her unconscious belief in the destructive magic of her wishes.

Interpretation of her fear of progress, lest she lose the therapeutic relationship, now led to a series of adaptive improvements, both at work and in her social life. She then began to consider an eventual termination of our work. She got her own apartment, a better job, and became orgasmic in coitus. Her biggest residual difficulty concerned the regressive pull she experienced within the context of any ongoing relationship; she felt she could defend her more "mature" adaptation only by giving up such affectionate ties. In the therapy, she now relived her conflict about leaving her mother: she realized that her helplessness had been a way of satisfying her mother's symbiotic needs as well as her own. She was afraid that mother would be hurt and unable to function without her, and she had similar concerns about pulling out of any other relationship. She relived the childhood feeling of being unable to give her mother *enough* in terms of her humiliation about the relatively modest fee she could afford to pay me, i.e., her present inability to give *me* enough. And yet she was very envious of her older siblings, who had been able to escape from the mother's orbit.

Eventually, she decided to stop coming regularly shortly before the summer break during the fourth year of treatment. She was afraid that she would be tempted to relapse into illness in order to have reason for coming back into treatment, but she discontinued her attendance on schedule, with an appropriate expression of grief. During the next year, she occasionally returned to maintain contact with me. She proceeded satisfactorily in her everyday life, but she continued to mourn the loss of treatment unabatedly. The prospect of losing touch with me altogether filled her with a sense of bewilderment and panic.

About 18 months after we discontinued regular therapy, the patient's grandfather died, leaving her a substantial legacy. She came back to report this, as if hoping that her wealth would make her irresistible for me. When these fantasies were disappointed, she became seriously involved with a man for the first time. In spite of certain limitations in this relationship, she became engaged and decided to follow him to another city. She returned for several visits, as if to ascertain whether I would oppose her plans, as her mother was doing, and thus gratify her transference wishes. She left town about two years after "termination" and went through with the marriage. She then called me to report that she felt lost and detached; she wanted to resume psychotherapy—with a woman.

I believe that this second example demonstrates the limitations of a psychotherapeutic approach to archaic personality disorders with special clarity. Once again, the derivatives of the Oedipus complex as well as the so-called "narcissistic" issues later highlighted by Kohut were amenable to interpretation and far-reaching modification, and these aspects of the treatment were permanently useful. But the principal vehicle of improvement turned out to be a silent (and therefore uninterpretable) transference bond, and the final rupture of that illusory merger necessitated a return for further treatment. This sort of outcome is also common in psychoanalyses conducted along rigidly traditional lines (cf. Firestein, 1978). Better results require consistent analytic focus on the patient's archaic psychological needs. In that regard, I wish to stress that the psychological issues brought to general attention by Kohut (1971, 1977, 1978; see also Goldberg, 1978) were not overlooked in either of the therapies I have presented thus far. The uninterpreted transference bonds that defeated my therapeutic efforts, however, transcended the realms of idealization and of subject-centered grandiosity that he has described.

In other words, these patients were not simply fixated on a set of archaic fantasies; they truly needed a therapeutic symbiosis—without continuing external assistance, they were unable to adapt effectively. They had failed in childhood to acquire some of the psychological skills essential to cope in adult life. Thus the archaic transferences they manifested in therapy, often reminiscent of the constellations of fantasies described by Kohut, merely echoed the manner in which these individuals had tried to compensate for their basic deficits in childhood by attaching themselves in a symbiotic manner to the people in their environment.[2] To put my point in still another way, the so-called "selfobject transferences" (Kohut, 1977; Goldberg, 1978) and the childhood conditions which they echo are not central to the psychopathology—they are epiphenomena, compensatory efforts to patch over a developmental deficit.[3]

Perhaps it is also pertinent to note that, with individuals whose problems involve matters that have traditionally been considered analyzable, "intensive psychotherapy" of the kind I have tried to illustrate through the two case reports can achieve satisfactory results, with or without the use of the couch, on a two- or three-session-a-week schedule. Comparably successful therapeutic outcomes have been widely reported and do not require further documentation here.

[2] The issue of so-called "symbiotic need" is discussed more fully in Chapter 9.

[3] My objections to Kohut's understanding of the "selfobject transferences" from the standpoint of his theory of psychic structure formation are elaborated in Chapter 4.

A full-scale psychoanalysis is essential in most personality disorders precisely because there are very few people whose pathology is derived principally from the childhood developmental phases referable to the familiar intrapsychic conflicts (see Gedo and Goldberg, 1973). In fact, it is the developmental deficits stemming from the earliest phases of maturation that require the detailed examination and painstaking repair now made possible by contemporary psychoanalytic techniques (see Gedo, 1979a). I should like to illustrate this conclusion by means of a highly abbreviated account of a series of clinical encounters with one patient over the course of 20 years.

Case 3

This woman originally sought my assistance in her mid-twenties after being rescued following a serious suicide attempt. She had carried out a long-standing intention to end her life when she realized that she could not get enough satisfaction from the sexual affairs through which she had tried to console herself for the lovelessness of her marriage. She felt tied to her emotionally aloof spouse, partly because his commitment to the relationship was absolute, although essentially asexual. He had recently completed his professional training and obtained a promising job in a successful law firm, and he was genuinely supportive of the effort to provide his wife the treatment she needed. The patient's relationship to her husband seemed to repeat her childhood dependence on a controlling but distant mother. She had realized that her mother was an inadequate person when she was about 11, and her chronic depression started at that time. Her father had left the home around the time of the birth of her only sibling, when the patient was four. He was successful in a business venture peripherally connected with the underworld and lived with a woman from that subculture. Although the patient had been raised to despise him, it had been her efforts in adolescence to force her father to discharge his financial obligations toward his family that had caused a rupture between them. The practical result of this breach was his refusal to send her to college. She still managed to obtain a degree through her own efforts in a technical field that did not challenge her.

We agreed to begin psychotherapy on a two-session-a-week schedule; with the exception of two maternity leaves lasting several months each, treatment was continued on and off for 10 years. She then returned to school to obtain an advanced degree in her field and was able to sustain herself without therapy while this hopeful effort lasted. Shortly after graduation, she returned to see me with the realization that her defect in self-esteem could not be remedied by actual accomplishments in everyday life. In the course of another year of weekly psychotherapy, we concluded that she was addicted to treatment precisely because her sense of worth depended on our relationship. I began to urge her to attempt a radical solution to this dilemma through a psychoanalytic effort, but she was understandably reluctant to make such an investment and opted, instead, to wean herself from treatment. She absented herself for a considerable period, but about 15 years after our initial contact, she became suicidal once again, and (out of consideration for her children) decided to accept my previous recommendation. Her analysis took about three-and-a-half years on a five-session-a-week basis, and covered approximately the same ground we had gone over in all the preceding years of therapy. The development and interpretation of an archaic mother transference in this setting did, however, permit the resolution of her addiction to therapy. A recent follow-up, almost 25 years after we began, confirmed that she is doing quite well, in spite of certain unavoidable misfortunes that place great burdens upon her. Clearly, it is not feasible to describe the course of these various treatment procedures here. Instead, I shall try to focus my discussion on a single issue: the problem of what made it impossible to resolve the archaic transference bonds without resorting to the psychoanalytic method.

The initial period of therapy, up to the delivery of the patient's first child, was characterized by intense conflict about motherhood. Without having children, she could find no meaning in life, but she was terrified that giving birth might lead to the destruction of her family, just as her brother's arrival had been followed by the desertion of her father. These issues were resolved in the context of an erotic transference; she was able to understand that her tendency to fall into hopeless competitions with males was actually a consequence of a prior retreat from the more guilt-provoking feminine ambitions of her oedipal years. The net result of this therapeutic work was a dramatic and permanent improvement in her capacity for self-assertion.

In spite of the encouraging success of this bit of psychotherapy, we could perceive a harbinger of things to come in the patient's acute depressive response to my summer vacation at the beginning of the second year of our work. After her delivery, she kept in touch through letters and phone calls until we resumed regular contact about eight months later. She then picked up the themes that had preoccupied her previously, as if the interruption had not occurred at all. In addition to the oedipal "father transference," however, there were now indications that she was also reliving a more archaic maternal transference, one that was characterized by unfulfilled longing, rage, and negativism. She nonetheless continued to make progress, especially in throwing off her compliance with her mother's unreasonable requirements. The most significant practical result of this change was the removal of a broad intellectual inhibition, which showed her to have great potential as an abstract thinker, a capacity that she eventually put to good use many years later. But this second period of treatment culminated in the birth of her second child, so that the importance of her intellectual liberation did not become immediately apparent. As her delivery approached, she tried desperately to negate her great need for the therapeutic relationship, but she was compelled to check in with me within a few weeks of giving birth. She felt so helpless about this need that she described her state as one of being hypnotized.

Regular treatment was resumed following a six-month hiatus. With the acknowledgment of her absolute dependence on treatment, the patient was able to repudiate certain patterns of behavior formerly necessitated by a similar symbiosis with her husband. She realized that her infidelities had actually been carried out to please him, and she was able decisively to shift the balance in their relationship so that henceforth major family decisions would be subject to her veto. Unfortunately, in spite of lengthy psychoanalytic treatment, her husband was unable to achieve sexual adequacy, and the marriage never came close to meeting her needs for intimacy. She felt her husband only wanted to exploit her, as her father had always insisted on taking advantage of women. However, she also experienced the frustrations of therapy as a repetition of the same pattern. She now gained the courage to demand that she be treated properly by everyone, and her outward behavior changed from masochism to a presence that most people felt as authoritative or commanding. In this context, she was able to recall certain childhood experiences with grandparents or other relatives that had been very positive; her negativism was brought forth by relationships that did not re-create these infantile satisfactions. She now developed a number of friendships, instead of allowing her husband to monopolize her or to push her into unacceptable sexual adventures.

Her inability to leave the unsatisfactory marriage

could now be understood as the repetition of her childhood loyalty to her needful mother. The latter could only be gratified through grandiose achievements; hence the patient's self-esteem was contingent on accomplishing the impossible. She was now able to grasp the full extent of her mother's psychopathology for the first time, including certain gross delusions involving the patient. She also realized the crucial importance of her early relationship to a step-grandmother, who counteracted her mother's influence to a large degree but died when the patient was four. She experienced mourning for this and a number of other childhood object losses at this time, and this led (early in the ninth year of therapy!) to a reliving of her erotic attachment to one grandfather in the transference. Her husband's actual resentment of her obvious attachment to me echoed her mother's active efforts to block any meaningful ties to other people in childhood. The reward for loyalty to mother had been inclusion within a megalomanic folie-à-deux. Yet the child had never lost her sense of reality and understood clearly that she did not actually have the capacity to satisfy her mother, either sexually or in other ways.

Following these insights, the patient decided to put childish concerns behind her, to concentrate on trying to get her satisfactions from achieving realistic goals, and to bring therapy to a close at long last. Although she continued to manage her everyday life with unprecedented competence, she became aware of fears of actual helplessness when she thought of getting along without me. At times she felt suicidal, as she had before the start of treatment. In this context, for the first time the maternal transference came into interpretive focus, but the reasons for her symbiotic dependency were by no means discernible. However, at this point she was grimly determined to stick to her plans to stop therapy, exactly 10 years after our initial contact. She warded off her feelings of loss by focusing on her angry dissatisfaction with the results of our work, and she tried to overcome the regressive pull by investing herself in a program to resume her professional training. Thus she discontinued treatment without any mourning. Her only distress related to the impossibility of achieving the grandiose ambitions she had absorbed from her mother. She did express considerable gratitude before leaving, however, especially for the help she had received in being a loving mother to her children.

As I have already stated, she returned to therapy upon completion of her advanced degree. Although she was by this time quite convinced that she possessed superior abilities, her basic self-esteem had scarcely improved. She did understand that childhood circumstances, rather than her current situation, had determined her sense of worthlessness. In the transference, she was still caught up in the endless repetition of her hopeless longing for a loving father. She grasped for the first time that neither of her parents had in fact rejected her; on the contrary, each in a different way had failed in such a disappointing manner that *she* had rejected *them*. Hence her continuing reliance on the therapeutic relationship was in part based on my having managed not to disillusion her. This fact was so vital to her that she was continuously tempted to jettison her therapeutic gains in order to justify and rationalize her need to continue seeing me. When, after an additional year of weekly visits, she realized this, she once again interrupted therapy, only to return two years later with a recurrence of suicidal impulses. At that point, we agreed to begin her analysis.

I shall not go into the details of that procedure, except to try to show through a single example the reasons for the ineffectiveness of our previous therapeutic efforts. Within a few weeks of instituting a five-session-a-week schedule, the basic maternal transference came into focus. This consisted in a panicky and rigid conviction that I was trying to destroy her; her 15 years of clinging to the father transference had defended her against this terrifying experience. Only after she had relived these childhood vicissitudes in the analytic setting could she begin to master her adaptive deficits; her lifelong negativism about accepting instruction from others had perpetuated these deficits at the same time as it protected her from being absorbed into her mother's psychotic world. And the conviction that her mother was full of malice toward her had also been a distortion, based on a little girl's inability to grasp the limitations of her primary caretaker. I want to underscore the fact that insight into these archaic transferences was by itself insufficient to alter the patient's self-experience; in addition, she had to correct a host of maladaptive behavior patterns she had learned in earliest childhood. As long as she adhered to these patterns, her self-condemnation had, in actuality, a great deal of justification in reality.

Summary

I have presented three case examples of complex personality disorders not regarded as analyzable by the criteria commonly accepted some years ago and therefore treated by means of intensive psychotherapy. All three treatments were reasonably successful, in terms of both achieving a number of important insights and markedly improving adaptation. In certain crucial respects, however, the behavioral changes did not prove to be lasting, although there was no reason to doubt the validity of the understanding that had been reached. Apparently, psychotherapy had not permitted us to grasp, to interpret, and to overcome some of the reasons for the patients' symbiotic need for a therapist.

In the last illustrative case report, I have tried to show that the nature of such archaic transferences is potentially analyzable. If the deficits that make these symbiotic attachments necessary can be corrected (generally by means of techniques that have not formed part of psychoanalysis as it has been practiced traditionally), the archaic bonds will be spontaneously resolved. Hence I believe that "intensive psychotherapy" is no longer the treatment of choice for the heterogeneous personality disorders that fall between the categories of neurosis and psychosis (in the stricter definition of these terms).

Instead, the optimal approach to the treatment of

these conditions is one that provides the opportunity to develop the archaic transferences to the full in a psychoanalytic setting proper. To this end, we must extend the model technique of psychoanalysis beyond the use of interpretations of unconscious contents or reconstructions of the subjective world of childhood, to include so-called educational measures designed to correct the personality deficits that render these individuals unable to cope on their own with the expectable vicissitudes of life.

CHAPTER TWO

Some Lessons of Psychotherapy for Psychoanalysis

With character problems that fall outside the boundaries of that analyzable grouping we have called the "transference neuroses," psychotherapies based on psychoanalytic knowledge have yielded equivocal clinical results. The resultant impetus to broaden the range of psychoanalysis proper has been accompanied by efforts to develop a variety of psychotherapeutic models less directly derived from the technique of psychoanalysis (e.g., Grinker et al., 1961; Tarachow, 1963). Unfortunately, the proponents of these measures have seldom worked out the criteria defining the suitability of any given therapeutic technique to a group of patients sharing replicable characteristics. Hence the question of what should be done if analysis is not indicated (either for intrapsychic or adventitious, external reasons) long remained a major area of confusion in the professional literature. Although, in practice, much effective therapy was doubtless performed, it was equally true that psychological treatment was all too often based on the assumption that bringing a so-called patient into the same room with a so-called therapist might magically elicit beneficial changes in one or both of the participants. Elsewhere (Gedo, 1964) I have labeled this strategy "the therapy of drift."

Perhaps the clearest of the treatment techniques developed in the context of the postwar psychotherapeutic boom came to be called "supportive" (see Luborsky et al., 1958). In these therapies, the relationship between the therapist and patient was not interpreted as an expression of the patient's unconscious fantasies; instead, transference was utilized as a vehicle of cure. Tarachow (1962) called supplying the infantile object in the present the first "overriding principle" of psychotherapy, as distinguished from psychoanalysis. In supportive treatment, that is, "the therapist assumes the role of a helper . . . for the learner, he becomes a teacher; for the guidance seeker, he . . . sets standards, demands adherence to values, and pronounces judgments . . . for the identity-seeker, he appreciates and identifies the patient's . . . essential attributes" (Grinker et al., 1961, pp. 94–95). Tarachow (1962) characterized these therapeutic interventions as the provision of stability via educating, informing, commanding, prohibiting, or manipulating the environment.

A consensus gradually developed (cf. Gedo, 1964) that supportive therapy is indicated for persons suffering from developmental arrest or distortion at primitive levels—the anal phase in terms of traditional libido theory, the psychosocial crisis of autonomy in Erikson's (1959) vocabulary, or the crisis of separation-individuation in Mahler's (Mahler, Pine, and Bergman, 1975). Many authors now prefer to call such patients "borderline" (cf. Kernberg, 1975). Supportive therapy often turns out to be interminable, even if lengthy interruptions prove to be feasible during the sunny intervals between life crises. In certain other instances, however, such therapy has been shown to produce surprising results. As Stone (1961) has observed, "many patients, otherwise inaccessible to or unavailable for thorough analytic work, can become satisfactory analytic patients on the basis of extended preliminary interviews" (p. 148). E. Rappaport (1960) coined the term "preparation for analysis" to encompass such contingencies. He explained these favorable shifts by assuming that treatment can teach certain individuals to view their pathological behaviors as ego-alien for the first time. Such learning may require long periods of work, involving verbal and behavioral confrontations with the patient's actual functional capacities. Glover (1960) also believed that psychotherapeutic measures could produce certain structural changes of this type; I would characterize such changes as the result of accepting the adult identity of a neurotic patient.

In reviewing various psychotherapeutic models (Gedo, 1964), I once reached the conclusion that successful treatments falling into the twilight zone between psychoanalysis proper and supportive therapy are of two distinct types. The simpler type ensues from the handling of the gamut of age-appropriate developmental crises throughout the life cycle, as exemplified by techniques designed to assist adolescents with the expectable turmoil of "growing up" (e.g., Gitelson, 1948). More difficult to conceptualize are therapies that tackle sequelae of poorly resolved developmental vicissitudes from the past and succeed in stimulating maturational progress of some kind. When this occurs, an analytic process may be set in motion; alternatively, we may witness the resumption of an interrupted developmental crisis that can be dealt with as if it were taking place in age-appropriate fashion. I have labeled the last of these possibilities "the psychotherapy of developmental arrest" (Gedo, 1966). Incidentally, the spontaneous improvements in adaptation occasionally observed in persons who have not engaged in any formal therapy may also be attributable to the undoing of developmental arrests by fortunate life experiences.

Psychological maturation, whether it occurs spontaneously or as a result of therapeutic intervention, does not imply that a satisfactory level of integration will eventually be reached. As is true in the course of expectable development in childhood and adolescence, there can be little significant change in the structured conflicts already embedded in the personality as a consequence of earlier vicissitudes. Nonetheless, maturation may shift the capacity to deal with this enduring pattern of intrapsychic conflicts; even though such a shift may not alter the degree of basic psychopathology, it may create dramatic adaptive changes. As Hartmann and Loewenstein (1962) put it, "Powerful identifications as they sometimes are made even by adult persons can produce such changes in individuals whose. . . superego has remained more open to change than is commonly the case" (p. 177). I should like to illustrate this point by means of some brief clinical vignettes.

Case 4

An 18-year-old college student sought help because she felt depressed and was in academic difficulties. She had done well until her mother's accidental death about two years before. A previous attempt at psychotherapy had foundered because she had been unable to accept interpretations of her behavior as self-punitive, but she had felt somewhat better while she had a temporary job with a man whom she could respect and rely on.

In her weekly therapeutic sessions she quickly discovered that her poor performance was in spiteful identification with her father. He had begun to disappoint her a few years earlier by showing contempt for women; he had completely lost her respect when he responded to his wife's death with depression and overt promiscuity. As she became aware of her vengeful reaction to these events in an atmosphere of mutual respect in the treatment, the patient's performance and mood improved dramatically. After a visit with her father, she resigned herself to giving up clinging to the past and to her grievances; for the first time, then, she began to live the normal social life of a college girl. She took the initiative for discontinuing therapy about four months after she had begun.

Two years later, she returned for a single visit to discuss breaking off an engagement to a man who had become anxious at the prospect of marriage. She was not depressed, nor had she acted out either spitefully or masochistically. She had made a notable success in her chosen field of study, and she gave the impression of being a self-sufficient young woman capable of deep feelings.

My view of this material was that severe stress in mid-adolescence had arrested this girl in a pervasive, hostile oedipal relationship to her father, whose own emotional resources were at that time insufficient to help his daughter master the situation. A real relationship with a man whom she respected, who could respect her, and who made himself available as long as she needed him was sufficient to set in motion her spontaneous emotional growth, and the adolescent process (cf. Wolf, Gedo, and Terman, 1972) was completed within a span of two years. This therapeutic relationship was a new experience for her; it emphatically did not represent a repetition of her previous experiences with her father. But there was never any doubt that she responded to me primarily in a heterosexual manner. Interpretations were not made; it was my emotional response to her as conveyed through my communications, both verbal and nonverbal, that served as the catalyst for the crystallization of her feminine self-esteem and identity. In other words, the therapeutic relationship had met the deficit created by her father's limitations and the loss of her excellent relationship with her mother. As Gitelson (1948) stated, in treating adolescents, our conduct must be emotion-determined: "Objectivity is not nough!"

Case 5

A 21-year-old college student started therapy on his return from an episode of running away to Florida, where he took the pseudonym of the conqueror of the state, Andrew Jackson. He knew that he had thereby attempted to rebel against the rigid standards of his militantly pacifist parents. He had been their exemplary child, and his older sister had been cast into the role of the delinquent one. He had joined his parents in condemning her for overt sexual escapades, but he was beginning to realize that she was ill and also needed professional help.

When he thought I was supporting his rebellion against his parents, the patient again ran away in a panic. On his return, he revealed his fear of his erotic impulses toward his seductive sister and appealed to me for a code of conduct to deal with such a situation. He confessed that he knew that their puritanical father had actually made impulsive sexual overtures to the girl. I made extensive and explicit explanations of my standards of sexual morality, and I urged the patient to act in a manner that would not make him feel guilty.

He next asked me for similar guidance on the issue of his aggressiveness in the context of his parents' expectations of his conscientious objection to military service. Once again, I frankly revealed my own (favorable) attitudes about national service, whereupon he decided to tell his parents that he *would* serve as a soldier, and in this context he had a vivid dream of rebirth in which his "Florida body" (i.e., his aggressiveness) was merged into his total personality.

There was marked improvement in his subjective state at this time, and he began to come less frequently. At the end of three months of treatment, he enlisted in the army. He wrote me a few letters while he served a satisfying period of enlistment as a musician in a military band. Upon his discharge, he made an appropriate marriage. Four years later, he was functioning well in a responsible position and reported satisfaction with his life.

I have taken the preceding two examples from the period of late adolescence because older patients who have sought my assistance have seldom presented themselves with relatively uncomplicated developmental crises. The two people I have described had solved the maturational tasks preceding adolescence relatively well. Whenever sequelae of unresolved problems from earlier developmental phases complicate a current crisis, their continuing influence will, of course, render the therapeutic work more complex. The next vignette illustrates such a contingency.

Case 6

A college professor in his early thirties entered therapy largely at the insistence of his wife. Great marital friction and inability to complete his dissertation were his main complaints. He had always known that his wife was a person with severe emotional problems, which he had hoped to alleviate by marrying her. Their difficulties had been present all along but had become much graver after the birth of their only child, about three years previously; this boy had a congenital malformation that needed surgical correction. The patient felt that he could under no circumstances leave his wife because of the consequences of such a change for the child.

The patient was the only child of a professional couple in a European city. His parents were divorced when he was two; he was raised by domestics, while his mother resumed her career. She never remarried, but his father did so and had little contact with the patient thereafter. The latter felt quite bitter about the father's obvious preference for a stepson and another child by the second wife. Both parents fled from Nazi persecution when the patient was 10; the families settled in different sections of the United States. During his adolescent years, the patient was often separated even from his mother, and he managed to behave in an extraordinarily competent and independent fashion. His academic record was brilliant, he did well in the army, and in his early twenties he achieved prominence in one of the intellectual competitive games. Marriage and a faculty appointment followed.

The patient's uncertain motivation for treatment and his aura of the eccentric genius led me to undertake once-a-week therapy with very modest goals. Discussing his wife's irrational behavior with me helped him to deal with her more calmly. He realized that she was upset with every success he achieved and that his reluctance to complete his dissertation was an effort to appease her. He identified with my scientific interest in her psychopathology and was able to decrease his attempts to cure her by acceding to her demands. He discovered that he had been denying his awareness of his wife's seemingly irreversible difficulties in order to avoid the issue of a possible separation. His self-esteem improved, and he was subsequently able to renegotiate his academic contract to his great advantage. In this context, he realized that he had failed to make demands in the past because in his department he wanted to be the favorite son, one who received every gratification without having to ask for it. This wish in himself, in turn, had impelled him to treat his wife with total indulgence.

These insights enabled him to change his behavior at home, precipitating a prolonged crisis with his enraged spouse. His awareness of his therapeutic orientation toward her was thus consolidated, and he now decided to leave her as soon as their son was old enough not to be damaged by the change. In the year of therapy to this point, my activities might have been characterized as the supervision of his psychotherapy of his wife. A great change now occurred: the patient realized with shock, relief, and profound emotion that he too had needs both in relation to his wife and to me, that he was neither invulnerable nor sufficient unto himself. As his tendency to project his own infantile wishes onto his wife and son diminished, he decided that the latter would not be devastated if he did not have both parents at his beck and call at all times. He thereby understood that the marriage could be dissolved at his own convenience.

The patient became aware of having, through his pattern of life, perpetuated a fantasy of omnipotence which simultaneously filled him with guilt. He connected the guilt with fantasied responsibility for the divorce of his parents. He now stopped talking about his wife during the hours and made an earnest effort to understand himself, especially his irrational guilt. This effort turned out to relate to the wish to leave his wife and to find a more mature woman.

A new theme now emerged: he recalled that the person who had actually raised him had been a young peasant girl hired by his mother. They had been extremely close, and he had wanted to be adopted into her family. It was this relationship, and his fantasies of its indefinite prolongation, that had given him the omnipotent feeling of possessing some *a priori* innate merit that made it unnecessary for him to be judged on his performance. Consequently, he had always avoided testing himself with a woman who could leave or reject him, and this explained why he had chosen as his wife a girl who was clearly too sick to do so. He had always managed to deny that his nursemaid had actually chosen someone else (she had married before their final separation), preferring to cling to the fiction that her feelings were for him alone, and that only overwhelming sociopolitical forces had rent them asunder.

While these matters were unfolding in the therapy, the patient succeeded in obtaining his doctorate and in having his bilateral inguinal herniae surgically corrected. He viewed these self-assertive steps as preliminary to leaving his wife and terminating therapy. He was able to tell her of his intention to separate after their son's impending corrective surgery, but he experienced irrational reluctance to take the initiative in broaching it to me. He realized that he was in this way reliving his inability as an adolescent to offend his mother by departing from her expectations in any way. In practice, the only matter about which he had disagreed with her was that of sexuality, and his transference reaction attributed her sexual morality to me. His fantasy that she would be devastated by a signal affirming his emotional separation from her was based on the fact that his mother had indeed broken down with a series of severe depressions over the past 15 years. As he relived this conflict in the therapy, however, he grasped the irrationality involved in assuming responsibility for her fate. As he realized that his reluctance to leave others was based on attributing to them the insecurity and loneliness he had suffered as a result of the need to be prematurely independent in his childhood, he was able to plan to end therapy open-endedly, allowing himself a reasonable interval to work through the resulting emotions. He experienced feelings of genuine loss and sadness about relinquishing the therapeutic relationship, but he brought the treatment to an end at a time of his own choosing.

Discussion

The treatment of both adolescent crises and a "situational reaction" in adult life share the cardinal requirement that the therapist enter into the patient's psychic world as a reality figure who furnishes an essential age-appropriate relationship. Although strong transference components may complicate the relationship, as in the last case example I have provided, and the emergence of such components will create obstacles to the accomplishment of the therapeutic task, the treatment process can be guided in the direction of "undoing the developmental catch" (Winnicott, 1965) by nipping transference developments in the bud through reality confrontations (cf. Bibring, 1954). In other words, in treatment designed to master specific developmental vicissitudes, the patient has to be reminded of the irrationality of the slightest transference manifestation, in order to focus the relationship unceasingly on the present and on the realistic aspects of the joint endeavor. This technique stands in marked contrast to that of psychoanalysis, which encourages the flowering of a transference neurosis before attempting to resolve it through interpretation based on its genetic antecedents.

By the same token, the emergence of tranference reactions in the context of psychotherapeutic transactions designed to provide stability through an object relationship appropriate to a previous phase of development (in the instance just cited, the phase of adolescence) raises the possibility that treatment processes might be devised to deal with both developmental arrests and intrapsychic conflicts in the same person, in succession. In other words, it is not only feasible to follow a period of preparatory psychotherapy with one of psychoanalysis proper, but possible to begin with a segment of analytic work, then go on to deal with the consequences of maldevelopment, perhaps to return again to the elucidation of further conflicts, etc.

Such complex treatment plans might be necessitated by the fact that most cases in which development is interrupted do not simply follow from environmental deficits (as in the cases I have described here); more frequently, the arrest is caused by an accumulation of functional handicaps which were in turn produced by much earlier developmental vicissitudes. In such cases, psychoanalysis must be attempted to correct the structuralization of maladaptive patterns (see Winnicott, 1965; Gedo, 1966), even though many of these patients would not be considered analyzable in terms of the criteria appropriate for the classical analytic procedure. Eissler (1953) was the first to suggest the systematic modification of psychoanalytic technique by means of supplementary noninterpretive modalities (which he called "parameters") in order to accommodate such individuals.

The use of therapeutic measures (i.e., those found to be optimal in repairing developmental deficits in psychotherapy) as "parameters" within a psychoanalysis proper was probably discouraged by the conclusions of Anna Freud's (1965) studies of childhood pathology. In her view, "corrective emotional experience is limited by maturational considerations. It has to happen approximately within the same developmental phase in which the damage to the libidinal process has taken place. Once such time limits have been overstepped, it is too late for correction" (p. 231n). Needless to say, on the basis of clinical experiences such as the one described in Case 6, I emphatically disagree with this hypothesis.

I have previously tried to demonstrate that there is no meaningful critical period for corrective experience in the treatment of arrested development (Gedo, 1967). Fortunately, I did not have to rely exclusively on clinical evidence from my own practice, because of the timely publication of an account of the treatment of a young concentration camp victim rescued from Auschwitz at the age of four (Ludowyk-Gyomroi, 1963). This therapy was undertaken about 15 years after the patient's development was interrupted but succeeded in undoing the arrest through methods that did not involve the reliving of a transference neurosis. Ludowyk-Gyomroi had purposefully tried "to adapt the analytic technique to the task of treating a person whose object relations did not proceed beyond the identifications of earliest infancy" (p. 509), and she freely utilized whatever intervention she felt would be helpful in an original manner. The most crucial of the many intuitive maneuvers she attempted conveyed to the patient "the analyst's idea that she [the patient]... was a separate person who had her own experiences, different from those of others" (p. 494). Astonishingly, this bit of education was entirely successful!

Yet amnesia for the first five years of life was never lifted by this treatment process. The patient gradually learned internal guidance, so that imitative behavior and adaptation through efforts to please others were outgrown. (For accounts of similar cases, see Zavitzianos [1967, 1971, 1977].)

Therapeutic outcome in such endeavors seems to depend on the extent and importance of childhood oedipal involvements. If these are minimal (or altogether absent, as in the case reported by Ludowyk-Gyomroi), the emergence of sexual feelings, either within the therapeutic relationship or elsewhere, can be dealt with as an expectable developmental advance without particular difficulty. If the childhood oedipal conflicts played an important role in structuring the personality, however, the resumption of development initiated by treatment will produce transference reactions that cannot be managed within a psychotherapeutic framework but require a complex psychoanalytic procedure involving a hierarchical view of the varied material derived from a number of distinct phases of development (see Gedo and Goldberg, 1973; Gedo, 1979a). These technical requirements place heavy demands on the analyst for skill and tact: it is all too easy to injure the patient's self-esteem by seeming to underestimate his adulthood in the process of accepting the child within him (cf. Ferenczi, 1933). Such requirements are even more demanding in terms of our cognitive capacities, for they involve simultaneous assessment of the meaning of all analytic material in terms of multiple developmental lines.

CHAPTER THREE

In Search of the Borderline: The Current Limits of Psychoanalysis as Therapy

In recent years we have witnessed extension of the field of application of psychoanalysis as a treatment procedure from the narrow area of the symptom neuroses to a vast range of character disturbances. This broadening of scope has led to certain disagreements about the appropriate limits within which analysis is the treatment of choice. To some degree, these differences of opinion stem from differing definitions of what constitutes the treatment technique called psychoanalysis. To date, there is no consensus about how far we can modify the traditional model of psychoanalytic technique, in which the activity of the analyst is confined to interpretation, without crossing the boundary line between analysis and a psychotherapy based on psychoanalytic principles. It is not my intention to deal with this particular controversy here. In order to discuss the practical limits of therapeutic psychoanalysis, however, I must specify that my own definition of the procedure, in agreement with the views of Freud (see E. Freud, 1960, pp. 316–317), is relatively inclusive. I hope that the clinical illustrations I shall provide will clarify my point of view on this score. (For a more detailed exposition, see Gedo [1979a].)

There is another issue relevant to determining the practical limits of psychoanalysis that must be confronted; this concerns the distinction between the two principal criteria of success in psychoanalytic endeavors, those we customarily designate as criteria of process and criteria of outcome, respectively. The former refer to the appropriate unfolding of typical phases in the analytic transaction, including a terminal one initiated by consensus between the participants about the achievement of reasonable therapeutic goals. Outcome criteria refer to the ultimate results of treatment. The latter are extraordinarily difficult to assess, not only because they generally require elaborate follow-up studies scarcely practicable in the social context of psychoanalytic work, but because they are very hard to differentiate from the effects of other influences on the life of the ex-patients. Let me attempt to illustrate these difficulties through a pair of brief case vignettes contrasting a successful treatment oucome with a disastrous one.

Case 7

The patient was a graduate student in the humanities who sought analytic assistance in his early twenties, chiefly because his sexual life consisted exclusively of masochistic masturbatory fantasies in which he was submitting to athletic men. It was only in the course of treatment that he revealed his severe difficulties in applying himself to his work, particularly in organizing and writing his research papers. He showed much greater concern about a series of social and political enthusiasms, mostly of a Christian-Socialist and pacifist nature, extremely idealistic and lacking in pragmatic programs.

We agreed to attempt psychoanalysis; the treatment lasted for over six years on a four-session-per-week schedule. After it came to an end, the patient was working effectively to obtain a degree as a librarian, and his interest had turned to women, with whom he was able to have sexual relations. He was no longer involved in quixotic political causes; he had been supporting himself for a number of years in a variety of jobs, having abandoned the quest for a Ph.D. when he discovered that scholarly pursuits did not really interest him. In summary, he was more realistic, more mature, more goal-directed, and his adaptation seemed reasonably adequate, although he was still limited in his capacity for personal intimacy. All in all, however, the outcome was satisfactory.

Case 8

This case also involved a young graduate student, a woman seeking a degree in social science. She sought help at the student health service after an unsuccessful love affair and was referred for analysis because her hysterical character structure appeared to preclude satisfactory sexual or emotional intimacy. We agreed to undertake this effort on a four-session-per-week basis. Within a few weeks, however, she became helplessly addicted to treatment, and her panic states during routine interruptions of our regular schedule (or whenever I failed to understand the associative material) alerted me to the fact that I had grossly underestimated the severity of her problem. In view of her intense involvement in a transference relationship which continued to yield useful insights, we decided to persevere in the analytic endeavor.

After four years of work, a lengthy vacation interruption precipitated a serious depressive reaction and a suicide attempt that necessitated hospitalization. Although I was able to continue the treatment during this emergency and beyond the patient's discharge from the hospital, these events disrupted the analysis. The patient's father, who had paid for her analysis until then, used these difficulties as a rationalization for withdrawing his support. Imminent loss of the therapeutic relationship made the patient feel suicidal once again, and I was forced to transfer her care to a public facility. When she left that setting, she concluded that she could not realistically resume our work, and she went to live in another city where certain relatives were willing to assist her in making a new start. About six months later, the patient committed suicide after sending me a letter movingly spelling out her reasons for doing so.

In accord with outcome criteria, there can be no question that this second case example illustrates one of the enduring limits of psychoanalysis: if the therapeutic regression entailed in the procedure activates archaic states of helplessness, certain patients (particularly those deprived of a supportive family matrix) will require the provision of a protective milieu. If it is feasible to coordinate this with continuing treatment, there may be a fortunate outcome, but, in accord with process criteria, this will not have been achieved by means of a psychoanalytic process as such. And once we begin to examine cases from that perspective, if we wish to be consistent, we have to use the same process criteria to assess those analyses in which a successful outcome is reached without recourse to auxiliary therapeutic measures. Let me underscore this point by returning to Case 7, and reviewing it from the standpoint of process criteria.

Case 7: A Further Discussion

The analysis in this case succeeded in elucidating a variety of problems related to the entire gamut of early developmental phases. This accumulation of insights produced very little change, however, either in the patient's overt behavior or in his subjective world, except for his dropping out of school and taking a job. The transference repeatedly went through a series of recurring phases, among which the most prominent were the following: much of the time, he experienced me as a depreciated, critical, and narcissistically exploitative paternal figure, one he could torment sadistically by his refusal to succeed, and especially by accentuating his feminine qualities. Periodically, he shifted into an ambivalent attitude, echoing his most important relationship of middle childhood, that with the husband of his beloved oldest sister. Thus he tried to entice me into exhibiting myself intellectually during the sessions, as he had actually seduced his brother-in-law to exhibit his muscles in the past. When he felt successful in enlisting someone in such a transaction, the patient became sexually excited.

Although, superficially, his fantasy concerned admiration of the other man, this attitude barely concealed a sense of triumph about having disgraced someone in this way. He had set out to conquer his brother-in-law when he was an oedipal child in order to reverse the crushing defeat of having lost his sister through her marriage. She had been his principal caretaker for a number of years, at least from the time their mother became severely depressed sometime after his first birthday. The most significant transference configuration seemed to involve repetition of the patient's reaction to this catastrophic event. Needless to say, he defended himself against the contingency of losing maternal figures in a variety of ways, and these defenses were generally successful. They generally failed, however, when he was confronted with the possibility of losing the therapeutic relationship; hence his resistance to progress in the analysis was principally motivated by separation anxiety.

Perhaps the clearest instance of such resistance occurred early in the sixth year of treatment, after the patient began to think of the eventual need to terminate his analysis. The associative material thereupon gradually dried up; he felt comfortable but continued to avoid situations in which he might have been less than adequate. For instance, he would have no dealings with women but fantasied being worshipped by young boys; dreams clearly indicated that he was afraid of heterosexuality because of the possible repetition of the traumatic loss of his sister in childhood. After several months of impasse, I indicated my growing pessimism about the possibility of concluding our work successfully.

Under the impact of the implicit threat that he might face separation because of the *failure* of treatment, the patient began to face his lifelong commitment to chaos, illogic, and immediate gratification as guides to action. We were then able to grasp the fact that throughout the work our dialogue had amounted to a covert debate about *Weltanschauungen* and not to a collaboration based on shared premises. Hence the emergence of overtly grandiose ideation had never been followed, as is usually the case, by renunciation of those illusions about himself. For instance, he could not contemplate having sexual relations because of his previously unconscious belief that he was Christ reborn. At the same time, he clung to equally unrealistic illusions about my alleged perfection, which were associated with his expectation that I would magically transform him into a peerless artistic genius.

All attempts to deal with this material were met with orgies of unreasonableness which finally convinced me that I was powerless to offer the patient anything of value. Although he reacted to my statements to this effect with conscious anxiety concerning his future, there was in fact no shift in his basic attitudes. He did make an effort to persuade me that I was in error, in order to justify continued treatment. When he realized that, unlike his mother, I had no personal need to perpetuate a symbiosis between us, he accused me of malice toward him and angrily demanded reparations. Nonetheless, he instituted urgent measures to prove me wrong by improving his adaptation, and all of the outward changes I described earlier took place during the last three months of our contact. He decided to stop the treatment when his insurance coverage for the year was exhausted because I continued to demonstrate to him that I had been unable to alter his underlying delusional ideas. He left affably, with no evidence of sadness or regret.

It is possible, of course, that my confession of therapeutic impotence may actually have destroyed the patient's illusions; inasmuch as these illusions had probably formed in reaction to his mother's depressive illness and in the context of his symbiotic relationship with her, the fact that I took responsibility for rupturing the symbiotic transference bond between us certainly had a powerful impact on him. Nonetheless, it is unlikely that his acceptance of a more realistic attitude about himself on a conscious level signified the total abandonment of his unconscious belief that he was a god. But even if we did achieve a change in this regard, the desirable result would have been brought about through direct use of my remaining leverage as a symbiotic object, not by means of interpretation and insight. In other words, such a transaction, insofar as it produced adaptive improvements, could not be part of a psychoanalytic process but would constitute its abandonment. In point of fact, I did my utmost to interfere with a nonanalytic resolution of that kind by insisting that the proper criterion for evaluating where we stood was not the patient's day-to-day adaptation but the latent meaning of derivatives from his unconscious. And to the very end of the treatment the dream material continued to betray his unaltered megalomania, although the unconscious meaning of dreams does not constitute decisive evidence on this score.

I trust that I have provided sufficient data to demonstrate that the limits of analyzability must be assessed simultaneously in terms of the completion of the analytic process and in terms of its practical outcome. The latter depends in part on a variety of uncontrollable external factors (such as the decision of a third party to terminate a financial commitment, as in Case 8). Such events defy classification. When adventitious factors play no significant role in determining the therapeutic results, unsatisfactory outcomes will, of course, reflect difficulties that should also be apparent from study of the analytic process. I should like to underscore this point by presenting one final clinical illustration.

Case 9

A talented actor who had tried psychotherapy on several occasions consulted me upon quitting his most recent, ineffectual psychotherapeutic experience. He had started treatment in a state of panic when his wife had thrown him out after she became sexually involved with her prominent attorney. Although he eventually adapted to the situation, he had stayed in treatment because he became obsessed by doubts. He was preoccupied with the pros and cons of cutting his losses by leaving town and starting a new life wherever his professional opportunities might be optimal, or of embarking on a campaign to restore his marriage. He left his previous therapy because he felt he was being pressured in a dogmatic way to accept the psychiatric view of rationality. In line with his lifelong sense of fraudulence, the patient did not feel that either of his alternative programs of action authentically reflected his own wishes.

On the basis of the severity of the characterological problem, I recommended psychoanalysis, to be arranged wherever the patient decided to settle. Probably in order to keep all of his options open, he then chose to remain in town and asked me to undertake responsibility for the analytic attempt. At the same time, he rescued the only child of his marriage, an 11-year-old son, from dangerous neglect by the boy's mother. He proceeded to raise the child with the intrusive overconcern that had characterized his own upbringing by what he called a "typical Jewish mother."

Actually, as we were to learn in the course of the analytic work, the patient's mother was hardly typical by any standard. She lived an isolated life in the setting of a characteristic ghetto, contemptuous both of her working-class husband and the uncouth products of the

American melting pot around them. She considered herself to be a member of the Russian intelligentsia, a claim her son eventually came to see as untenable, although he thought her bright enough to have fit the part. But she was not able to use her abilities to any purpose, for she was lost in the romantic haze of her girlhood in tsarist times. She had a paranoid attitude toward her neighbors' alleged envy of her status and was constantly suspicious regarding her husband's alleged propensity to be unfaithful. Although the patient had no knowledge of any philandering on his father's part, the latter certainly absented himself a great deal, especially after the birth of a second child, the patient's only sibling. This brother was six years younger than the patient but never constituted a serious rival for his mother's preference. As one might expect, he grew up to be much better adjusted than the patient, a sober and prosaic person like their father.

In his childhood, the patient identified completely with his mother's attitudes: he felt that he had maternal responsibilities toward his brother, he viewed his father as a villain, and he experienced the neighborhood children as inferior savages. When he started school, these attitudes provoked considerable retaliation, and he was forced to come to terms with the world of actuality through superficial compliance with social demands. It was the need to pretend that he was different from his mother that launched him on his acting career, initially by gaining acceptance as a clown and a group mascot. This uneasy compromise between the world of his mother and that of others persisted as long as he lived in the parental home. When, in his early twenties, he left to attend a famous drama school in New York, he experienced confusion and panic. He was able to persevere with his training because he obtained adequate psychotherapeutic assistance. In this context, he became involved with a girl for the first time. After some initial difficulties with erectile potency, he felt more or less adequate with this depreciated person. The relationship dragged on for some years, and it was in the context of this relationship that he became preoccupied with his first interminable obsession. He felt he could not marry the girl because such a decision would kill his mother, and he was afraid to end the affair because of his conviction that this alternative would drive his mistress to suicide.[1]

This era of confusion came to an end when the patient met his future wife one summer while he was working in a country playhouse. Although their relationship began because he was able to impersonate a man-of-the-world rescuing a damsel-in-distress, her wish to get married ended his obsessional indecision about his previous affair; it also ended his excessive concern about his mother. His indecisiveness began to manifest itself mostly around issues involving his career, because this was the one area of life about which his iron-willed wife had no strong opinions. She was soon undeceived about his façade of adequacy (even his sexual potency gradual-

[1] Although she was in fact relieved to be rid of him when they finally separated, this woman many years later did commit suicide.

ly disappeared over the years), and she responded to her disappointment with impotent outrage or imperious demands that he change. Until the charismatic man for whom she abandoned the patient came along, however, she was never able to take the initiative to get out of the marriage. Even at the time the analysis started, moreover, she had no interest in divorce; she took the position that she was being forced to meet her own needs as best she could, pending the requisite changes in her husband.

Following his decision to stay in Chicago (which also involved getting a long-term job in television), we persisted in the analytic effort for about six years, with absolutely no result. I shall specify my reasons for deciding that the enterprise was hopeless shortly; here I wish to record only that the patient accepted this judgment without surprise or resentment. He continued to consult me, although with decreasing frequency, for about another year; the therapeutic relationship remained unimpaired, and he finally discontinued his visits only because we were in agreement about their futility. Thus, when we gave up almost eight years after we started, this man was in the very position in which he had presented himself. He still wished to restore his marriage, but his character problems continued to make him unacceptable to his wife. In the meantime, he had been living with another woman whom he held in contempt, and he was afraid to leave this woman lest she commit suicide. The parallel to his situation during his years in drama school is obvious. He considered the treatment to have been a worthwhile investment because it had helped him to raise his son without committing all of the errors his mother had perpetrated with him. The boy had left for college, where he was surviving better than his father could when left to his own devices. The security of the therapeutic relationship had permitted him to persevere with his work better than ever before so that his income had markedly improved. These benefits could no doubt have been achieved through simpler therapeutic measures, however, and the analysis as such must be rated as much ado about nothing.

Let me try to describe this fiasco from the perspective of the analytic process. In the manner typical of obsessional characters, the patient attempted to project one side or another of his ambivalence onto me, and he responded to my efforts to point this out by begging for, or insisting on, direct advice from me. Insofar as I avoided this nonanalytic role, he sought such assistance from his wife, who never hesitated to intervene. If she was unavailable, the patient overcame his sense of helplessness through frantic skirt-chasing, an activity for which his professional training gave him excellent preparation. It is of some interest that, in the context of a sadistic perversion, he seldom experienced any problem with his potency. But most of the analytic material was focused on his longing to restore the relationship to a grossly idealized version of his wife as well as his continuous effort to disavow the fact that she was either paranoid and overtly grandiose or severely depressed. Without the fantasy of fusion with an omniscient woman, the patient felt overwhelmed, almost literally unable to organize his own behavior. My efforts to correlate these dynamics with their presumable antecedents in the childhood past with his mother regularly met with contemptuous dismissal. In fact, none of my pronouncements sounded sufficiently dogmatic or sufficiently insistent to merit serious attention in his scheme of things. He was able to grasp the fact that he wished for a magical cure and that he could not endure the humiliation of facing his actual limitations. Indeed, it was his refusal to acknowledge these limitations that exasperated his wife to the point of leaving him.

During the second year of treatment, the summer vacation period brought this tenuous equilibrium to a crisis point, largely because his wife and I were away at the same time. By the time we resumed work, his panicky sense of needing my assistance was covered over with mistrust and arrogance. Abetted by the taunts of his wife to the effect that he sought treatment in order to indulge his infantile propensities, he then refused to lie on my couch or to attempt to free-associate. For all intents and purposes, the analysis had failed, although, of course, I did not realize this at the time. I tried to deal with the resistance in terms of the blatant homosexual anxieties it circumvented, and the correctness of this view was confirmed by subsequent events. To be precise, the patient began an intense search for an ongoing relationship with a woman, while he secretly maintained the symbiosis with his wife. The fact that the mistress-to-be was supposed to replace me as a secondary resource when this symbiosis was disrupted was apparent from his choices: he initially tried a number of mental health professionals, and when he found them relatively intolerant of his peculiarities, he turned to a European scholar of an upper-class background of the kind he attributed to me. He was able to manipulate this psychologically naïve girl most of the time, and eventually she agreed to keep house for him. In sexual relations, he treated her as an animate tool (which was acceptable to her because she was entirely indifferent to sexuality), and he was potent and experienced unprecedented pleasure from the sexual act. After some years, she became dissatisfied with her depreciated status and left him for awhile. He reacted with an agitated depression of alarming intensity, losing over 40 pounds within a few weeks. This syndrome disappeared abruptly as soon as he succeeded in ensnaring her once again. I infer that his reaction to my lengthy vacation during the second year of our work had been very similar.

In spite of my consistent efforts to interpret the function of these formidable resistances, the patient was never willing to pay heed to my judgment that his wide-ranging disregard of the requirements of the analytic work would defeat our enterprise. What was even stranger, neither my concerns nor the evident stalemate we had reached discouraged him in the least from persevering with the treatment; he made it perfectly clear that he would regard any move to stop on my part as an outrageous abandonment. In effect, he demanded a cure and insisted that I provide one by complying with *his* procedures instead of using those of Freud. I focused increasingly on this issue, but I was unable to make him take me seriously for a very long time.

The impasse was finally broken by a shift in the relationship with his wife. The latter became disillusioned with her lover and, in desperation, offered to resume the marriage. The prospect of unremitting exposure to her arbitrary tyranny now filled the patient with dismay and impaired his illusion about her perfection. In this context, he became motivated to investigate the analytic stalemate. His negativism could now be understood as a characterological attribute, an automatic reaction to the danger of losing his sense of autonomy through his propensity for symbiotic fusion. This set of automatized behaviors had always had its ideational counterpart in a conviction, hitherto unconscious, that he was the only person in the world who knew the basic truth, i.e., that he alone understood the impossibility of attaining reliable knowledge. He had been enacting this nihilistic delusion in his contemptuous disregard of the analytic necessities; in challenging me to cure him magically, he was demanding *proof* of my superior knowledge and power.

Faced with this information, I told the patient that I had no hope of influencing him through my therapeutic tools, and our "collaboration" petered out, as I have already described. In this instance, in contrast to my first clinical example in this chapter, the patient did not even bother to disclaim his delusional convictions. There were no outward shifts in his adaptation—he managed to perpetuate his status quo by stringing along his wife and his mistress through a series of false promises and outright lies. Moreover, as far as I could judge, the patient was not disappointed by my admission of failure.

Within the confines of a brief report, it is difficult to substantiate the adequacy of my efforts to allow this patient to overcome his grandiose ideation. It is possible, of course, that the poor result may have reflected a countertransference problem on my part. In terms of the actual procedure, however, the treatment was carried out in exactly the same manner as in those cases in which the uncovering of grandiose ideation is followed by its therapeutic resolution. As I have tried to demonstrate elsewhere (Gedo, 1977a, 1979a), it is often sufficient to make these archaic attitudes conscious to bring about their elimination; in other instances, it may be necessary to offer a reconstruction of the childhood circumstances in which they arose, including the specific reasons for the adoption of the grandiosity, before it can be relinquished. These measures did not suffice in Cases 7 and 9 which I have summarized in this chapter. I should add that these cases represent the only instances I have encountered in two decades of analytic practice in which formerly *unconscious* attitudes turned out to be unalterable by the voice of reason after being brought forth from repression.

Discussion

I believe the clinical material presented in this chapter highlights two of the current limits of analyzability: first, the emergence of actual states of helplessness in the course of treatment; second, the continuing influence of unalterable but disavowed delusional convictions. I do not believe, of course, that my own clinical experience is sufficiently extensive to rule out additional factors, but it is significant that in the treatment of about 50 individuals by means of the analytic method over the past 20 years I have encountered only the two limits mentioned. I realize that the claim about the broad range of usefulness of psychoanalysis as a therapy implicit in this statement may sound excessive. Perhaps it will not provoke disbelief, however, if I reiterate my conviction (see Gedo and Goldberg, 1973; Gedo, 1979a) that the standard technique of psychoanalysis must be systematically altered in planned ways if the procedure is to be applied to conditions other than the neuroses in the strict sense of that term. What I wish to emphasize here, however, is our incapacity to devise effective analytic methods to deal with the contingencies described in the clinical material presented in this chapter.

In order to avoid potential misunderstandings, I should also clarify my terminological choices with regard to nosology. It should be apparent that our traditional categories have little or no relevance to the issues I am considering here. More specifically, I share Meissner's (1978) doubts regarding the usefulness of the concept of "borderline states." The archaic transferences and other primitive psychic phenomena allegedly characteristic for this group of patients (see Kernberg, 1975) are exceedingly diverse. At any rate, with regard to nosological schemata, the decisive question is the pragmatic one: Do they help us to make meaningful distinctions about the possibilities for treatment and respective prognoses? In my experience, our existing diagnostic categories are not serviceable in this regard: individuals who fit the "borderline" category often turn out to be analyzable (for one illustration, see Chapter 6) and, as Cases 7 and 9 in this chapter may show, others who might be diagnosed as "neurotic personalities" sometimes turn out to be beyond the therapeutic reach of psychoanalysis. Under the circumstances, our only secure borderline is that of analyzability itself. (For a review of the major literature on "borderline states," see E. Shapiro [1978].)

What, then, are the implications of this kind of boundary demarcating our therapeutic capabilities? For one thing, it cannot, as I have already observed, be correlated with traditional psychiatric syndromes. In no sense of the term were any of the patients I have described "psychotic"; specifically, they suffered from no defect in reality testing. Although some of their behavior was determined by primitive attitudes, their own considered judgments about these "ego-alien" mental contents were essentially rational. The two patients in Cases 7 and 9 discovered their grandiose ideation only as a result of the analytic work, and the same was true about the other patient's helplessness. Yet the rational, conscious surface had amounted to a "false self" in Winnicott's (1954) sense, and the true, basic core turned out to be unalterable through verbal treatment methods.

Moreover, the pathology in these cases did not conform to the archaic syndromes described by Kernberg (1975) or Kohut (1971), although it had certain features in common with both. If we agree on my definition of psychoanalysis as a treatment procedure, however, Kernberg's "borderline conditions" and Kohut's "narcissistic personality disturbances" are analyzable disorders, unlike the cases I have described here. From the fact that *these* analytic failures occurred in instances that our nosology cannot accommodate, we can infer that the therapeutic limits of psychological intervention actually coincide with the boundaries of the individual's capacity to acquire new knowledge. The specific grandiose fantasies uncovered in the cases that were ultimately found to be unanalyzable differed from those encountered in many others in failing to yield to rational reconsideration. They proved to be unmodifiable precisely because they involved the inability to acquire valid knowledge: convictions such as one patient's assumption of divine wisdom or another's epistemological nihilism. And the helplessness to which the other patient regressed also prevented the assimilation of new information because it involved (temporary) loss of the capacity to use verbal symbols. Had it been possible to weather these episodes without disruption of the therapeutic relationship, the prospect of resuming effective analytic work with this person would by no means have been hopeless.[2]

[2] Perhaps it may be pertinent to add the reminder here that erroneous beliefs constitute delusions only if they cannot be corrected, i.e., when such beliefs are accompanied by some thought disorder or some supraordinate idea about the individual's infallibility.

My conclusion that the practical limits of analyzability are determined by the patient's capacity to process the information he might receive from the analyst is congruent with the commonly held clinical impression, hitherto unexplained, that the prognosis of analytic treatment cannot be predicted on the basis of the overall severity of the presenting psychopathology. Many patients who seem maximally impaired, disorganized, or desperate are able to use the procedure successfully—even those with grandiose illusions about themselves, if these illusions do not concern the acquisition of knowledge. Conversely, the assimilation of new information is prevented either by the regressive loss of the capacity to process the meaning of human messages or by impairment of the function of correcting erroneous beliefs.

SECTION II

CRITIQUE OF SELF PSYCHOLOGY

In retrospect, the four decades of analytic evolution since the death of Freud can be divided into two periods of about equal duration: the era of ego psychology, dominated by the work of Heinz Hartmann, and a more recent period of theoretical speculation, clinical experimentation, and lack of consensus. In my judgment (Gedo, 1975b), the most significant factor in creating this ferment has been the work of Heinz Kohut (1971, 1977, 1978; Goldberg, 1978). Kohut's contributions have also generated a movement within the psychoanalytic community often referred to as "self psychology."

Whatever the ultimate verdict of scientific opinion may turn out to be about the specific details of Kohut's proposals, there can be no question about the importance of the issues to which he has addressed himself. Nor do I doubt that through this courageous effort Kohut has, more than anyone else, helped to open hitherto neglected avenues for the expansion of psychoanalytic psychology. The magnitude of his contributions has been recognized not only by those who have accepted much of his viewpoint, but also by others, including myself, who do not concur with most of the answers he has provided for the crucial questions he has raised.

I attribute greater significance to Kohut's work than to the contributions of numerous other recent psychoanalytic innovators (such as the British theorists of object relations, to mention only the most influential) because, at its core, Kohut's work presents a valid empirical discovery, testable by any practitioner of psychoanalysis:

the realization that certain weighty disturbances of mental functioning have no direct connection to the intrapsychic conflicts of the oedipal period but can nonetheless be successfully treated by the classical psychoanalytic method. The psychological problems in question seem to occur with particular frequency in individuals whose character is suffused with narcissistic features; hence Kohut (1968, 1971) assumed that he had defined a syndrome of "narcissistic personality disturbance," a nosological entity he attempted to differentiate from neurotic disturbances proper (which he continued to attribute to faulty resolution of the Oedipus complex) on the one hand, and covertly psychotic disorders (often called "borderline conditions") on the other.

Given the bitter controversies subsequently generated by Kohut's proposals, it is ironic that their author initially presented them in impeccably conservative guise, as a small—if pivotal—modification of the libido theory (Kohut, 1966). He hypothesized independent lines of development for narcissism and object love (i.e., love for oneself and for others), in disagreement with Freud's assumption that, originally, libido is entirely narcissistic and is only transformed into love for others through later maturation. Kohut postulated that subject-centered grandiosity and illusory idealization of the caretakers are normal way stations along the line of development of narcissism; he assumed that optimal maturation of this libidinal component eventuates in its transformation into the attributes of creativity, wisdom, humor, and empathy. By means of this theoretical schema, Kohut attempted to fit his novel observations into the existing

Freudian paradigm (as modified by Hartmann [1939, 1964]). I suspect, however, that by 1968 he was already aware that his data, if valid, transcended that paradigm. In the years preceding the publication of *The Analysis of the Self* (1971), he often spoke about his disinclination to disrupt the psychoanalytic community by depriving it too abruptly of its traditional conceptual framework. Consequently, that seminal book still presented its revolutionary message under a camouflage of familiar terminology.

The crux of Kohut's clinical contribution has been the description of a series of archaic transference constellations which he believed to be characteristic of "narcissistic personality disturbances." These constellations were all variants of the early forms of narcissism postulated in his developmental schema. Or, more accurately, his theory of development was a direct outgrowth of the assumption that the various archaic transferences—many of which had already been noted by previous observers—were interrelated in the sense of constituting repetitions in the analytic situation of the early childhood vicissitudes of narcissistic development. Another implication of Kohut's theory was equally important: because these developmental narcissistic issues were presumed to be unconnected to the fate of object love, the occurrence of these archaic transferences could no longer be explained (as had previously been the case) on the basis of anxiety-driven regression from oedipal conflicts. In other words, narcissistic fixations were given vastly greater weight in pathogenesis than they had been accorded in classical theory.

Kohut subdivided the narcissistic transferences he had observed into those characterized principally by subject-centered grandiosity (he called these the "mirror transferences" because of the patients' insistence on receiving external confirmation of their worth) and those centered on idealization of caretakers. The implications of the emergence of such reactions in the analytic situation and their optimal therapeutic management will be discussed in detail in Chapter 4. Here it should be noted that, in Kohut's view, establishment of these more or less stable narcissistic transferences implied the development of an intense object relationship with the analyst—one that did not consist of loving a separate being, but implied a relationship in which the other was subjectively experienced as part of the patient himself. Kohut asserted (1968, 1971) that accurate interpretation of the vicissitudes of these archaic bonds in the transference permits insight and gradual mastery of fixations at these primitive levels of object relations.

Whatever the merits of these formulations, they encouraged a growing body of analysts to follow Kohut in experimenting with the analytic method in ever-broader fields. Patients with problems of delinquency, addiction, or perversion, as well as characterological difficulties including depressive, masochistic, and paranoid features, were added to the roster of potentially analyzable individuals. The results of such work have been reported in a casebook prepared with Kohut's collaboration (Goldberg, 1978) and are subjected to detailed scrutiny in Chapter 5. However daring these innovative proposals of Kohut's were, his work of the 1960s, capped by his Brill Lecture (1972), in which he formulated a theory of aggression as the organismic response to narcissistic injuries, received a generally favorable reception as the vanguard manifestation of the progressive mainstream of American psychoanalysis.

When, in 1973, I had occasion to assess the impact of Kohut's work on the contemporary psychoanalytic scene, I predicted that "Kohut's contribution is likely to have even more profound effects on psychoanalysis as a scientific discipline than it has had on clinical practice [although he] has largely refrained from spelling out the improvements in psychoanalytic psychology made possible by his new clinical findings" (Gedo, 1975b, p. 319). By this, I expressed my belief that Kohut had demonstrated that our existing clinical theories did not have the universality we had formerly attributed to them but rather described special cases that should be fitted into a new, larger schema. In collaboration with another student of Heinz Kohut, Arnold Goldberg, I undertook to develop a hierarchical model that would provide such a schema (Gedo and Goldberg, 1973).

The fundamental disagreement between Kohut's more recent views and my own standpoint emanates from the foregoing assessment of the relation between Kohut's discoveries and the preexisting clinical theories of psychoanalysis. He has become progressively bolder in claiming that his hypotheses constitute a new paradigm for psychoanalysis (Kohut, 1977), and the christening of that paradigm as "self psychology" has marked the inception of the disruption of the psychoanalytic community that Kohut feared a decade earlier. To date, Kohut has stopped short of dismissing Freud's psychology of intrapsychic conflicts altogether, although he has made it clear that he would prefer to reformulate its findings in accord with the concepts of self psychology. Nevertheless, his writings of the 1970s continue to differentiate the problems described by Freud (which Kohut has begun to term the conflicts of Guilty Man) from those he claims to have discovered (and which he designates the dilemmas of Tragic Man). Thus Kohut has been consistent in his views about nosology: he has continued to distinguish three groupings of psychopathology of progressively diminishing severity—problems of guilt, of tragedy, and of incomplete self-formation. My theoretical objections to this approach and its actual clinical limitations form the subject matter of Chapter 7.

In Section III, I shall try to demonstrate how Kohut, in his late work, has effectively repudiated his previous adherence to Freud's libido theory and, despite the continued references to "self" in his discourse, has proposed an entirely new theoretical framework that must properly be classified as an object relations theory. Certain metapsychological limitations of his theory construction will be discussed in Chapter 8. What should be stressed here is Kohut's continuing conservatism at the metapsychological level—in contrast to such theoreticians as George Klein (1976) or Schafer (1976), and, of those more receptive to clinical innovations, Basch (1976) or myself (Gedo, 1979a).

Kohut's more recent system focuses on the formation and subsequent predominant influence of a mental structure (the "self") that represents a stable configuration of nuclear ambitions and ideals brought into being as a consequence of the transactions between the infant and its primary caretaker (the "selfobject" who is still subjectively experienced as part of the child). The cohesiveness or stability of the "self" differentiates analyzable syndromes from covert psychoses; in the "narcissistic" disturbances (those of Tragic Man), this stability is not absolute and experiences of "fragmentation" will occur in stressful circumstances. Unfortunately, Kohut has never spelled out the specific relationship between the structured, subjective goals and values that he sees as the constituents of the self and the narcissistic transferences that actually form the subject matter of his "self psychology."

In Kohut's view, the denominator common to the stresses that impair self-cohesion is the absence of an empathic milieu. This emphasis on the importance of empathy is the most enduring theme throughout his writings. As early as 1959, he focused on empathy as one of the characteristic observational tools of the psychoanalyst; we have observed that, in his papers on narcissism, he conceived of the capacity for empathy as one of the fruits of optimal maturation in the narcissistic realm. I have the impression that empathy, as the essential ingredient of both successful mothering and effective psychotherapy, has become ever more important as an element in Kohut's thinking. In Chapter 6, I shall take up the controversial aspects of that point of view, especially the implicit notion that the capacity to detect the inner psychological states of others through identificatory processes has curative powers in itself.

Kohut (1975a, 1975b) has conducted a campaign to combat the "tool-and-method pride" that, in his opinion, has ritualized psychoanalytic technique. He has even called into question the primacy of insight as the active principle that accounts for the therapeutic action of psychoanalysis. Combined with his advocacy of the analysand's entitlement to unceasing empathy, the contraction of the cognitive factor in Kohut's theory of technique threatens to push "self psychology" into a realm of psychological intervention that is beyond the boundaries acceptable to most psychoanalysts. We can only hope that the tendency in some quarters to confuse the capacity to grasp the analysand's emotional states and/or motivations with some type of nonspecific, benign concern will not gain general acceptance.

But I wish to close these introductory remarks on self psychology on a more positive note. The critique that follows may give the impression that I deplore Kohut's overall influence on the current course of psychoanalysis. I should reiterate that the contrary is in fact the case —I regard his paradigm as one of the vital catalysts that have reinvigorated our intellectual life at the close of the first century of analytic history.

CHAPTER FOUR

The Psychoanalytic Management of Archaic Transferences

In the opening section of this volume, the possibilities of expanding the scope of psychoanalysis in various directions (and the limits of those possibilities) were discussed without considering the nature of the psychopathology for which prospective patients might seek assistance. In actual practice, perhaps the main area in which real expansion has taken place has been that of the systematic therapeutic handling of personality disturbances that have their genesis prior to the establishment of an infantile neurosis in the oedipal phase of development (cf. Kohut, 1971; Kernberg, 1975; Settlage, 1977; Gedo, 1979a; see also Chapter 5 in this volume). In spite of general agreement among these authors about the capacity of such patients to experience intense, archaic object relations within the analytic transference —experiences that presumably involve the repetition of

---

Portions of this chapter were previously published in the *Journal of the American Psychoanalytic Association*, 23(1975):485–505 and 25(1977):787–803, and are reprinted here by permission.

crucial infantile transactions with the original caretakers, albeit in forms distorted by later developmental vicissitudes—these syndromes have continued to be referred to, in Freud's terminology of 1914, as "narcissistic." It seems clear, however, that in current usage the latter word has lost its original meaning, that of turning sexual cathexis away from others and onto oneself, without the development of a consensus about what it refers to in phrases such as "narcissistic personality disturbance."

Although an exhaustive survey of the various points of view on this matter would take us too far afield, (but see Moore, 1975; Stolorow, 1975; Panel, 1973), any fresh look at the psychoanalytic treatment of archaic modes of personality organization should begin by considering at least the most influential proposals about it, as embodied in the contrasting positions of Kernberg (1975) and Kohut (1966, 1971; Kohut and Wolf, 1978). Ostensibly, both Kernberg and Kohut employ the concept of narcissism within the framework of the libido theory, but their writings reveal wide divergences in their approach to Freud's metapsychology. Kernberg apparently looks upon many profound character disorders as the consequences of "pathological narcissism." Although he is not entirely explicit about what he means by this term, in the overall context of his work it appears to signify some disorder of drive organization, particularly in the realm of constitutional aggressiveness, which, in turn, interferes with early object relations. In other words, Kernberg seems to adhere to a concretistic conception of narcissism that belongs in the realm of "id psychology" or perhaps even that of somatopsychic processes.

By contrast, Kohut insists that narcissism, which he defines rather loosely as a combination of self-love and self-hate, is a universal developmental line; in Kohut's theory, pathological derivatives from its infantile vicissitudes are therefore seen as focal arrests in development and/or regressions. From a clinical point of view, Kohut regards "narcissistic personality disturbances" as consequences of environmental failures that have traumatically interrupted the normal developmental progression. Until 1972, this progression was defined as the maturation of narcissism from subject-centered grandiosity, through the idealization of parental imagoes, to "transformations of narcissism" into creativity, wisdom, and humor. Like Kernberg's conception, Kohut's initial hypothesis implied that narcissism is a discrete pathogenic force, but one that may mature more or less successfully, depending on the quality of early object relations.

One reason for the confusion created by Kohut's work is that he has alternated between his original conception of narcissism as a variety of libido and another hypothesis, quite inconsistent with the first. According to this second view, predominant in Kohut's writings since 1972, the term "narcissism" is to be understood metaphorically, and the pathology of "narcissistic" disturbances is to be conceptualized in terms of a "psychology of the self." At the same time, Kohut was slow to define what he meant by the term "self." In his earlier writings (cf. Kohut, 1970), he used the word to designate the mental representation of one's own person. More recently (1977), he has alluded to a "broader" definition of self as a bipolar structure involving ambitions and ideals, as these are mediated by the individual's skills (see also Kohut and Wolf, 1978). The implications of this definition for an understanding of narcissism remain obscure, however.

I have summarized my understanding of these disparate conceptions of narcissism in order to show that, once we have abandoned Freud's definition of 1914, idiosyncratic uses of the term will only lead us into a Babel of confusion. With regard to the treatment of archaic personality configurations, we should avoid talking past each other by labeling them with words that have lost any precise connotation; instead of dealing with a wastebasket of "narcissistic disorders," we would do better to begin by studying specific vicissitudes of the transferences encountered in analyzing these patients. Only in that manner can we avoid constructing fictive nosological entities, i.e., referring to a variety of configurations by a single name.

If there is agreement about anything concerning archaic character types, it is about the frequency of a transference constellation in which we face insistent demands for affirmation of the patient's exceptional worth, for delighted acceptance of his exhibitionism, and for self-abnegating renunciation of any acknowledgment of the patient's actual dependence on the analyst. The triad of vanity, exhibitionism, and arrogant ingratitude is probably characteristic of the states Kernberg calls "pathological narcissism"; in popular usage, of course, this is precisely what the word "narcissism" has come to mean. According to Settlage (1977), this set of attitudes is the expectable reaction of a child after the "rapprochement crisis" of the middle of the second year of life if the caretaker is unable to deal empathically with the toddler's initial confrontation with his relative helplessness and dependency. By contrast, Kohut (1971) asserts that these manifestations of subject-centered grandiosity are universal and phase-appropriate, presumably for the latter half of the second year of life (see M. Tolpin, 1971). In other words, Kohut views the "grandiose self" as a phase of healthy self-assertion rather than as a pathological response to trauma. On the contrary, he claims that regressive retreats to more primitive states of withdrawn megalomania are brought about by unempathic responses to these natural reflections of the child's (or analysand's) desirable expansiveness.

Because of the nature of the demands made upon the analyst in this type of transference, i.e., in view of the implicit lack of mutuality and the clamor for continuous reflection of the patient's value, Kohut (1968, 1971) has given it the general designation "mirror transference." This ambiguous term has sometimes been misconstrued, as if it implied that the analysand, rather than the theoretician, conceives of the analyst as a mirror. The term has other disadvantages: by portraying the analyst as an inanimate object, it underplays the essential role of his judgment and perceptiveness in the process of reflecting the "facts" of the analysand's performance; by stressing the visual pathway of perception, it may lead the unwary to overlook exhibitionistic demands enacted within the analytic setting through the medium of other sensory channels. Although such considerations have long been familiar, it may be useful to give one illustration of the subtle ways in which exhibitionistic wishes may be acted out entirely beyond the realm of the visual sphere.

Case 10

A sophisticated, middle-aged social worker, long familiar with the procedures of psychoanalysis and with their rationale, sought assistance because of chronically low self-esteem, unresolved by previous analytic work. As the transference unfolded, she settled into an attitude of unremitting hostility, echoing her childhood competitiveness with her father. Far from seeming to look for acknowledgment or approval in the analysis, she lost no opportunity to demonstrate her contempt for my opinions. Although this was in part a defensive attitude (one already manifest during the oedipal period), her actual behavior was by no stretch of the imagination "exhibitionistic."

It took many years of persistent and systematic effort to discover a completely different aspect of the transference, one that was covertly repeating facets of the childhood relationship to the mother. We discovered this by investigating her difficulties in adhering to the basic rule, which she depreciated as analogous to her father's senseless compulsive systems. Among her numerous violations of the letter or spirit of our agreement about procedure, she insisted on making anxious efforts to organize the material of her sessions in advance. The meaning of *her* compulsive system was finally revealed through a dream in which her beloved lady piano teacher compelled her to play by sight-reading. Her associations concerned a chronic inhibition about such spontaneous performances, based on tremendous stage fright in the context of wishing to dazzle a maternal figure.

This insight led to the recovery of deeply embarrassing memories of early childhood experiences in which, whenever she had performed poorly, her mother had reassured her by asserting that she was better than anyone else because she was born a princess. In a paradoxical way, then, her poor performance as an analytic patient had been an exhibitionistic assertion of her superiority; princesses are exempt from the judgments of their servants.

The foregoing example illustrates not only the multiplicity of perceptual channels involved in the enactment of a grandiose fantasy within the analytic situation; it also demonstrates that, in such circumstances, the analyst is not used to convey factual data but to exercise human judgments. Hence the mirror alluded to in the term "mirror transference" can only be the magical one of fairy tales which bears accurate witness to the purport of all behaviors presented to it. Problems in the management of these archaic modes of relatedness result from the inability of many patients to tolerate the unfavorable verdicts of an impartial witness, in large measure as a consequence of the fact that their childhood caretakers bore false witness to their behavior, as my case example illustrates.

In effect, no consensus has yet been reached about the appropriate analytic response to the transference manifestations of a grandiose self—even in the casebook devoted to explicating Kohut's recommendations (Goldberg, 1978), differences among various contributors appear in this regard (see this volume, Chapter 5). There is general agreement, of course, about the necessity of responding to these infantile claims with maximal tact and empathy; any failure in this regard is inevitably followed by humiliation and outrage. To put this in allegorical terms, when patients are offended, they respond with the destructiveness of the Wicked Queen when her magic mirror confronts her with the unpalatable truth. The difficulty of managing these transferences without provoking such complications must never be underestimated, if for no other reason than because individuals afflicted with such archaic fixations almost always have a need to re-create the atmosphere of the circumstances that traumatized them in the first place. The following example is offered as an illustration of this dilemma.

Case 11

A young professional man entered analysis because

of dissatisfaction with his performance in every area of living. It gradually became apparent, however, that he was not interested in learning how he might do better; unconsciously, he expected magical assistance to change the response of the environment to his objectively inadequate performances. Only in the seventh year of a long analysis did we gain insight into the meaning of this seemingly senseless behavior: the patient, convinced since middle childhood that his destiny would transform him into a prophet, was ceaselessly monitoring his experience for signs of this development. Any effort on his part would have obscured the advent of the divine miracle he had been awaiting for decades. The repetitive enactment of would-be miracles within the analytic setting prior to this discovery had put severe strains on my capacity to accommodate the patient's requirements.

Perhaps the most obvious—and in retrospect perhaps the most tragicomic—example was my response to the patient's fantasy that he could turn into a serious operatic singer. Needless to say, he had never had any musical training and had no intention of acquiring any. From time to time, he attempted to test out whether his transformation into a star performer had been accomplished by singing an aria from the couch. In view of the fact that he could not carry a tune, the effect was bizarre and exceedingly unpleasant; but the aspect of these enactments that I found most difficult to bear was the patient's demand that I confirm his excellence. It was not possible to avoid being pulled into this delusional system through silence; any failure to respond positively was correctly understood by this sensitive man as radical disagreement with his hopes.

To put this in a different way, the patient did not, in fact, suffer from a failure in reality testing; he was merely utterly unable to evaluate his own performance. It should be kept in mind that his expectation of a miraculous transformation was unconscious. The confrontation with my dysphoric reception of his songs that we could not avoid filled him with disappointment and anger— which he tended to act out by prolonging his dreadful exhibitions indefinitely, unless I stopped him by actually protesting my unwillingness to tolerate such acts of aggression. It was scarcely a surprise to learn that his older siblings had nicknamed the patient "the aggression baby" when he was still quite young. But that was hardly the central aspect of our reconstruction of the relevant childhood ambience. What the patient had been ceaselessly recreating was an atmosphere in which he had been contemptuously neglected by his parents, perhaps because he had been the last in a long line of unwanted children. However, before this insight could be communicated to the patient in a manner that forestalled his provocations, we had to go through many months of agonizing tension. Nonetheless, accurate interpretation eventually succeeded in resolving the archaic transference and led to a satisfactory analytic termination.

Although a clinical problem of this kind puts an uncomfortable emotional burden on the analyst, the example given above actually constitutes a relatively simple variant of the emergence of archaic claims in the analytic setting. As Kohut (1971) has correctly stated, the grandiose infantile ambitions in question very often have been warded off by means of various defensive measures and cannot be brought into the open without long, systematic analysis of the resistances. In spite of this fact, one frequently encounters much overt arrogance, vanity, and selfishness on the part of such individuals from the very start of their treatment. The coexistence of such surface characteristics of "narcissism" and deeply repressed archaic grandiosity is attributed by Kohut to a "split" in the personality.

I would prefer to say that these patients alternately disavow the significance of one side or the other of their experience: their attitude of open self-aggrandizement is based on a refusal to acknowledge the presence of severe difficulties associated with archaic constellations which often include grandiosity; when the latter supervene, on the other hand, there is a similar defense against seeing the significance of the surface characterological attributes. A great variety of symptoms may come to the fore when the "narcissistic" surface collapses, generally under the impact of the disruption of some covert symbiosis upon which it was contingent. The difficulties that emerge are, in turn, derivatives of the repressed infantile self-organization. Although these considerations add a degree of complexity to the task of elucidating the course of any particular analytic experience, they do not, in fact, substantially alter the principles governing the therapeutic encounter. Nonetheless, it may be useful to illustrate the problems involved in treating such patients by means of a highly abbreviated case history.

Case 9: Another Look[1]

A man in his mid-forties sought treatment because he was unable to reconcile himself to the failure of his marriage. He had provoked his wife in various ways for many years; she could not get rid of him, however, until she found another man, whereupon she insisted that the patient leave. For reasons of her own, she did not seek a divorce, and the patient became obsessively preoccupied with the question of whether he ought to attempt to win her back. In spite of his panicky uncertainty about this and his continual pleas for immediate guidance, his behavior in general continued to be characterized by chilly hauteur, contempt for everyone (with the exception of his wife), and unscrupulous exploitativeness.

As the analysis went on, the patient realized that his relationship to his wife, whom he regarded as the source of all wisdom, was essentially unaltered by her affair, because she was no more ready to abandon their symbiosis than he was. He settled into an equilibrium consisting of the disavowal of the need for treatment, except for short periods of panic which supervened when he felt cut off by his wife. With persistent effort, it became possible to demonstrate that the patient's obnoxious characteristics echoed those of his messianic spouse. Prior to his marriage, he had been chronically anxious and confused, al-

[1] This is the same patient discussed in Chapter 3.

though there were hints that during the early school years he had adopted his mother's attitudes of superiority toward neighbors.

I shall not repeat the account of this analysis here; suffice it to say that the treatment process was exceedingly difficult. After a number of years, it became possible to focus on those aspects of the personality which were subjectively suffused with feelings of helplessness. In these circumstances, the patient was able spontaneously to articulate his fantasies of personal omniscience, such as his conviction that he alone understood the impossibility of attaining any knowledge. He also revealed fantasies of magical power, e.g., his belief that he could indefinitely violate all of the ground rules of psychoanalysis and still profit from the procedure.

Whether the demands of the archaic self emerge in the transference directly or only after systematic analysis of the defenses that have warded them off, the technical problems posed by them are basically identical. To put the issue in terms of the metaphor of the mirror in the story of Snow White, the analyst must make some judgment about who is fairest of them all. As my case of the aspiring "opera" singer demonstrates, the issue often cannot be avoided, either through silence or by means of efforts to look into the reasons behind the needs for affirmation. In these regressed states, patients will often accept no substitutes for gratification; moreover, their need to repeat the childhood traumatization through reenactment may also impel them to insist on straight answers. Consequently, the analyst's conviction about the appropriate emotional response to such infantile expectations will prove to be decisive for the further course of treatment. Each of the principal participants in the debate about appropriate technique in the analysis of personalities who develop archaic transferences has taken a different position on the matter, at least implicitly. Perhaps the only point on which there might be consensus is that analytic technique requires us to state only the truth —it is not permissible consciously to enter a folie-à-deux with a patient falsely convinced of his excellence.[2]

My reading of the implications of the alternative hypotheses offered to explain the significance of grandiose fantasies in early develoment is as follows. I assume that Kernberg's view, which looks upon infantile grandiosity as ipso facto pathological, suggests an interpretive approach that focuses on the defensive aspect of "narcissism," with special reference to its function in warding off infantile aggression, e.g., by forestalling the occasion

[2] It is very strange, under the circumstances, that there is no consensus about the application of this unquestioned principle in different circumstances: many analysts would hesitate to offer confirmation when a patient asserted something favorable about himself that the analyst considered accurate. This reluctance has been rationalized on the ground that such statements might covertly gratify one or another unconscious wish, e.g., some derivative of the Oedipus complex. It is very likely, in fact, that most patients would squeeze such a meaning out of the situation—if they have the need, they will squeeze blood from a turnip—but the elaboration of *that* fantasy is merely grist for the analytic mill, not an undesirable complication. And refusal to acknowledge the truth if it is favorable for the patient will usually create serious difficulties; such acts of omission *actually* depreciate the analysand. One wonders what purpose is served by elaborately avoiding truths about the skills, wisdom, or beauty of people who are manifestly competent, wise, or beautiful.

to envy those who are more fortunate. Adherents of Mahler's developmental theories would also assume that the emergence of grandiosity in the transference serves defensive aims, but their hypothesis stresses that subjective experiences of helplessness and mortification have preceded and necessitated this defense. The logic of Kohut's viewpoint, on the other hand, dictates interpretation of the infantile ambitions embedded in the grandiosity as expectable attitudes in early childhood, now reawakened by the analytic process. In this system, mortification (either in childhood or in the course of analysis) is seen as the result of unempathic responses to the child's (or patient's) healthy expansiveness.

The three approaches I have outlined are not necessarily mutually exclusive if they are put forward as clinical theories that do not claim universal applicability. In a particular clinical instance, however, only one of the three approaches can be valid. In our present state of uncertainty about the actualities of psychological development in the first two or three years of life, our conduct of psychoanalytic treatment should certainly not be guided by rigid theoretical presuppositions about this period. To the contrary: the controversy can be resolved only on the basis of unprejudiced inferences made through the inductive method, i.e., inferences based on observations of transference developments. I wish to underscore this point by presenting some condensed data from one of several analyses I have conducted that do not seem to give support to any of the foregoing hypotheses.[3]

[3] I should add, perhaps, that I have also had clinical experiences which did substantiate either some of Kohut's formulations or the ones developed by

Case 12

A young woman of upper-class background entered analysis following an episode of confusion and excitement, partly induced by experimentation with various drugs. Her disorganization occurred when, for the first time, she tried to live on her own in Chicago, far from her family; it had promptly abated as a result of some weeks of daily visits to a psychiatrist, who then recommended analytic treatment. The confusion had resulted from frantic efforts to keep up with a multitude of varied enterprises undertaken without forethought or planning. She was extremely humiliated by the need for psychological assistance but never lost a firm sense of the necessity to proceed with the work. Whenever we had the opportunity for some weeks to pursue the therapy without interruption, she was able to put her life into order; she then became interested in a variety of new projects. She threw herself into these with uncritical enthusiasm, only to fail over and over again because she would undertake too much. She could never renounce a part of her program in order to salvage the rest. For her, there was absolutely no conflict about the rashness and

---

Settlage on the basis of Mahler's work. In my judgment, the hypotheses of Kernberg about narcissism have not been stated in a testable manner. Inasmuch as it is not possible to find a person born without the constitutional predisposition for aggression, Kernberg's formulations necessarily apply to everyone. Thus, the judgment that a patient has an abnormal quantity or quality of aggressiveness (or of narcissism) is a post hoc evaluation based on the very data it is supposed to *explain*, i.e., the presence of psychopathology in the adult.

grandiosity of her customary behavior, and she fully credited her private judgment that she ought to have been able to accomplish these ends.

It took over a year of analytic work to help the patient to manage her sense of humiliation and failure about each of these episodes sufficiently to be able to look into the actualities of the behavior that produced them. We eventually succeeded in determining that she had been systematically taught to believe that she should be able to accomplish literally anything that she set her mind on. She had also been given the impression that her fabulously successful father was practically omnipotent and that these larger-than-life capacities were entirely expectable in her patrician circles.

It should be noted that neither the patient nor any other member of her family had any defect in reality testing—on paper, she had as sober an understanding of the laws of nature as anyone else. Her grandiose fantasy involved the ambition to be emotionally invulnerable; it had crystallized in this form during the oedipal period under the impact of continual sadistic harassment by her father. But it was clear that her attitude was not simply a reaction to this strain-trauma; rather, in this respect as in almost all others, her thinking was a direct reflection of that of her mother.

As we came to realize, the patient's personality had an uncanny resemblance to her mother's. In part, this was based on identification, but although she had idealized her mother as a nurturant caretaker in early childhood, there was more to their similarity than the unconscious identification with an admired model. There were indications that even the maternal grandmother had some of the same attitudes of *noblesse oblige*. In the mother's case, this social code had turned into a governing ideal, and her self-esteem was quite fragile as a result of her own inability to live up to these perfectionistic standards at all times. Consequently, she had been quite unable to teach her daughter any sensible scale for measuring one's worth, and she had insistently indoctrinated the child with grandiose notions. About these attitudes, the patient had little or no conflict; she had a childlike naiveté in these matters, and she always welcomed more sensible methods of rating herself as extremely helpful additions to her capabilities. (For further details of this analysis, see Chapter 12.)

The foregoing examples of emergent grandiose fantasies in a transference setting permit a few summary statements about the psychoanalytic management of archaic transferences. In each of the preceding case examples, the transference manifestations constituted the repetition of transactions from earliest childhood. In Case 10, the cavalier disregard of the necessity for free association re-created the infantile conviction of aristocratic privilege fostered by the mother. The patient in Case 11 enacted a fantasy developed around the age of five that he would inherit the mantle of the Prophets of Israel. In Case 9, two layers of grandiosity were recaptured in the analysis: the borrowed megalomania that had characterized the patient's relationship with his mother and, after long therapeutic work, a very primitive attitude of omniscient nihilism, acquired in earliest childhood. In the last example (Case 12), the patient's grandiose rashness had been learned from the mother at the very dawn of consciousness.

How do these findings fit into the various developmental schemata I reviewed earlier? Two of the patients (Cases 11 and 9) demonstrated primitive grandiosity as a regressive response to childhood traumatization, as suggested by various authors, but the data did not permit a decision about which competing hypothesis best fit the cases. In one instance (Case 12), the archaic ambitions seemed to have developed and to have remained unaltered because the primary caretaker had falsely assured the child that she was indeed the fairest in the land; in my judgment, this example does not fit into any of the familiar theoretical frameworks. The remaining example (Case 10) concerns someone whose mother fostered the choice of regression into grandiosity as the optimal response to life's vicissitudes; this case best fits into Kohut's description of regression into archaic omnipotence when expectable ambitions have been frustrated.

All in all, each of the proposals from the literature had a limited range of applicability, but none could explain the full scope of the case material. In fact, the one feature that recurs in each of the four cases is the finding that the primary caretaker of every one of these patients during the earliest years had systematically resorted to grandiose fantasies in her own thinking. Two of the mothers (Cases 10 and 11) were passionately committed to eccentric religious belief systems which involved illusions of personal omnipotence, although these illusions were felt to be contingent on difficult esoteric rituals; several (certainly the mothers in Cases 10 and 12, and probably also the one in Case 9) overtly espoused claims of biological superiority that were poorly founded, given the evidence of their own performance. In some instances, there were additional clues about more serious thought disorders in the family, including the occurrence of overt schizophrenia in the patient's siblings.

I believe the clinical data I have summarized suggest the need for extreme caution in making assumptions about normative criteria of early development with regard to grandiose ideation. In the absence of carefully controlled infant observations specifically focused on this problem, we would be well advised to confine our hypotheses to those special cases in which maldevelopment at these archaic phases comes into focus in the analytic transference. In my judgment, the data best support the inference that, when the child initially becomes capable of symbolic thinking, i.e., somewhere around 18 months of age, the prevalence of his magical ideation will be decisively influenced by the quality of the familial matrix. I think it is entirely likely that grandiose fantasies may not be "endogenous" at all but are entirely *learned.*

How, then, should the analyst respond to the archaic narcissistic claims he encounters? I do not believe that any generalization is as yet warranted. Obviously, whenever possible, he should confine himself to the elucidation of the current and past significance of the archaic claims for the patient; as I have tried to show (particularly in Case 11), an exclusively interpretive approach is, in many instances, not feasible in practice.

I should like to review briefly my actual procedure in the four illustrative cases. In Case 10, the analysand's grandiosity led her into magical performances in the course of professional work that periodically resulted in disastrous failures. I persisted, in spite of the lengthy rages provoked by this policy, in consistently pointing out the disavowed magical ideation at the root of the patient's behavior, including the enactments in the analytic situation. Only the cognitive grasp of the actualities of her performances permitted the patient to gain insight into their sources in the identification with her mother. In Case 11, the patient enacted his grandiose fantasies in a manner that ensured their frustration within the transference. Systematic attempts to analyze the sources of the need to repeat this pattern ultimately led to the discovery of the disavowed illusion of impending prophetic illumination. The superficial arrogance of the patient in Case 9 had been evident to him for many years; in the analysis, the underlying megalomania emerged from repression. This clinical development did not yield to the voice of reason; the treatment ended in failure because of my unwillingness to share and confirm the patient's delusional view of his position in the world. In Case 12, only a veneer of embarrassment covered the patient's naive fantasies of automatic preeminence, and these fantasies were readily given up when their genesis in her mother's attitudes was brought to her attention.

On the basis of this range of clinical material, I would tentatively conclude that, in analyzable instances, infantile grandiose claims will yield to genetic reconstructions of the context in which they took root in early childhood.[4] In many cases, this genesis will be found to have been traumatic; in others, it is a result of expectable identifications with the caretakers. In my experience, it is unusual for a patient to insist that his archaic exhibitionism be gratified; in my opinion, such insistence may well be a sign of the delusional nature of the archaic ideation. Quite emphatically, what patients need from analysis is understanding of the reasons for having become fixated on these attitudes of primitive entitlement. If, in the process of conveying this insight, the analyst is forced into the position of making judgments like those of the magical mirror of the fairy tale, it is imperative that he remain an accurate witness.

In the preceding portion of this chapter, I have considered the therapeutic problems presented by the archaic transferences characterized by subject-centered grandiosity, conditions Kohut (1971) has grouped under the heading of "mirror transference." I have made no attempt to follow his classification of these contingencies into smaller categories because my clinical experience has failed to support his contention that there is a developmental continuum from primitive states of merger, through transferences in which subject and object are re-

[4] Cf. in this connection my discussion of the limits of analyzability in Chapter 3, especially pp. 77–81.

quired to be exactly alike (Kohut has called these "twinships" or alter-ego transferences), to mirror transferences proper. I shall discuss this disagreement in greater detail in Chapter 5. Here, I shall confine myself to consideration of the second major group of archaic transferences described by Kohut, those characterized by idealization of the object.

These conditions, like the mirror transferences, sometimes involve regression to states in which psychological boundaries between subject and object become blurred. However, idealization is also seen in situations referable to much less archaic periods of childhood. Hence idealization has generally been regarded as a reaction formation against the hostile aspects of the ambivalence inherent in the object relations of the oedipal child, as may very often be the case (cf. Kohut, 1971, p. 75). Its appearance within the transference has therefore been viewed as a resistance against the acknowledgment of hostile-rivalrous attitudes; in accord with the primary technical principle of dealing with transference resistance through prompt interpretation, the routine management of transference idealization has consisted of pointing out its defensive aim. Such intervention can be counted on to undermine the idealization and to bring the patient's hostility closer to awareness; i.e., it is generally effective in promoting the analysis of the hostile components of the Oedipus complex.

Kohut (1971, p. 88) has cautioned against making *premature* interpretations of this kind if we are uncertain about the exact nature of the emergent transference. If the analysand is about to mobilize archaic idealizing needs, interpretation of their manifestations as a defense may prematurely push him to deal exclusively with oedipal issues, to the neglect of more archaic problems. Recently, Kohut (1979) has published a lengthy case history which, in his opinion, exemplifies an error of this kind. A view of psychopathology sufficiently complex to depict the various ways that different clusters of conflicts may be interrelated in the same personality was first proposed in *Models of the Mind* (Gedo and Goldberg, 1973, especially pp. 153–168).

At any rate, the successful management of emerging idealization should follow from a classical psychoanalytic technique, one that avoids the application of formulas or routine interpretations. Proper technique might well be compared to old-fashioned infantry tactics, summed up in the motto of Bunker Hill: "Don't fire 'til you see the whites of their eyes!" Incidentally, the emergence of the oedipal transference does not, by itself, validate an interpretation that the idealization of the analyst is a defense; it only shows the Oedipus complex to be part of the configuration of the personality. It is necessary to be able to weigh the relative importance of fixations at more archaic levels and at the oedipal one and to assess the manner in which complex defensive structures have become layered within the character.

If the predominant psychopathology does not fall into the oedipal realm, interpretation of transference idealization as a defense will be largely incorrect: the infantry will have used up its ammunition before the enemy has come into view. The patient's expectable reaction in such circumstances will still be primarily hostile, that is, he will respond with appropriate outrage to the disappointment of having been misunderstood. If the analyst should wish to disclaim responsibility for such an iatrogenic impasse, he may be tempted to compound his sins by further misinterpreting the patient's anger as confirmation of his hypothesis that the main issue is that of oedipal hostility.

According to certain authors, including some adherents of Kohut's viewpoint (cf. Goldberg, 1978, pp. 148, 156, 245–260), avoiding premature interpretations of the meaning of idealization within the transference is tantamount to the indefinite acceptance of the latter and its therapeutic utilization as a direct carrier of improvements in adaptation. It is true that the establishment of a stable idealizing transference often leads patients into unprecedented states of well-being, contingent on the availability and continued "perfection" of the analyst (cf. Kohut, 1971, p. 10). But the very core of Kohut's original technical recommendation was the utilization of the inevitable, spontaneous, recurrent *disruptions* of the "narcissistic equilibrium" achieved in these transferences for the purpose of arriving at reconstructions of the traumatic effects of childhood disillusionments with idealized parental objects. By means of such genetic interpretations, the patient may understand and master his need for continuing idealization of omnipotent others (Kohut, 1971, pp. 95–96, 207–208).

Those who would exploit an idealizing transference

to promote direct adaptive changes are in fact reverting to the psychotherapeutic methods developed by Aichhorn (1951) for the management of delinquent youths. Actually, Aichhorn did not advocate that the therapist allow the unimpeded unfolding of the transference in all such cases; only with delinquents who would otherwise fail to develop meaningful contact with him did he actively foster the emergence of idealizing potentialities in order to gain therapeutic leverage. Such a tendentious effort is alien to the analytic approach; a psychoanalyst should no more encourage idealization than he should attempt to prevent it by automatically interpreting its emergence as a resistance.

Kernberg (1974), another theorist who differentiates "narcissistic" pathology from sequelae of the Oedipus complex, also views idealization as a defense. However, he does not see it primarily as a defense against oedipal hostility; he stresses its defensive use against awareness of *primitive* aggression. It would seem that Kernberg's conception of idealizing transferences may refer to a set of clinical contingencies different from the ones Kohut included in his use of the term (cf. Ornstein, 1974). Kohut has never proposed a specific designation for defensive idealizations; I believe it may be best to borrow Segal's (1974) terminology and differentiate defensive idealizations from primary ones by calling the former "pseudoidealizations." Conceptually, pseudoidealizing transferences are reaction formations after the traumatic destruction of childhood idealizations. On occasion, these defensive efforts are only partially successful; in instances of this kind, the simultaneous occurrence of pseudoidealization and disillusionment is maintained through disavowal.

Kohut has emphasized a different vicissitude following traumatic childhood disillusionments, that of regressive retreat to archaic grandiosity or, perhaps less frequently, to forms of archaic idealization akin to hypomania. He has implied (1971, pp. 137–142) that a significant proportion of patients who develop transferences predominantly in the sphere of subject-centered grandiosity (what he calls "mirror transferences") actually sustained their original fixations when traumatically disillusioned with the infantile idealized object, and that these syndromes therefore involve regressions from the idealizing sphere to that of grandiosity.

If we accept the possibility that idealization is a universal attitude in early childhood, it follows that the establishment of a genuine idealizing transference presupposes that any defensive pseudoidealization has been overcome. This therapeutic achievement, in turn, involves the mastery of the childhood depressive affect that made the defensive structures necessary in the first place. If the split in the self-organization that perpetuates the paradoxical coexistence of pseudoidealization and disillusionment has also been part of the syndrome, the disavowals that maintain it must first be eliminated by systematic interpretive work.

Roughly speaking, Kernberg's technical recommendations about the management of idealizations have implications similar to those proposed by Kohut. The real difference between their views involves the *origin* of the hostility we uncover by undoing pseudoidealizations: where Kohut (1972) sees "narcissistic rage"—which he understands as a reaction to the frustration of the child's appropriate developmental needs—Kernberg sees instinctual aggression, generally in the form of envy. Although Kernberg does not share Melanie Klein's acceptance of the death instinct, he does seem to regard the child's aggression as a primary given.

The difference between Kernberg and Kohut with regard to technique therefore consists of their respective responses to the rageful patient: Kohut (1975a) stresses the rage-assuaging properties of correct empathy and insists that analytic focus on a primary envy-hostility complex is unempathic and provocative. Because patients may experience such analytic interventions as a repetition of the unempathic behavior of the parents early in childhood, they may respond not only with hostility but also with renewed disillusionment and its accompanying depressive affect. I should like to clarify these issues by returning to a discussion of Case 10, the first case illustration offered in this chapter, after some amplification of the clinical data.

Case 10: A Further Discussion

The patient resumed analysis after obtaining a divorce because she still "felt like a wreck," although ridding herself of a husband of dubious character had proved to be a great relief. She attributed the courage to seek the divorce to her previous analysis, which helped her see that she had greatly overestimated this man. In the end, however, she was only able to leave him when she managed to get out of that treatment after it reached an unpleasant impasse. Several earlier therapeutic attempts had also failed; on those occasions, however, she had either clung on after losing hope until dismissed by the therapist, or had deluded herself into believing that she was "cured," as the therapist claimed.

The analyst she was finally able to leave was an older woman of aristocratic bearing. Initially, she had experienced mounting enthusiasm for this person, and the relationship had provided her with an unprecedented state of inner joy. This feeling of peace and self-satisfaction had curdled and was replaced by grief and outrage, as she gradually came to feel that the analyst was displeased by early evidence of growth in the patient. Although this sequence clearly repeated a series of early childhood transactions with the mother, as we were to learn in the course of a lengthy analysis, the patient's perception of her analyst was probably accurate. The clearest instance of displeasure the patient was able to relate was the analyst's haughty statement, when the patient was elaborating ecstatic fantasies of moving into close proximity to her, that the former's immigrant husband would not fit into that exclusive community. The patient's subjective reaction was echoed in a dream reported shortly after she resumed treatment.

In this nightmare, she was driving in a beautiful landscape and suddenly found herself in territory where everything was tilted: the water level of the lake ran uphill at a steep angle, etc. Her associations led to pinball machines, which are not supposed to be tilted to enhance the player's chances to win. The dream was interpreted as an expression of fear that the new analysis would once again place her at an unfair disadvantage. The validity of this interpretation, made on the assumption that the nightmare quality of the dream resulted from the helplessness induced by a passive experience in the previous analysis, was subsequently borne out by a series of dreams on the same theme. In these dreams, the patient was tilting the world to her own advantage, with pleasurable affect.

The account of this analytic failure provides us with a clear illustration of the consequences of a therapist's grossly disillusioning performance for a patient who has an idealizing need. In this regard, it is not even to the point that the enthusiasm for the analyst had only been a pseudoidealization, accompanied by disavowed fears and suspicions about the significance of her perception of the analyst as pretentious and arrogant. The analyst's inadequate handling of the transference proved to be a traumatic disillusionment nonetheless; when the analyst then conceptualized the patient's rage as evidence of the latter's envy of her social position and professional prestige, rather than as a reaction to therapeutic errors, an irretrievable impasse resulted. The impasse was the result of countertransference problems. These data further suggest that Kernberg's method for the management of idealizing transferences may run the risk of creating comparable difficulties through interventions planned on theoretical grounds.

Kohut (1971, p. 267) has described such countertransference reactions as resentment based on a feeling of being belittled when a patient's idealization begins to wane. In other words, in such instances the analyst has looked upon the initial idealization as if it were a realistic response to his actual qualities. However, Kohut has stressed that a more common countertransference difficulty in response to idealizing transferences is an incapacity to tolerate the idealization because it stimulates the analyst's covert, ego-alien grandiosity.

One of the ironies of the story of the patient I have described was the fact that the analyst's alleged "reality," that of her superior social status, was quite without foundation. The analysand was the child of a highly successful and wealthy professional man of American pioneer stock, and her mother bore the name of one of Europe's most distinguished families—although princes they were not! She was the first child of this couple, and she recalled her early childhood as a period of general satisfaction. During her fourth year, her mother gave birth to her twin sisters, a circumstance that apparently overstrained everyone's emotional resources. When the babies were about 18 months of age, the patient witnessed an accident, unequivocally produced by the mother's negligence, in which one of the toddlers was permanently crippled in a horrible manner. The mother became obsessed with the need to make reparation to this child, withdrew from the rest of the family, and gradually underwent a change in personality. She became a Rosicrucian, preoccupied with clairvoyance, and she grew more and more negligent of the household.

In spite of these developments, in later childhood the patient continued to admire her mother; she could not regard her with disfavor until midadolescence. At that time, she abruptly broke away from home to escape the mother's persistent pressure on her to act out sexually. It would seem that the vicissitudes of the transference in the first analysis, as well as the outlines of the relationship to her delinquent husband whom the patient had invested with a romantic aura, had repeated the childhood refusal to accept the emotional reality of the mother's severe pathology. In contrast, the patient's relationship with her father was at best lukewarm, although not outwardly troubled. She had always been puzzled by his minor eccentricities; in the analysis, she grasped that they stemmed from excessive modesty and the need to avoid admiration.

The patient began her new analysis with the conviction that she needed an experience in which it would be her turn to be admired. She used this belief as a brake on her propensity to raise her therapists onto nonexistent pedestals; it soon became clear that, if no one would tilt the world she inhabited against her, she would have a need to do it on her own. Yet she continued to use her extensive repertory of defenses successfully to ward off her idealizing needs. Although she continued to complain that she felt like a wreck, in a split-off part of her personality she repeated the transaction with her former analyst with the financial manager of her estate. This man was full of optimism and charisma, and he was glib and superficially skilled at his work. Although she had been studying his methods for decades and was supposedly a sophisticated investor, she had never managed to learn from him how to handle her investments independently. He was, at least, more prudent than the first analyst had been and managed to avoid a rupture of their bond.

For a long period, the analytic work focused on overcoming her disavowal of the simultaneous but contrasting feeling states she was experiencing. She then began to understand that, without the belief that she would pyramid her estate into a great fortune with her advisor's magical help, she felt permanently wretched and deflated. We reconstructed the significance of her admiration of the bizarre mother as a source of security and self-esteem under the umbrella of the latter's clairvoyant powers. She had been unable to turn to her father as an alternative because of his obnoxious pseudohumility. She had to resort to a regression to grandiosity under the onslaught of a barrage of accusations, both from the mother and from the crippled sister, that every manifestation of anger on her part was a sign of her selfish envy of the maternal care required by the sick child. The first analyst's interpretations of her anger as motivated by envy had repeated this childhood brainwashing rather precisely.

The successful completion of this reconstructive task ushered in the development of a genuine idealizing transference. This did not involve placing the analyst on any kind of pedestal: in fact, it had more to do with idealizing the analytic process than the person who performed it. It also lacked the overtly enthusiastic quality of the patient's response to her former analyst. As a matter of fact, it was a process that remained largely silent; its presence had to be inferred from indirect evidence. She began to toy with the idea of discharging her investment counselor, whose actual performance no longer seemed so distinguished to her. In this connection, she had a dream in which she no longer felt interested in financial speculations because she possessed a set of solid gold tableware. To this, she associated the ownership of the best available tools for feeding oneself, i.e., her analysis. The validity of her interpretation was confirmed when, upon being asked by a friend to compare her two analytic experiences, she found herself bursting into tears of relief, hope, and gratitude. In genetic terms, the imagery was related to the memory of the mother as an ideal nurturing figure in early childhood.

I believe this clinical material demonstrates the distinction between pseudoidealization and a true idealizing transference. The former repeats a phenomenon occurring relatively late in the sequence of events forming the personality and therefore tends to bear the imprint of its more recent origins: it will usually involve a whole person, one who is acknowledged as an independent source of initiative even if the qualities attributed to him are illusory. By contrast, the idealizing transference repeats a more archaic mode of experience; typically, the omnipotent other is a symbiotic object whose availability and perfection are therefore taken for granted. This is why an idealizing transference tends to be silent; insofar as it becomes explicit, it will have an impersonal quality. In other words, it will focus on the functional capacities rather than on the specific person of the symbiotic object—e.g., analysis as a set of golden tools.

The mobilization of a relatively archaic configuration such as the idealizing transference generally requires a therapeutic regression, analogous to those that make the analysis of the oedipal transferences possible. Such regressions take place in the face of more or less intense resistances that usually have to be interpreted to be overcome. This aspect of the management of idealization may be profitably illustrated by an excerpt from the analysis of a patient who had recently gained insight into the defensive function of her ubiquitous, lifelong pseudoidealizations.

Case 13

The patient reported a dream which she characterized as having the flavor simultaneously of a nightmare and of slapstick. She was in the Egyptian section of a local museum; there were a series of mummies, one of which was a female midget who was lying in a stone crib. Miraculously, the midget was resurrected, jumped out of the crib, and went into a series of mischievous antics. The curator rushed in and, in order to calm her, addressed the midget by name; the patient recognized this name as her own.

She associated the setting to that of the analysis where she lies on the couch and reexperiences childhood feeling states. The analyst is the curator: he has miraculous curative powers; he can calm her overexcitement and overcome her lifelong feeling of inner deadness by treating her as a person of value—a museum piece. Many other ramifications of this complex dream must be omitted here. Suffice it to say that, among others, one meaning of the dream was that the patient needed to protect herself against the dreaded repetition of a series of crushing disappointments in people whom she had tried to idealize in the past. She did this by mocking the whole analytic procedure as well as her own gullibility through the black humor of the dream—precisely because the analytic work had progressed to the point where her real idealizing transference was about to be mobilized. We see that the burgeoning idealization once again does not focus on the person of the analyst but on his actual skills, in this case, his expertise in recognizing the genuine worth of his charges. In other words, he is admired for his ability to manage the archaic transference, a process that cannot be described in detail here. But the interpretation can be documented by means of a dream reported about five sessions later.

In the second dream, the patient was watching the take-off of an enormous airplane, like a 747. It rose steeply and rapidly; the only occupant was the patient herself. Suddenly the plane began a sharp 360-degree turn, like a graceful bird or a stunt flyer. She was terrified that it would crash, but the machine completed its loop and kept flying. Her associations recalled a family adage about mood swings: whatever goes up, must come down! She had always looked upon airplane flight as miraculous; she thought the dream again referred to her mistrust of the analysis, like the resurrection of the mummy in the previous one. She had been reading Susan Schaeffer's *Falling*, a beautiful novel about analysis, and like the girl who was being analyzed in the book, the patient could not foresee avoiding a fall.

The dream was interpreted as an indication of beginning mastery of the overexcitement that had always led her to collapse into mummylike states in the past, and of her hope that the analysis could become airborne. Although she was still inclined to mock this hope as illusory, the flight of airplanes is no miracle, like a resurrection; it only seems so if one confuses the air with a vacuum or if the machine lacks fuel. Although she felt somewhat depleted during the weekend interruption, she had in fact managed to reach the Monday "refueling" session in a better emotional state than had been customary for her.

In contrast to the image of the analyst in the previous dream—that of the pseudoidealized magician who pretends to wake the dead—in this dream, he is not explicitly represented. Instead, his presence must be inferred, like the air and the fuel that make the flight of airplanes possible. The intervening work had brought the patient's grandiose and exhibitionistic tendencies into focus: she is now the greatest and most beautiful of flying objects. Significantly, in one sense she is still inanimate, a mere machine, and the grandiosity implicit in the image of stunt flying endangers her—she is really threatened with a fall. At the same time, a core of humanity is portrayed in the image of herself as passenger.

The example illustrates the fact that the onset of the genuine idealizing transference is often correlated with parallel progressive movements in mobilizing other aspects of the archaic psychological world, such as the reawakening of grandiose ambitions. Hence it is not unusual for the patient to suffer his most painful disappointments in the analyst because of the latter's failure to deal optimally with the issues of exhibitionism and shame-propensity, the most difficult aspects of the "mirror transference." If these difficulties are managed with tact, the establishment of the idealizing transference produces not only improvements in tension regulation —a golden mean between a living death and overexcitement—but provides the opportunity to sort out and integrate hitherto unconscious, archaic ambitions. This is a slow process, cumulative over long spans of time and dependent on the avoidance of traumatic disillusionments.

Minor disruptions of the idealizing transference provide sufficient opportunities for interpretation of the childhood need for parental objects who do not fail in important ways. Such interpretation should go hand in hand with the patient's increasing acceptance of the analyst's actual, inevitable limitations. Progress is indicated by a gradual sharpening of focus in idealizing more discrete aspects of behavior and values, instead of global *gestalten*, and by increasing refinement of judgment about what is truly admirable. And these changes do not involve any loss in the capacity for enthusiasm for admirable others.

As I have stated in the introduction to this section, I regard the description of at least two sets of archaic transferences as the most important clinical contribution of "self psychology." In my experience, these constellations may emerge in the course of all analyses and are by no means confined to any particular group of patients; in other words, I do not agree that their detection permits us to make a diagnosis of "narcissistic personality disturbance." In this chapter, I have tried to discuss some technical problems related to the occurrence of these constellations whenever they arise.

My point of view is clearly at variance with that of Kohut and his followers. They view these transference patterns as pathognomonic for a distinct nosological entity. The putative delineation of this new psychopathological grouping was seen as an exception to the Freudian paradigm of sufficient moment to justify the erection of a new conceptual framework. There can be no objection to such an enterprise, of course, and there are a number of other reasons for undertaking the revision of psychoanalytic theory (see Gedo, 1979a). Unfortunately, "self psychology" has been presented as an independent fragment of clinical theory without any effort to correlate it to existing analytic propositions. This neglect of internal consistency has been especially regrettable because Kohut has not attempted to replace traditional psychoanalytic psychology in its entirety. Because he and his collaborators have not specified how much of the body of analytic theory self psychology is meant to supersede, a situation of extraordinary conceptual confusion has resulted. Nor has the chaos been avoided in the clinical arena, as I shall try to demonstrate in the next chapter.

CHAPTER FIVE

Reflections on Some Current Controversies in Psychoanalysis

Among current controversies in psychoanalysis, one of the most significant has been generated by the work of Heinz Kohut (1971, 1977, 1978). Although first presented simply as a clinical discovery about a specific group of narcissistic personalities, his ideas were greeted with unusual skepticism (e.g., Panel, 1973). "Traditionalists" who insisted that the narcissistic syndromes in question are variants of the oedipal neuroses seemed to regard Kohut's propositions as the entering wedge for a radical revision of psychoanalysis. Kohut has responded to such suspicions ambiguously: he continues to proclaim his acceptance of the greater part of the analytic heritage, viewing his own theories as supplements necessitated by the broadening field of applicability of psychoanalytic treatment. At the same time, however, he has become bolder and bolder in presenting his viewpoint, which he

This chapter was previously published in the *Journal of the American Psychoanalytic Association*, 28(1980):363–383, and is reprinted here by permission.

now calls "the psychology of the self," as a new paradigm for psychoanalysis.

Unhappily, controversies of this kind have seldom led to sober, scientific evaluations of the reliability of observational data, the adequacy of theoretical inferences, or the congruence between these inferences and analytic theory as a whole. The disputes about Kohut's work have been no exception: we have witnessed the formation of hostile ideological camps engaging in global condemnation of, or cultish enthusiasm for, Kohut's "system." Yet, selected assessment of his manifold ideas should be possible, for both his point of view and the traditional one have been clearly articulated, and analyses conducted in accord with these differing premises have been reported in satisfactory detail, most recently in two edited compilations of clinical material (Goldberg, 1978; Firestein, 1978).

The Chicago casebook (Goldberg, 1978) describes six analyses based on Kohut's principles. In addition to severe subjective discomfort, all patients suffered from combinations of addictions, perversions, and delinquencies. All but one also lapsed into hypochondriasis in stressful circumstances; in analogous situations, the remaining patient experienced exacerbations of certain somatic symptoms. The severe and pervasive psychopathology precluded a diagnosis of neurotic personality. Closer study reveals that this selection of cases does cover a *range* of archaic syndromes. Perhaps the most impaired patient was Mr. E., a man with openly grandiose ideation who had paranoid reactions when traumatized.

Mr. B., who had no capacity to manage his own tensions, occasionally became disorganized by stimulation; consequently, he kept his human contacts to a minimum. In contrast to these patients, Mrs. R. was merely *afraid* of disorganizing experiences, and Mrs. A. never seemed to be threatened with deeper regression, perhaps owing to the adaptive aspect of her psychosomatic illness. Similarly, Mr. I. maintained his stability by resorting to a variety of perversions. Probably the least impaired was Mr. M., whose rigid self-control was seldom shaken.

However we might classify these patients nosologically, they had in common an actual or potential need for a symbiotic partner—in Kohut's special terminology, for a "selfobject." To illustrate: the addiction of Mr. I. to sexual experiences was almost immediately transformed into an addiction to psychoanalysis; Mr. B., previously addicted to barbiturates, became aware of an imperative need for his analyst as soon as her early interventions succeeded in calming him. However, in several instances, the developmental deficit became manifest only after much analytic work was accomplished. In the case of Mr. M., the symbiotic adaptation was regressive, necessitated by traumatic circumstances in later childhood; in other words, the symbiotic need was his parents', and the crucial problem in his analysis was the elucidation of Mr. M.'s decision to comply with that external pressure.

The casebook is entitled *The Psychology of the Self* to indicate the centrality of the issue of self-cohesion in the "narcissistic" disturbances (see pp. 4–5 and Kohut, 1977, pp. 93–94). The need for a symbiotic partner, well-documented in five of the reports, betrays the tenuousness of the self-organization; from another perspective, the regressive syndromes supervening whenever the "self-object" was functionally unavailable are understood, in Kohut's terms, either as direct consequences of "fragmentation" of the self or as emergency measures to ward off such a catastrophe. Therefore these reports enable us to deduce what Kohut may mean when he refers to "the self"—a term he has been reluctant to define too precisely (cf. Kohut, 1977, pp. xv–xix, 206–207, 310–311).

In *The Restoration of the Self* (1977), Kohut acknowledged that in all his previous writings he had used "self" exclusively to refer to "a content of the mental apparatus" (p. 207n). In clinical terms, this usage refers to the individual's self-representations, both conscious and unconscious. Kohut then called attention to a second meaning of "self," one he termed "broader" and that I would identify as more abstract. In this broader sense, Kohut uses the concept to refer to combinations of a person's ambitions and ideals (Kohut and Wolf, 1978, p. 414), i.e., to aspects of the subjective world. It has been difficult to discern in what sense these constitute an entity that may undergo dissolution; in contrast, the examples in the casebook make an operational definition possible.

This is clearest in the case of the most vulnerable patient, Mr. B., who became literally helpless and disorganized without appropriate external assistance. The author of this report (the only one prepared from another analyst's written notes) equates these states with fragmentation, a view echoed by the analyst of Mrs. R.; this patient feared psychological disorganization, which she concretized as the fragmentation of her *body*. Given these clinical assumptions, it seems legitimate to infer that "the self" in Kohut's broader usage should refer to a supraordinate psychological organization and not to the representation of a concrete person. In fact, the term "self" and its synonyms have often been employed in just this sense ever since the idea of supraordinate organization was adumbrated decades ago as the synthetic function of the ego (Nunberg, 1930; see also Lichtenstein, 1961; Gedo and Goldberg, 1973; G. Klein, 1976).

Most of the contributors to the casebook seem to have realized that it makes little sense to label disorders in the capacity to organize behavior "narcissistic," and this terminology of Kohut's early work (1966, 1968, 1971, 1972) has been more or less abandoned by his supporters. Unfortunately, this desirable semantic change has not been accompanied by its necessary correlate: the elimination from their theoretical discourse of concepts derived from Freud's conception of narcissism as one set of libidinal vicissitudes. This anachronism is especially regrettable in view of Kohut's clear statement (1977, p. 224) that disorders of the "self" do not lend themselves to drive-psychological explanations.[1] Yet the developmental theory underlying most of the new formulations in the casebook is that proposed by Kohut over a decade

[1] In my opinion, the so-called "narcissism" of such individuals consists of vanity, selfishness, and arrogant ingratitude—character traits that may be acquired in a number of complex, diverse ways.

ago as an emendation of Freud's hypotheses about narcissistic libido.

This hidden armature, holding the confusing array of Kohut's propositions together for better or for worse, is not mentioned in the casebook. In the Introduction, Goldberg states that the heart of Kohut's contribution is the empirical discovery of a number of archaic transference constellations. In my experience (see Gedo, 1975a, 1977a), important preoedipal transference configurations characterized by archaic idealization or grandiosity are indeed frequently encountered in analytic practice, so that Goldberg's judgment may well prove to be correct. He fails to specify, however, that the "predictable routes" (p. 6) traversed by these transference patterns in both progressive and regressive directions were mapped out by Kohut as stages along the line of development of narcissistic libido. The casebook uses this developmental schema as an established law of nature, although no evidence has ever been offered to justify it. The clinical material here is *organized* according to Kohut's hypotheses and is therefore unsuitable for testing them. There is no inductive reasoning in this work; as one contributor acknowledges, "I was unable to 'hear' the significance of what the patient was saying until I had the conceptual assistance of a new analytic *discovery*" (p. 203; italics added).

Actually, the observational data offered as supportive evidence for the self-psychological perspective require the revision of Kohut's original developmental schema. For example, the analyst reports data suggesting that Mr. I. simultaneously attributed magical powers to him and exhibitionistically demanded praise for himself. In Kohut's terminology, this means that archaic idealization coexisted with a mirror transference proper. Yet in Kohut's original schema these conditions should not coexist; idealization of the parent is allegedly a developmental achievement contingent on the taming of personal grandiosity (see Kohut, 1971, p. 97). In his more recent work, Kohut (1977) sometimes simplifies his developmental propositions, speaking of the crucial significance of an earlier phase focused on the "mirroring mother" and a later one related to the "idealized father" (see 1977, p. 50). The clinical material suggests that Mr. I.'s megalomania was actually the result of persistently confusing his own person with an idealized other: until a few weeks before termination, he continued to experience the analyst as omnipotent (see p. 95), and he fantasied that they were going through the same somatic vicissitudes (p. 88). These and similar data undermine Kohut's assumption that archaic, subject-centered grandiosity is the earliest expectable stage of "narcissistic" development. The material suggests instead that the most primitive transferences evoked in analysis probably involve idealizations. Kohut's view that the latter represent a relatively late stage in development suggests an apparent confusion of genuine idealizations with reaction formations eventually erected against disappointment in the caretakers that I have termed "pseudoidealizations" (see Chapter 4). In the case of Mrs. A., for example, persistent self-depreciation reflected depreciation of the mother (p. 277). A silent idealizing transference was masked by the patient's clamor about her (adult) disappointment in her mother. But the implicit criticisms of the analyst (in the mother transference) amounted to a repetition of an early childhood disappointment with the mother as idealized caretaker and the defensive disavowal of this disappointment.

As for the proposition that there is an expectable pathway from states of "merger" through those of "twinship" to "mirror transferences," one can only say that no material in the book supports the concept of merger or twinship transferences as independent entities. Several patients tended to confuse their own person with idealized others; this significant finding illuminates the limited cognitive capacities of certain people when they regress into archaic states, but it does not document the usefulness of the concept of "merger." A "twinship" was detected only once in the course of the six analyses (p. 246), and it is difficult to grasp how that interpretation was reached. Thus, the casebook demonstrates only two constellations stressed by Kohut: first, naive idealizations; second, insistent needs for affirmation of the patient's actual functioning.

These needs for validation raise a technical issue that was handled in divergent ways by various members of the Kohut research group. The analyst of Mr. M. takes great pains to show that the appropriate handling of the "mirror transference" requires *only* interpretation of the specific wishes that express the underlying need for affirmation, i.e., that such handling does not require gratification of those wishes (p. 146). The point is convincingly supported by the data: Mr. M. was forthright in requesting only recognition of his realistic assets (p. 144), and when the analyst failed to give even that (interpreting the wish instead), he made decisive progress in spite of his anger.

In contrast, the analyst of Mrs. A. repeatedly refers to the necessity to recognize the patient's need to be told that she is "terrific" (e.g., p. 203) despite the fact that Mrs. A., even as a child, scarcely comes across as a praiseworthy individual. The patient had sufficient sense, however, to state more than once that she could not stand to be evaluated *incorrectly*, either by her mother or by her analyst.

The difference I am pinpointing does not have to do with the handling of the transference as such (although many therapists have used Kohut's writings as justification for treating patients by means of providing them with "narcissistic" gratification); the divergence concerns the proper manner of bringing a missing experience of childhood to the patient's attention. Should the child have been *praised* for being whatever he was, or should he have received conditional acceptance along with clarification of his limitations? Kohut (1977, p. 151) seems to agree with the analyst of Mrs. A. in preferring the first alternative.

As a repository of evidence for Kohut's scientific hypotheses, the value of the casebook depends on the technical adequacy of the analyses reported. Such matters are difficult to evaluate, especially with regard to the emotional contribution of the analyst. The authors claim

(p. 444) that no major countertransference obstacles were encountered in these cases. But did the presence of many of the analysts within the research group encourage thorough exploration of these painful topics? It is very striking that only the case report prepared from written notes contains any mention of the possibility that the analysis may have come to a premature end because of the analyst's "too ready willingness to soothe or reassure," experienced by the patient as a repetition of "the mother's hanging on to him for reasons of her own" (p. 432). Ever so gently, the author of this chapter suggests that Mr. B.'s analysis was therefore incomplete. I myself have similar questions about a number of other cases in the book, especially those of Mr. M. and Mrs. A.

The case of Mr. M. is also extensively discussed in Kohut's 1977 book. There it is used to illustrate Kohut's concept of "compensatory structures"—patterns of behavior acquired after the formation of a primary developmental defect that may permit satisfactory adaptation in spite of those deficits. Kohut argues that the therapeutic goals of analysis have been achieved if it succeeds in strengthening these compensatory functions to a sufficient degree; i.e., he believes that interruption of the analysis when adaptation has sufficiently improved amounts to a genuine analytic termination. In the context of this argument, Kohut explains that the treatment of Mr. M. failed to touch upon the sector of his personality derived from those earliest transactions with his caretakers that produced his later psychological handicaps. This assertion about the limits of Mr. M.'s analysis is substantiated by the data in the casebook.

On the other hand, the clinical evidence fails to support Kohut's argument that, because of the patient's vulnerability, an attempt to deepen the analysis by discouraging early termination would actually have been dangerous. The reasons given for these fears are purely arbitrary, based almost entirely on the assumption that the patient's adoption at the age of three months meant that he had had an insuperably deficient infantile matrix, so that his later development was necessarily built on quicksand. On the face of it, this is an implausible idea, one that regards the human infant as incapable of adapting to various common vicissitudes. The only other evidence offered for Kohut's pessimistic position is the patient's own statement, in justification of his wish to discontinue treatment, that he was afraid of becoming addicted to analysis. But the casebook abounds in data demonstrating that addiction to treatment (not to speak of *fears* about becoming dependent on it) is neither a contraindication to psychoanalytic efforts nor a particularly unfavorable prognostic sign—witness the cases of Mr. B. and Mr. I., who did become unconditionally dependent in that way almost as soon as their analyses began. Kohut contradicts his own position (1977, p. 195) when he makes the correct judgment that Mr. M. was actually less impaired than was Mr. I. Yet, as supervisor, he did not find it necessary to exercise caution in pursuing the analysis of the latter wherever it might have led. It may well be that the therapeutic results in the case of Mr. M. were indeed adequate from the patient's point of view, but the claim that an analytic termination was reached is not sustained.

As for the treatment of Mrs. A., the analyst reports that for a number of years she did not manage it adequately; actual deterioration of the patient's adaptation and a threat of analytic interruption led her to consult Kohut. In view of her admirable candor in describing all this, we can accept the analyst's belief that these difficulties resulted from an erroneous theoretical stance toward the material; there is no need to specify the personal factors that lead us all into such mistakes. Whether or not one accepts the interpretive schema adopted on Kohut's recommendation, however, serious questions arise about the influence of years of misunderstanding on the subsequent fate of the analytic relationship.

To recapitulate, then, at least half of the illustrative protocols in the casebook are flawed as models for the natural unfolding of the analytic transference. Nor did one of the most skillfully conducted of these analyses, that of Mr. I., reach a natural termination; unfortunately, after several years of fruitful collaboration, the patient's life circumstances apparently required setting an arbitrary time limit for the analytic work.[2]

Only the cases of Mr. E. and of Mrs. R. were reasonably complete and beyond reasonable criticism in

[2] It is probably only a side issue, but worth noting, that the analyst (and the casebook group as a whole) was (and were) nonetheless satisfied with the outcome. It is, however, very much to the point that this is the example chosen to report in detail on the *terminal phase* of an analysis conducted in accord with Kohut's principles. In my judgment, this material is discussed with unrealistic optimism—an attitude otherwise absent from the casebook.

terms of technique. Yet, even these analyses share one feature with the others: the assumption, explicitly stated in the Introduction, that Kohut's description of the typical "selfobject transferences" permits those who use his hypotheses "to arrive at valid genetic reconstructions." That is exactly the manner in which all of these treatments were carried out—the detection of a specific transference configuration was used, in a global way, to postulate the occurrence of an equally global, typical, childhood emotional constellation. Such inferences may or may not turn out to be valid in specific instances (and, valid or not, they may exert a beneficial therapeutic influence), but the procedure does exclude the possibility of discovering instances that would suggest any alternative explanations.

The casebook fails to make explicit its assumption that "narcissistic" disturbances and the familiar oedipal ones constitute two distinct clusters (Kohut, 1977, p. 225). Kohut calls these the problems of Tragic Man and of Guilty Man, respectively, and he claims that both are seldom found in the same person. The casebook demonstrates the basis of his belief: in none of the six analyses was an oedipal conflict detected. But the interpretive technique used clearly precludes the detection of *any* significant childhood constellation beyond the ones described by Kohut, once one of the "selfobject transferences" has been recognized.

It is therefore extremely instructive to compare these protocols with the ones prepared by Firestein (1978) in his study of analyses terminated under the aegis of the

Treatment Center of the New York Psychoanalytic Institute. Many of the patients in the New York study seem indistinguishable from those in the Chicago casebook; in New York, significant oedipal problems were found in every case, but no other sources of psychopathology were discovered. Such discrepancies are very painful and embarrassing.

It is, of course, useless to speculate about what might have been found if any of the cases I consider to have ended without an analytic termination had been handled differently. At the same time, I accept the group's evaluation of Mr. E., a person on the edge of total decompensation when he undertook treatment. The analyst properly designated his personality organization as one of "arrested development," and the data suggest that this arrest occurred early in life, probably before the expectable onset of the oedipal phase. Mr. E. is therefore one of those rare individuals who seek analysis for grave problems unconnected to oedipal issues. Such people do exist, they can be analyzed, and (in spite of the schematic approach to reconstruction), this account may serve as an adequate presentation of such work.[3]

In spite of the reductionism of their clinical theory and of the inevitable imperfections in performance by

[3] Perhaps a word of caution may be in order about this. In Mr. E.'s case, the arrest in development (and even some later regression) came about as a result of traumatic events; the character structure of the primary caretaker may have had less bearing on the child's difficulties than in many comparable instances. Consequently, Mr. E. did not present the analyst with the defensive character structure that usually makes it so complex a task to work with such impaired individuals. At the same time, the minimal resistance makes the case history unusually easy to follow—translucent, so to speak.

the inexperienced analysts whose work appears in the casebook (at least four conducted the analyses as students), valuable therapeutic achievements were made in every case. These results tend to support Kohut's claim (1977, p. 282) that "even a comparatively small improvement in self pathology" will produce a "vast increase in well-being." Most impressive in this regard were the lasting beneficial consequences of close attention to difficulties in tension regulation (in the form of either a desperate need for stimulation or a propensity to become overexcited in disruptive ways) encountered more or less obviously in each case.

In this regard, the best example is that of Mr. B., whose alarming disorganization was rapidly ameliorated without dealing with any psychological content. His capacity to forestall such episodes was gradually improved as he learned about the nature of this deficit and acquired ways of self-management through planning. Very little else was achieved in this analysis, yet the outcome was most satisfactory from the patient's viewpoint; indeed, it produced a revolution in his life. Although it is more difficult to single out the consequences of ameliorating the problem of tension regulation in the case of Mr. E., the resulting adaptive benefits were equally striking in that analysis. The same might be said about Mr. I., except that the artificial time limit imposed on him so disappointed and angered him that even these solid gains appeared to be in question at termination. Although the issue was less crucial in the other three cases, it did play a part in all of them.

The deficit in tension regulation detected in these individuals is one of Kohut's more significant empirical discoveries (1971, pp. 229–235). He has attributed this developmental defect to the lack "of a strong central self" (1977, p. 163). He has failed to show what this deficit has to do with a "psychology of the self," however, and his findings seem, rather, to confirm the validity and importance of Freud's definition of "actual neuroses," i.e., syndromes of psychoeconomic imbalance, essentially without psychological content. Kohut has ascertained that these conditions (the very existence of which has often been called into question) are most likely to occur in persons suffering from developmental disturbances. The casebook supplies copious evidence for the importance of attending to the actual-neurotic core of any psychic disorder.

If the appropriate management of psychoeconomic disturbances does not quite amount to a revolution in psychoanalytic technique, as Kohut's more enthusiastic followers would have us believe, other characteristics of the approach demonstrated in the casebook are more original. Most important for therapeutic effectiveness was the constant alertness for transference developments in which the analysand lived out his symbiotic needs—in Kohut's terms, for the occurrence of "selfobject transferences." These archaic transactions were consistently correlated with psychological vicissitudes at early developmental levels, and the latter were taken *seriously* as etiological factors accounting for later maladaptation.

In the case of Mr. E., for instance, understanding

the need for the analyst's availability as an organizer of the patient's behavior led to reconstruction of a persistent childhood symbiosis with the mother that had left him unprepared for independent functioning. These insights permitted formulating the therapeutic task as the completion of an interrupted developmental process. The analysis of Mrs. A., long unproductive, was salvaged in part when the analyst grasped that the patient's negativistic response to her attempted therapeutic activities represented the repetition of fruitless childhood struggles to escape enmeshment in a symbiosis required by her mother. Relinquishment of a hostile identification with these aspects of the mother's behavior accounted for most of the adaptive changes effected by this treatment. In the case of Mr. I., the patient's confusion of his own person with that of the analyst shortly before termination (p. 88) belies the authors' assertion that the symbiotic adaptation had been transcended. But this failure does not cast doubt on using the need for symbiosis as the main criterion for evaluating this case.

For purposes of comparison, we may conveniently turn to the case reports of Firestein (1978), who did a follow-up study of eight analyses, also conducted by students. As a group, the analysands at the New York Treatment Center are scarcely distinguishable from those described in the Goldberg casebook, although there are fewer references to addictive or hypochondriacal propensities in Firestein's accounts. It should be noted, however, that these reports are much briefer than those of the Chicago group and are deliberately focused on the process of termination. At any rate, if Firestein's sample did perhaps consist of personalities slightly less impaired, this minor difference should lead us to expect better analytic results for the New York patients. The comparison is instructive because these analyses were conducted, to judge by the reports, in a specific tradition that is the polar opposite of Kohut's emphasis on archaic issues. The work was focused on the derivatives of the Oedipus complex; more archaic manifestations were interpreted as defensive efforts to ward off the oedipal anxieties. No evidence of technical deficiencies or countertransference difficulties can be found in Firestein's accounts, nor does the author evaluate the outcome of these analyses. It is my impression that the candidates who performed the work were superior students, who conscientiously carried out whatever they had been taught to do.

It is therefore quite striking that the outcomes were so uniformly disappointing, in spite of the fact that only one of these cases had to be discontinued for adventitious reasons. In none of the cases did the analysand decide on termination unilaterally; these analyses satisfied our usual process criteria. The follow-up interviews revealed a host of residual difficulties: a number of the patients had to seek subsequent treatment relatively soon after the analyses ended; others sorely missed therapeutic assistance or led empty, isolated lives, *felt* ill, etc. At best, with painful effort, some patients managed to function somewhat better. I do not mean to imply that the insight gained about a variety of oedipal conflicts and fantasies was useless; in most cases it relieved certain sexual inhibitions and anxieties about vocational success. Moreover, the nonspecific supportive effects of "being in analysis" almost always diminished the patient's current turmoil, and the practical results of several years of relative peace were generally lasting and significant. Nonetheless, these people remained psychologically ill, and not simply in the sense of our customary equation of illness with the human condition.

Even Firestein's brief accounts provide enough data, however, to suggest that much more could have been accomplished through different therapeutic strategies. The misconceived emphasis of this work is most obvious in the case of Shirley T.: her masculine identification, her perverse fantasies and behavior, and her use of pregnancy to relieve distress were arbitrarily assigned exclusively oedipal meanings. After six years of analysis, she was resisting change lest the treatment come to an end; she felt aggrandized by the relationship, as if it provided her with a penis. She sensed that without analysis she might become promiscuous. When the analyst suggested termination, she voiced the illusion that she was not simply a patient for him. Should we be surprised that a year after treatment ended this woman was drinking to excess, or that her sadomasochistic battles with her husband were worse than ever? That she had overt erotic fantasies about the analyst or that she improved when she once again became pregnant? At follow-up she described the nature of her illness clearly: she needed analysis to repair her self-esteem; it "invigorated" her. In other words, her symbiotic needs were overlooked in a seven-year treatment, although even her presenting history might have alerted an unprejudiced observer to the probability that the all-too-obvious oedipal material was largely a vehicle for the expression of pathological object needs.

The five-year analysis of Frank B. dealt mainly with the passive erotic wishes within a father transference; the defensive aspects of these obtrusive preoccupations were not investigated; the temporary emergence, early in the analysis, of a delusional mother transference was apparently ignored. As soon as some behavioral improvements were noted, the analyst suggested termination. His supervisor later stated that this move was indicated *because* the patient was addicted to treatment. It is a staggering assertion: the analytic treatment of a symbiotic need is that of dismissing the patient! At follow-up, two years later, Firestein found a man full of grief and rage, a person who felt castrated by the loss of a relationship to an idealized other. Obviously, this is what Kohut calls a "selfobject," and the patient's subjective sense of not being intact is the "fragmentation" so often referred to in Kohut's work. Fortunately, Firestein's objectivity helped direct this pathetic man back to his former analyst for further help.

I do not want to belabor the point: suffice it to say that the Oedipus complex, interpreted in a plausible manner in each case, remained unresolved in every instance because the developmental antecedents that determined the fixation on it had not been dealt with. In contrast, even the relatively inadequate analyses reported in the Chicago casebook had more favorable outcomes after focusing on certain pregenital issues. It is true that follow-up data on the Chicago cases are scanty, but they are much more encouraging than analogous information about Firestein's sample before his formal follow-up interviews. To put this the other way around, the situation at follow-up was by no means surprising in any of these instances.

For example, three years after termination, Charlotte E. recalled little about her six-year analysis. As always, she continued to be effective as a professional, but she was claustrophobic and led an isolated life. She was barely able to curb her masochistic inclinations, and she continued to project her hatred onto others. She reacted to the loss of the analytic relationship with a feeling of emptiness. The analysis had been characterized by a sadomasochistic struggle within the transference; the patient saw this opportunity of venting venom as a safety valve against the psychosis she feared. When a termination date was set, she tried to restrain her vituperativeness, but it persisted to the end. Her sexual excitement in the sessions must have been autoerotic, not directed at him, as the analyst arbitrarily assumed. The patient was overtly dissatisfied with the outcome, except for the prestige of having been "analyzed."

Joseph V. was overtly paranoid about his analyst and developed colitis after many years of treatment. He told Firestein that he was relieved about leaving analysis and that he had then sought nonanalytic assistance.

What are we to conclude about Firestein's matter-of-fact report that the faculty member who had supervised the analysis was satisfied with this termination? It would certainly be preferable not to attempt psychoanalysis with such a difficult patient, instead of indulging in complacency about poor results.

Am I, then, seconding Goldberg's claim (1978, p. 3) that analyses conducted in accord with Kohut's recommendations produce enormous benefits unexplained by classical psychoanalytic theory? Scarcely! The therapeutically effective procedures reported in the casebook were fitted into Kohut's explanatory schema rather arbitrarily. In particular, I am very skeptical about the concept that repair of a developmental deficit takes place via "transmuting internalization." For Kohut, this term means the gradual acquisition of hitherto missing, adaptively essential psychic structure through repeated reliving of certain childhood experiences in the transference (1977, p. 30). The transactions he regards as crucial are the development and resolution of the "narcissistic transferences." I do not see how such a sequence of events could repair a structural defect.

It seems to me that Kohut's hypothesis reverses the causal chain: I think it is the structural deficit that forces the individual into his persisting symbiotic adaptation. Hence the imperative need for external assistance can disappear only if these missing functions are acquired. Personal grandiosity or mistrust of potential instructors (because of previous disillusionments) interfere with the capacity to learn; overcoming such pathological fixations is therefore the usual prerequisite for structural repair. But the actual acquisition of essential skills is not to be confused with these preliminary therapeutic steps. New functions are gained not because of object loss followed by identification (a process that would lead only to the untenable, gross transformations Kohut correctly views as unhelpful [1977, p. 263]); they are *learned* in the context of a satisfactory and age-appropriate human relationship (see Gedo, 1979a).

The effectiveness of several analyses in the casebook was principally based upon correction of a deficit in the capacity to regulate tension, i.e., on direct instruction in identifying either excessive or insufficient stimulation and in taking appropriate steps to correct (later to forestall) these conditions. Traumatic disillusionment with the analyst (whether more or less reality-based or as a transference repetition) makes it impossible to accept his efforts to discuss these matters; an attitude of omniscience interferes with the learning process in the same way. The data suggest that many patients require that the analyst extend his therapeutic armamentarium beyond reading the patient's unconscious; thus the Goldberg casebook does not confirm his claim that "the activity of the analyst is *interpretation*" (p. 9).

The casebook group disavow the fact that their procedures involved radical departures from traditional technique by subsuming these activities under the rubric of managing a "mirror transference." They equate any symbiotic need with Kohut's postulated "merger transference." Kohut himself now speaks of merging with the omnipotent object (1977, p. 85), a usage that relinquishes the distinction between merger and archaic idealization. Perhaps these phenomena have not been classified as idealizing transferences because Kohut sees the latter as relatively late occurrences, generally within the relationship to the father (1977, pp. 10–11). When such events are forced into the category of mirror transferences, it is automatically assumed that they express untamed grandiosity; i.e., the group attributed improvement to the presumed renunciation of grandiose fantasies, the presence of which is postulated without convincing evidence (see Goldberg, 1978, pp. 123, 131).

A further consequence of these assumptions is an actual disregard of silent idealizations. It is claimed, for example, that the idealization with which the analysis of Mr. I. opened was worked through within two years, to be succeeded by a mirror transference. Yet during the terminal phase, his subjective states fluctuated according to his estimate of how well the *analyst* was doing (p. 85)—conclusive evidence for the persistence of idealization. The narrow interpretive focus led to the patient's complaints about his residual problems being disregarded. Even when he revealed that he had been attributing godlike powers to the analyst (p. 88), this issue was allowed to go uninterpreted. Kohut (1977, pp. 264–265) has similarly commented on the disregard of residual idealization in the analysis of Mrs. A. (coded in his book as Mrs. Y.). On the other hand, in the case of Mrs. R., the issue of idealization was handled explicitly and with appropriate persistence.

It should cause no surprise that similar transferences were generally overlooked in the cases reported by Firestein. For example, when Martha R. was told that her analysis should soon be terminated, she revealed that she had been violating the basic rule in various ways through the four years of treatment. The fact that this delinquency had gone undetected apparently convinced her that the analyst was lacking in omnipotence, so that she did decide to end the work rather abruptly. Thomas F., who had mystical experiences before starting treatment, decided on termination after four years of analysis. At that point, the work focused on primal scene material—exile from the parental bedroom or from analysis. At the end, the patient revealed that analysis satisfied his lifelong search for a transcendental power. His lengthy silences during the last part of the analysis had concealed that he was experiencing the worst time of his life, with a "demon trying to break out" of him—the demon of disillusionment, I assume.

The primitive idealizations that persist after an analysis that fails to deal with these issues explicitly, whether it focuses on the Oedipus complex or on the mirror transferences, cast doubt on the viability of a separate category of "narcissistic disorders." The casebook still uses these dubious nosological distinctions; Kohut's own recent volume (1977) is more cautious on this score, but he still differentiates conditions characterized by structural conflicts from those in which the cohesion of the self is as yet unstable. Because the self-cohesion disturbances are diagnosed on the basis of the spontaneous unfolding of "selfobject transferences," we must ask whether any child in the oedipal phase is capable of transcending the need to idealize others and/or to seek affirmation from them. It is clear from the clinical data in both books that Kohut does not, in fact, believe that these needs are entirely overcome before adolescence, if then (see Kohut, 1977, pp. 122n, 230). In actuality, anyone with unresolved childhood problems has to be seen, in this system, as suffering from a disorder of the self. The actual trend of Kohut's thinking appears in passages (e.g., 1977, pp. 187–189) in which oedipal fixations are explained on the basis of parental failures in response to the child's "narcissistic" needs.

Theories that attribute the structuralization of conflict to environmental influences alone leave a number of loose ends. The explanation of perverse behaviors *simply* as the "erotization" of other psychological needs or wishes, for example, seems insufficient. Even if perversion were a "sexualized replica of the original healthy configuration" (Kohut, 1977, pp. 172–173), the reason for this erotization would still need to be understood. It is not at all clear why a fantasy of incorporating masculine power via fellatio should be sexually exciting, to cite one example Kohut has used (p. 201). In spite of their length, the case reports in these books are not convincing about the fate of the patients' perverse activities, especially their fetishistic propensities.

To turn to more general issues, it is important to note that Kohut's entire system of thought departs in a subtle way from our customary intrapsychic framework:

he now tends to view psychic life within the dyadic model of object relations (cf. Chapter 8). Kohut seems to regard the symbiotic needs of childhood as primary; I believe they are only secondary adaptive devices—the child falls back on the caretakers only insofar as he is too immature to cope. I fail to see that normally developing children require the experience of "merger" or the unconditional admiration of their caretakers.[4] They do need to learn a reliable system for evaluating their own performance (Gedo, 1977a).

Kohut's viewpoint not only influences the way in which analysts who follow him reconstruct certain crucial aspects of childhood; it has also led him to look upon empathy as more than a tool of observation: he conceives of it as an agent of healing. This idiosyncratic view of empathy as a quality of *behavior* that should characterize the conduct of the analyst is related to Kohut's promulgation (1975b, 1977, pp. 65–66) of a new value system for psychoanalysis, different from Freud's absolute quest for knowledge. Yet, any other hierarchy of values cannot possibly be associated with *science*—literally the enterprise devoted to the acquisition of knowledge. Without it, we are ever in danger of turning psychoanalysis into a healing cult (Rieff, 1966).

The nature of Kohut's new system of values remains unspecified and must be inferred from the therapeutic choices he advocates. In my eyes, these preferences attempt to justify man's entitlement to a gratifying milieu. Does Tragic Man forever bemoan the Fall?

[4] The best illustration of this difference of opinion may be the case of Mrs. A. (in Goldberg, 1978, see especially pp. 230–231). The analyst viewed this patient's obnoxious clamor for approbation as the expression of a legitimate childhood need; I would have interpreted it as an identification with the most undesirable aspects of her mother's character.

CHAPTER SIX

On the Use and Abuse of Empathy in Psychoanalysis

Unresolved epistemological controversies about the proper designation of psychoanalysis either as an explanatory system or as a psychology of understanding (see Hartmann, 1927; Eissler, 1968) may appear to have little relevance from a clinical point of view. In actuality, however, the resulting uncertainty underlies our difficulties in trusting the validity of specific interpretations (see Habermas, 1968; Thomä and Kächele, 1975; Arlow, 1979). In this respect, the frequent appeals to the analyst's empathy as the primary guide to the meaning of the analysand's communications (Kohut, 1959) may constitute an effort to paper over the difficulty of fitting our data of observation into theoretical schemata (see Waelder, 1962).

Although we have failed to achieve consensus about the use of the term "empathy" in psychoanalysis, I would prefer to avoid detailed consideration of this semantic problem here. Freud's occasional references to *Einfühlung* (1921, p. 108; 1925, p. 273) related the process to identification with the observed; Kohut (1959) defined empathy simply as vicarious introspection. In this latter sense, it comes close to the Kleinian concept of projective identification, but in the service of adaptive rather than defensive aims. To these familiar ideas, I will only add that what may be projected onto the observed can consist either of a self-representation or an object representation. To be more precise, empathy focuses on the observed object's potentials for action (cf. Schafer, 1976) and yields predictions that are based on past experiences of human potentials, including one's own.

It is self-evident that the tendency to equate empathy with kindness or human warmth, or with the use of any particular set of psychoanalytic propositions, however valuable the latter may be, is a grotesque misuse of the concept. It is matched by a comparably serious error: the use of the word "empathy" as a screen hiding the fantasy that the observer's intuition is infallible.

The claim that psychoanalytic empathy leads to a more reliable understanding of others than does undisciplined intuition is based on the assumption that a preparatory analysis will give the prospective analyst sufficient access to hitherto unconscious motivations to prevent inappropriate intrusions of the latter into the analytic transaction. In practice, this aim of psychoanalytic training is probably achieved reasonably well. In supervising the work of advanced candidates, I have seldom encountered countertransference problems or gross identifications with analysands grave enough to cause difficulties in grasping the meaning of the associative material. In order to focus more specifically on the role of empathy in clinical work, I shall therefore confine my discussion to those instances in which there are no significant personal obstacles in the way of unimpeded empathic functioning. The question I wish to examine here is whether interpretations are in fact optimally formulated through the exercise of empathy.

I assume that analysts would concede without difficulty the possibility of arriving at valid interpretations on the basis of other, nonempathic criteria. As an illustration, I shall give an instance of alternative interpretations conceived by means of the method I believe to be most common, that of preconsciously fitting a set of observations into a familiar cognitive pattern through the process we have called "evenly hovering attention" (Freud, 1912). Such deductive inferences may not fully satisfy those who evaluate our clinical procedures from the viewpoint of the philosophy of science, but they are the common currency of our ordinary discourse (Waelder, 1962).

A recent colloquium on the management of difficult cases reviewed some work I published on that subject (Gedo, 1975a, 1977a). The discussion focused on clinical material I had cited to illustrate the phenomena of idealization within archaic transferences, including a sequence of dreams in which the analysand attributed magical curative powers to me. The manifest content of one of these dreams involved a pilotless jetliner in which the patient was the sole passenger; this enormous airplane was going through a series of impossible stunts (this clinical material is described more fully in Chapter 4, pp. 128–130). My interpretation stressed the impersonality of portraying the analysis as a miraculous mechanical device, a feature I have found to be characteristic of primitive idealization. At the seminar, we eventually concentrated on the fact that my interpretation left out of consideration the probable sexual meaning of the dream symbolism. My skeptical interlocutors, it should be noted, did not ask whether the patient's associations lent support to one hypothesis or the other, nor did they inquire about the subjective (or empathic) cues that might have led me to select the one I had used. It is of interest, in my judgment, that the challenge to my interpretation would be perfectly valid if it were based on the recognition that it could not pretend to be an exhaustive exposition of the significance of the dream. As the analysis subsequently revealed, the patient in question was certainly extremely ambitious in the sexual sphere, and the airplanes in her dreams did usually turn out to have a phallic meaning. But my critics were not willing to circumscribe the scope of their criticism: as far as they were concerned, the pattern of meaning I had highlighted was invalidated by the detection of a sexual theme in the latent content of the dream. Somehow, for them, a sexual miracle was of interest only because it concerned sex, not because it was a miracle. In point of fact, the precise meaning of the patient's intense penis envy only became clear five years later in the analysis, and it turned out to be rather unusual: she was convinced that the phallus made its possessor independent of others, and because she was without a penis, she felt herself incapable of self-sufficiency. Her belief underscores the fact that all that is sexual does not pertain to lusting for people.

I have described the foregoing incident not because I believe most analysts would endorse such an either/or reductionism in psychoanalytic conceptualizations, but because, in its very naiveté, such reductionism is particularly revealing about the thought processes involved. Optimally, we are sophisticated about keeping in mind the multiple functions (or manifold meanings) of every piece of behavior, but we generally continue to fit our data into the framework of established schemata, however many of these we may apply simultaneously. Whether pattern matching is the optimal, or even an adequate, method for choosing the appropriate interpretation from the available alternatives is, of course, a different and more complex problem. It would be perfectly reasonable to suppose, for example, that the analyst's empathy should be exercised precisely at the point where such a choice is to be made. Whenever he becomes aware of his own subjective response to the analysand's associative material through introspection, that affective state must be regarded as a highly significant element of the overall pattern to be understood, as Gardner (in preparation) has recently shown in convincing detail. Unfortunately, the kind of self-awareness required to use one's own responses as guides to the meaning of analytic material is not always available to the analyst; in particular, it may not be easy to differentiate such affective signals from inappropriate countertransference reactions. I should like to underscore this point by means of some clinical material that I shall return to in other contexts as well.

Case 14

Some years ago, I attempted to analyze an observant member of a closely knit, rigid religious community who sought help during a depressive crisis. Her marriage had failed; her children, who were then in college, were in turmoil; and she had invested herself totally in propagating the faith, an enterprise in which her expertise as a journalist was very useful. This way of life effectively placed her outside of the money economy, but health insurance coverage permitted her to undertake treatment. She felt desperate enough to proceed with therapy in spite of some disapproval among her coreligionists—a negative attitude that did not, however, reflect the views of the leaders of her religious group. One of her chief concerns was her inability to live in accord with certain precepts of her community. As a result of this failure, she alternated between acts of heretical rebelliousness, performed in what may have been altered states of consciousness, and a condition of profound loss of self-esteem, remorse, and expiatory self-abnegation.

She was a middle child in an extended family raised during the Depression on a large farm in the heart of the wheat country. Her father, descended from pioneer Yankee stock, was therefore a man of property, although he was penniless at that time. Her mother was an immigrant from Scandinavia, an energetic person who made her way to the New World on her own as an adolescent and managed to obtain training as a nurse. The patient's parents were married while her father served in the army during World War I; when they settled on the farm, the mother turned out to be unacceptable to the community because of her foreign ways. Moreover, the marriage was extremely strained, and the parents separated when the patient was five. At that time, the mother took her children and went to live in the nearest large town. As a result of this move, the patient was raised in an urban setting, receiving a good education and opportunities for a professional career.

All of the patient's siblings were more severely impaired psychologically than she. Her relative psychological health was almost certainly the result of her father's constant refusal to have anything to do with her. He had the delusion that she was not his child, a delusion that caused her desperate hurt and sorrow. By the same token, she was the only one of the children he did not molest sexually. He kidnapped his youngest child when the latter was about two years old; this brother's eventual suicide in adolescence would become the most shattering event in the patient's life. Naturally, the patient had been extremely close to her mother, a reliable person, of unwavering convictions; her faith in her mother's *Weltanschauung* was finally destroyed when she saw how fatuous and unhelpful it proved in relation to the difficulties that culminated in her brother's suicide. Shortly before this, she had still chosen a husband on the basis of her mother's preferences. Following the tragedy of her brother's death, she went through a lengthy spiritual crisis that ultimately led her to join the esoteric religious community which had been the center of her life ever since. Her mother had never been able to accept her conversion; she continued to preach to her daughter the need to return to her own brand of Christianity as the sole path to salvation.

Needless to say, I undertook the analysis of a prophetess—for the patient's "heresies," if they had been adopted by her coreligionists, would have amounted to nothing less than a radical reform of her community, which also fell short of the City of God—with no firm expectation of success. I anticipated some difficulty in accommodating her fanaticism, and this concern turned out to be well founded. But *this* problem was actually trivial in comparison to the effects of the patient's continual misunderstanding of the ground rules of the analytic procedure in terms of the rituals of a healing cult. There were also expectable frictions regarding my refusal to endorse the self-condemnations that proceeded from her departures from orthodoxy; on such occasions she regularly projected her "badness" onto me and assailed me for being bad just as her mother had assailed her for decades. But these patterns of irrationality were never too puzzling, and I needed no prominent affective signals to understand them or to make use of them analytically. The analysis eventually revealed that unconsciously she was not an ugly duckling (i.e., a heretic) but—a hitherto undiscovered identity—a religious innovator. Her acceptance of this view as a valid assessment was shown by a dramatic amelioration of her conflicted, inconsistent behavior, greater self-acceptance, a return to secular employment, and the disappearance of her fanaticism.

In actuality, this analysis proved to be extremely taxing for a reason I found very surprising: I was confronted with recurrent incidents of covert uncooperativeness about various aspects of the psychoanalytic procedure. The patient's uncooperative actions generally occurred without premonitory signs, and they involved procedural matters that presented no problems for her at other times. For instance, she might suddenly respond to some metaphorical expression I had used on a concrete level, or, vice versa, she might take a literal statement as a metaphor. Although I had encountered regressions in the capacity to use language for the communication of shared meanings in the course of analyses prior to this one, the regressive incidents in the case under discussion affected me in a new way. In the past, such events had generally struck me as puzzling and potentially illuminating—in other words, as grist for the analytic mill. With this patient, I responded with anger, as if she had deliberately made a fool of me in a malicious manner. I had sufficient confidence in the steadfastness of my analytic posture to use my affective response as a relevant observational datum: I would therefore usually inform the patient that she was mistreating me in some irresponsible way, and I would insist that she cease this childlike enactment and investigate its purport by means of the associative process. Although my interventions were likely to lead to further delinquent provocations, an indication that I might really get annoyed was always sufficient to regain the patient's cooperation.[1] I had the impression that her renewed cooperativeness occurred not because she felt intimidated but as a result of per-

[1] For a full discussion of the rationale of the therapeutic use of the analyst's affective responses, see Chapter 11. This example is particularly instructive with regard to that issue, because one might be tempted to assume that allowing the patient to see the success of her provocativeness would constitute a transference gratification of major proportions. The actual transaction turned out quite otherwise: the patient understood rather precisely that she was being shown how people might respond to her behavior in ordinary life situations. In other words, she could distinguish affects generated by investment in our common endeavor from personal reactions on my part. Whenever she was in doubt about this, I did not find it difficult to reestablish my basic analytic neutrality, e.g., by stressing in a very calm manner that I had no interest in influencing her in any way unless she requested my continued assistance with such an aim of her own.

Merton Gill (personal communication) has objected to another aspect of my technique, namely, my *insistence* that the patient resume the associative task. In such circumstances, Gill reports he would confine himself to inquiries about the meaning of a refusal to do so. This difference reflects Gill's adherence to the traditional technique of analysis with patients who were not traditionally considered "analyzable" from the standpoint of that technique. I tried to register my objections to the inconsistency entailed in this position in the title I chose for my most recent book—*Beyond Interpretation* (1979a), i.e., whenever the behavior of the analysand lies "beyond the pleasure principle," it cannot be dealt with through intellectual explanations alone.

Gill has raised another question about my procedure that I regard as more cogent than his first criticism. He writes, "in the process of exploring what the patient's subjective experience actually is, the therapist must always assume that, from the patient's point of view, the therapist has done something (or failed to do something) which. . . is a plausible explanation of why the patient is responding as she is." This statement is unobjectionable, but Gill underestimates the difficulty of maintaining rational discourse with patients who are literally unable to pursue goal-directed behavior. The emergencies I am trying to describe do not permit us to engage in the elucidation of fine points. As Napoleon remarked about ending the tyranny of the Paris mobs, "Give them a whiff of grapeshot!"

ceiving for the first time what effect her behavior was having on someone else.

I think it should be noted that I was quite unable to arrive at an accurate understanding of this disruptive pattern of behavior through empathic channels. I had no notion of the patient's motives for "attacking" me in this way, only the conviction that I was being deliberately assaulted. I could not imagine what was leading this devotee of holiness into these unprovoked episodes of irresponsibility. Needless to say, it was necessary to engage in some self-inquiry on each occasion the patient "attacked" me to make sure that her aggressive activity was indeed unprovoked. Judging by the fact that occasionally we did discover that I had inadvertently injured her in some way, it is unlikely that we were simply overlooking the proximate cause of her behavior in these specific instances. Moreover, her usual reaction to my therapeutic errors was one of hurt and disappointment, rather than the assaultive misbehaviors in question.

Thus I was at a loss for some time, and we had to settle on a consensus that we were confronted with a deeply meaningful set of patterned events that, for the time being, defied comprehension. After some months, it became possible to cut short the enactment of the aggressive sequence by calling attention to its recurrence in its earliest stages and enlisting the patient's curiosity about it. In this context, her associations gradually came to cluster around her early relationship to her psychotic father, and she came to realize that his behavior had regularly made her feel shocked, bewildered, and angry as I was reporting she now made me feel. Prototypical of these transactions was a screen memory of being invited, as a most exceptional favor, to go along with all the other children on an excursion in father's pick-up truck. She was told to climb in at the back, but when everyone else was aboard, her father pulled away, laughing, and she was left behind.

The recovery of this and similar childhood memories suffices to demonstrate that a valid interpretation of the transference phenomena depends entirely on the spontaneous emergence of specific cues that only the analysand can supply. In this instance, the key element needed to complete the gestalt, i.e., to read the "figure in the carpet," was the fact that as a child the patient had been completely bewildered by her father's sadistic acts because they occurred only when she did not expect them, i.e., when they were entirely unprovoked. Until this feature of the pattern was clarified, it was necessary each time to look for a precipitating event, or, at the very least, to suspect the presence of a countertransference problem. Such caution remained advisable at all times, but, once the requisite information became available, the correct interpretation could be discerned by the analysand. If it is customary for the analyst to articulate such conclusions, this is justified only by considerations of efficiency.

Let us retrace our steps in order to take up the main thread of this discussion once again. The clinical material I have summarized illustrates the manner in which the analyst may employ his affective reactions to apprehend more fully the significance of the therapeutic transaction. This process presupposes a capacity for continuous self-inquiry in order to screen out idiosyncratic responses that are basically irrelevant to the analysand's activities. I believe that the analyst's appropriate affective reactions are the signals that Freud (1912, pp. 115–116) had in mind when he characterized psychoanalytic work as the transmission of information from the unconscious of one person to that of another. It is essential to differentiate this aspect of the analyst's necessary self-awareness from his empathic functioning. Empathy refers to the capacity to detect the other person's state of mind through identificatory processes. I must reemphasize that this did *not* take place in the example I have provided.

Am I claiming, then, that empathy played no part in the therapeutic work I have reported? Not at all. I believe that it did not operate in the process of learning the meaning of the behaviors I have selected to highlight in the case thus far. Perhaps it would be easiest to show its influence by asking a hypothetical question: what would have constituted an example of *unempathic* handling of these transference crises? There are, of course, countless possibilities, but the one contingency we cannot include among them is that of offering an erroneous interpretation. For a very long time, this patient gratefully accepted all interpretations as signs of benevolent concern, and she did not even begin to question their truth value. One does not look a gift horse in the mouth—particularly if one has never seen a horse before! I suspect that the most unempathic approach I could have chosen would have been to disavow my feelings of being injured by the patient's actions (on the basis, let us say, of characterological masochism or some related personal difficulty) because this would-be saint experienced intolerable remorse about her transgressions. Such remorse pointed to her urgent need to learn that her transference enactments were most meaningfully assessed in terms of a compulsion to repeat (although we had no immediate way of knowing what was being repeated), rather than continuing to be judged on a moral scale.

In other words, I see my analytic interventions around this issue as "empathic" insofar as they were based on my preconscious conviction, previously reached through introspection as well as experience with a variety of individuals, that a person of high moral standards needs urgent assistance to raise his actual performance to a level closer to the ideals he has set for himself, that in the service of this aim one must confront the patient with the reality of his attacks on the analyst, and that the guilt of such a person will be kept within tolerable bounds (i.e., it may not require expiatory activities) if the victim of his aggression responds with vigor.[2] I think it is important to note that these assumptions about the analysand did not bring us closer to formulating an interpretation of her puzzling behavior, although

[2] The appropriate analytic intervention had, once again, to go "beyond interpretation," just as the patient's behavior in the treatment setting transcended the boundaries of the "basic rule." (See also the preceding footnote.)

they turned out to be absolutely correct. In my experience, such assumptions are most likely to be valid when they concern human universals close to psychobiological bedrock. Insofar as cultural, characterological, or experiential factors make us significantly different from our analysands, our efforts to do unto them as we would wish others to do unto ourselves are bound to miscarry when we are dealing with complex analytic issues, especially when these involve obscure subjective meanings. I shall try to provide an illustrative example of such a miscarriage of empathy shortly.

Kohut (1959) has defined the arena of psychoanalytic psychology as the world of subjective motives we can apprehend by means of introspection and empathy. In *Beyond Interpretation* (Gedo, 1979a), I have argued that our subject matter transcends the subjective realm, that in our essential concern about issues such as tension regulation or the establishment of a coherent hierarchy of personal aims, we deal with objective adaptive needs that can never be detected by such methods, but have been inferred from the cumulative analytic observations of almost a century. In other words, such knowledge is the fruit of the methods of natural science. When Kohut (and like-minded theorists) attempt to tilt the epistemological debate in the direction of viewing psychoanalysis primarily as a psychology of understanding, some attempts to disclaim the implications of this position (1977, pp. 304ff) notwithstanding, his emphasis threatens to substitute the subjective demands of patients in states of regression for our collective scientific judgment about the appropriate goals and methods of psychoanalytic treatment. Further, Kohut has placed greater stress on empathy as the cardinal tool of analytic observation than on introspection (Kohut, 1975a, 1975b; see also Wolf, 1976), discreetly implying that we are capable of identifying the analysand's subjective motivations instead of being confined to the perception of our personal responses to his behavior, especially his affects (see Modell, 1978).

It may well be that some authors would call the analyst's capacity to "read" the patient's affects in this manner "empathic." There can be no serious objection to this, although I would prefer to confine our use of the term to inferences about others based on identification with more complex behaviors, i.e., with the motivational matrix giving rise to their affects. However we resolve this semantic question, it is clear that we have no power to read unconscious meanings through the channels that permit us to detect affective signals. Perhaps this circumstance lies behind the common tendency (cf. Kohut, 1977, p. 281) to extend the concept of empathy from an observational process to an agency of healing. In this expanded (and misleading) sense, the analyst pretends not only to understand what the analysand wants, both consciously and unconsciously, but also genuinely to espouse the legitimacy of the infantile wish. Although we may empathically grasp how people feel when their infantile wishes are frustrated (or, for that matter, gratified in one way or another)—for that is indeed the psychobiological bedrock on which our common humanity rests—it is certainly no part of any truly psychoanalytic effort to assist people to gratify any of their wishes, infantile or otherwise, with the single exception of their presumed wish to achieve self-understanding. Some infantile wishes are more "legitimate" than others, and it must be seriously doubted whether any analyst is able wholeheartedly to empathize with the peremptory and unreasonable demands that some analysands place upon him. For example, I do not believe that any psychoanalyst could honestly have joined my prophetess during her episodes of monstrous misbehavior in viewing herself (through a screen of paranoid distortions) as a holy innocent, as she insisted that I do. But in pushing their position to such a logical extreme, I may be caricaturing the views of the advocates of "the healing power of empathy."

To recapitulate the argument: although introspection and empathy are indeed vital tools in the performance of psychoanalysis, emphasis on the use of these unique, subjective observational pathways must not lead us to overlook that the most common intellectual activity of the analyst is actually the matching of sets of primary data to (more or less familiar) patterns or schemata. Introspection assists in this task by screening out those percepts which do not pertain to the psychological world of the analysand but threaten to overlay the present with the shadow of the analyst's own past. It should also yield data about the patient's activities by way of the appropriate affective responses they have evoked in the analyst. Empathy plays its part in the enterprise because it may produce valid assumptions about some aspects of the analysand's inner life about which no direct information is as yet available. This avenue of observation may easily mislead us, however, because people tend to be alike only about the most fundamental features of human existence.

Among others, Modell (1978) has called attention to the similarity of psychoanalytic and historical inquiries, as the latter were conceived by Giambattista Vico. In both disciplines, we rely on the capacity imaginatively to place ourselves into the position of other human beings. Yet Modell also believes that every psychoanalytic explanation must simultaneously include consideration of the person's biological state, as that is reflected in the affective realm. In other words, Modell, with whom I am in agreement, sees affective life as the psychobiological bedrock about which empathic insights are potentially available to the analyst. In practice, of course, most analysts attempt to use empathy in a far broader area, with variable results.

If our analytic technique permits the correction of misunderstandings through the appropriate monitoring of the resultant feedback, errors caused by the misapplication of empathy are no more damaging, in principle, than any other mistakes would be—analytic work is only possible if both participants accept the analyst's right to be wrong. However, it is probably unrealistic to count on the ability of most analysands to counteract the powerful suggestive effect of incorrect interpretations (cf. Glover, 1931) or the ability of most analysts to overcome the narcissistic mortification of acknowledging therapeutic mistakes. Hence complacency about the overuse of empathy in our clinical work is quite out of place, and we would do well to face the fact that the best analytic approach to the investigation of unconscious meanings is to enlist the analysand's cooperation to undertake the task of introspection to the maximum extent. When this is achieved, the analyst's role can approach that of a technical advisor and recipient of transference projections (see Gardner, in preparation; Gedo, 1979a). From this perspective, it may be no exaggeration to state that the most difficult analytic self-denial is the necessity to curb our natural human propensity to take the measure of others by means of empathy,[3] that is, to delay closures until the analysand finds his voice and is able to speak for himself. I should like to illustrate this problem by returning once again to the case of the religious devotee.

Case 14: A Further Discussion

I have already described the episodes of incomprehensible delinquency this patient displayed from time to time, and my refusal to try to interpret their meaning, a policy that led to the spontaneous emergence of relevant associations about the past that made it possible to discern the significance of these episodes through pattern matching. Here I shall add an instance of my inability to

[3] I am indebted to Samuel D. Lipton for the acute observation that this process is parallel to the necessity to learn in the course of childhood not to rely on (pseudo)-empathy to understand the nature of inanimate objects, animals, etc.

exercise such restraint at a crucial juncture in the treatment. Through the resultant "error in empathy," the patient became disorganized, so that the analysis was temporarily interrupted. This was not the first occasion on which such an impairment of self-cohesion occurred in the course of our work; in fact, these were initially rather frequent events. They were generally brought on by any alteration in the schedule of our appointments and were gradually mitigated as the patient learned to anticipate this effect of separations between us. The disruption I shall now relate was the only real "iatrogenic" episode of this kind.

The patient's conviction that she was a heretic was closely connected to her childhood belief that her father was justified in excluding her from the family. Consequently, recovery of these repressed or disavowed memories resulted in her taking a more and more realistic view of her religious community, with increasing conflict about accepting anyone else's interpretation of its creed as Revelation. One sign of the imminent liberation of her thinking from "orthodoxy" was her increased vehemence about the desirability of submitting to authority—including, of course, that of her new-found psychoanalytic guru. Her attitude about the analytic procedure was drawn into the conflict in a number of predictable ways; among these, I was most concerned about the displacement of the intense proselytizing pressure of her religious community onto psychoanalysis. She began to feel like a prisoner, trapped in an endless series of analytic obligations, and her rebelliousness about such tyranny now took the form of covert but fairly transparent wishes to escape. The transference situation was reminiscent of the position of her youngest brother in childhood, after the father captured him and kept him trapped on the farm, away from his mother. The source of my disquiet about this went beyond the content of the fantasy, although I did feel uncomfortable about being mistaken for the Reverend Jim Jones; the problem was acute because the patient seemed progressively less able to maintain the realization that her experience of the analysis did not correspond to any objective reality.

In these circumstances, I made the cardinal error of assuming that she could profit from an insight that many of us would have needed in a similar situation: I reminded her that man is born free, and if everywhere about us we see him in chains, his condition of servitude is generally self-imposed.[4] To my astonishment, she

[4] I was, of course, attempting to lay the groundwork for an interpretation of her attachment to me in the father transference. In this report, I am not able to be precise about the exact wording of my intervention; it was aphoristic and ambiguous (I believe such an approach is indicated during preparatory stages of interpretive activity concerning novel material), but the metaphor I used may have been different. There is no question that the patient grossly misunderstood my meaning; on this basis, some readers have questioned whether the example actually demonstrates a miscarriage of empathy. In my opinion, it does so because at other times this patient was fully able to understand my metaphoric expressions. (The earlier example has, I trust, clarified that her failure to do so was usually an enactment within the negative transference.) In other words, the analysis went off the rails not because the patient failed to follow my meaning but because my interpretation was irrelevant to the crisis at hand. It is more difficult to substantiate the claim that my incorrect interpretation was reached via empathy, rather than through alternative channels. Because this is a question of my inner psychological experience, I am afraid I must ask others to take my word for it.

took this message to mean that I was urging her to enact the "corrective emotional experience" of liberating herself by walking out on the analysis. She enthusiastically proceeded with this plan of action, in such haste that I could do nothing effective to safeguard the continuity of the work. Even worse, she misinterpreted my feeble efforts to do so in the context of the father transference as an irrational and/or malicious trick, similar to her father's frequent maneuvers intended to tease and disappoint her. She did resume therapeutic contact with me after a lengthy interval, so that we were eventually able to piece together some meanings of this strange sequence of events.

One important issue we uncovered that seemed related to the disruptive effect of my insistence on differentiating the present from intense parental pressure for the patient's loyalty in the past was the primacy of her ambivalence about her mother that she evidenced in the clinical situation at the time of the interruption. The childhood idealization that characterized their relationship, later transferred to the religious community she joined and to the analysis, had come about as a reaction formation to an earlier disillusionment. Just before she bolted from treatment, the patient had recovered a memory from the period immediately following her parents' separation, when her mother's customary self-assurance deserted her and she regularly consulted a faith healer whose practices struck the child as completely bizarre. The fact that the flight from analysis was in reaction to a repetition of the original disillusionment with mother was already discernible in her attitude for several weeks prior to the rupture. During that time, as I have mentioned, she began to regard me as an infallible Wise Man, with an exaggeration so crude that the praise felt like an insult. After she fled, she wrote me a flowery letter of thanks about the marvelous assistance I had rendered her. Although it was obvious that these were reaction formations against perceiving me as a depreciated figure, the first clue that this issue was in any way related to a *maternal* transference was the emergence of the memory about the faith healer. This association occurred in the last session before the interruption, following the unfortunate intervention which demonstrated my lack of omniscience to her.

From a more general perspective, we might say that evidence for the genetic background of the focal conflict was not available, so that the sole guide for therapeutic activity was the analyst's empathic capacity. As it happened, the empathic effort led to a definite therapeutic error; the outcome of the empathic intervention proved that, in this instance, it would have been very much better to have done nothing. Is this, then, an example of what we generally mean when we speak of "errors in empathy"? Perhaps so, although in the strict sense of the term it was not an error resulting from a failure to appreciate our common humanity but an *unsuccessful* attempt to understand by means of the empathic process. To put this in another way, I see the error as the unavoidable result of having recourse, in a seeming emergency, to the only instrument available. In fact, the empathic instrument did make it possible to detect the patient's frantic need to idealize my authority, but it could not yield the specific data that would have clarified the source of her fear of disillusionment. Consequently, my interpretive intervention amounted to a perseveration on an issue that had been relevant on previous occasions, and its inadequacy merely confirmed the patient's fears.

Of course, one might simply regard the need to intervene in a situation of such uncertainty as "unempathic" in itself. In my experience with this patient up to the crucial moment, however, analytic inactivity had been too difficult for her to bear, largely because of her past as a neglected child. Nor had she ever been able to take statements about my lack of omniscience at face value, so that I do not think she would have accepted any temporizing on my part as a delay made necessary by unavailable information. In other words, I do not believe that any easy answer for this technical dilemma was possible. In hindsight, it might have been best to offer some interpretation that had a greater chance of being on the mark, even if the price for such accuracy had been to restrict myself to a very low level of potential relevance. If successful, such a trivial intervention could have bought enough time to permit subsequent efforts to enlist the patient's cooperation in investigating the sources of her crisis of ambivalence. Of course, I regarded the intervention I did make as rather banal, and I *had* intended it as a temporizing move!

In conclusion, I think the moral of this clinical case is

plain: the less we have to rely on empathy in psychoanalytic work, the fewer therapeutic errors will follow. What has commonly been viewed as empathic performance on the part of the analyst is, in actuality, the outcome of a different set of mental operations. By screening out his own personal responses and refraining from assuming that the analysand is nothing but an alter ego, the analyst exercises a kind of self-restraint that deserves to be regarded as genuine altruism. When, as a consequence of such altruistic behavior, the analysand achieves new insights about himself, the psychological world of the analyst may expand into novel areas of experience. He may then begin to understand aspects of humanity that were alien to him before and subsequently utilize this new knowledge to achieve a broader range of empathic contact with his patients in the future.

CHAPTER SEVEN

Epigenesis, Developmental Lines, and Psychopathology

In recent years, the principal issues of controversy in the realm of the theory of psychopathology have revolved around competing conceptions of personality development. These differences have involved both the application of the principle of epigenesis to the psychological field and the problem of integrating the influence of manifold developmental lines on the ultimate crystallization of personality structure. In general terms, the first set of questions has led to disagreements about the eventual effects of early developmental vicissitudes on the solutions to the crises of later phases, while the second cluster has divided those who believe that separate developmental lines give rise to distinct psychopathological entities from others who view both "normal" and pathological adaptations as final common pathways serving all of the multiple functions we classify, for heuristic purposes, in terms of specific lines of development.

It may be most convenient to document the practical consequences of the controversy concerning epigenesis by citing the contrasting positions of certain authors about the analytic treatment of persons suffering from archaic transference constellations. Kernberg (1979), for example, asserts that he has never encountered such a patient who, with appropriate psychoanalytic management, failed to reexperience the conflicts of the oedipal period in later stages of his analysis. In other words, he implies that early developmental transactions never prevent the occurrence of the normative crisis we have designated the "Oedipus complex"—at any rate, not in individuals intact enough to be considered for psychoanalytic treatment. On the other side, van der Leeuw (1979) reports that many of his patients with such archaic problems present a defensive facade of pseudorelatedness to others but actually live in a truly narcissistic universe. I assume that these disparate conclusions represent more than the selection of patients with differing characteristics; I suspect one author or the other has misunderstood the clinical data on the basis of *a priori* theoretical assumptions. As I have reported elsewhere (Gedo and Goldberg, 1973; Gedo, 1979a), my own clinical experience has supported van der Leeuw's explanation of archaic problems, although I believe that cases of the kind he mentions are, in fact, quite rare (for illustrative examples, see Ludowyk-Gyomroi, 1963, and Case E. in Goldberg, 1978). In most instances, archaic pathology does not arrest further development, and subsequent oedipal experiences, which are all the more difficult to master because of the legacy of earlier problems, generally complicate the clinical picture by leading to the formation of an infantile neurosis and its sequelae. (Settlage [1977] has expressed roughly similar views in his continuing debate with theoreticians who minimize the import of relatively early experiences.)

The manner in which our theoretical preconceptions structure our understanding of such clinical data is demonstrated with the utmost clarity in a recent case report by Kohut (1979). He describes two periods of analysis with the same patient, separated by some years, in the course of which Kohut's theoretical views underwent radical change. During the first analysis, he saw the observational material essentially in classical oedipal terms; during the second time of treatment, he understood the same phenomena as defenses against underlying "narcissistic" issues. However, Kohut does not clarify the issue that I regard as central here; it is unclear from his report whether he saw the results of the first analysis as genuine solutions to significant oedipal problems that left certain nonoedipal issues unresolved, or whether he thought his initial formulations had been incorrect. The clinical material presented does not enable the reader to assess the likelihood of either alternative. Elsewhere, Kohut (1977) seems to take the stance that the development of significant oedipal love and hate for the parents is contingent on prior consolidation of certain mental structures (what Kohut has called "the self")—in other words, he apparently shares the views of those who attribute maximal importance to earlier phases in the epigenetic sequence. If I assess Kohut's position as somewhat equivocal on this score, it is because he has consistently placed much greater emphasis on a different conception that contradicts this view. This countervailing idea sets up a nosology based on the differentiation of problems involving conflicts about love and hate for others from problems produced by the inability to satisfy personal ambitions or ideals (Kohut and Wolf, 1978). Kohut (1977) has called these categories the problems of Guilty Man and of Tragic Man, respectively, and he has stated that he has seldom encountered analytic patients who needed assistance with significant difficulties in both areas. From the standpoint of this latter perspective, his 1979 report on his two analyses of the same patient might be read to mean that only the "tragic" aspects of the material had been authentic.

A nosology organized according to preponderant issues that can be followed through the life cycle as "developmental lines," such as Kohut's postulation of Tragic versus Guilty Man,[1] confuses the conceptual categories we have devised for heuristic purposes with the actualities they are intended to clarify. In other words, developmental lines exist only in the observer's scheme in things; *in vivo,* every bit of maturational progress brings about simultaneous advances on all fronts of behavior. The gestalt of human behavior constitutes an inseparable unity, and it is *in principle* inconceivable to have pathologies affecting only discrete and specific

[1] Actually, Kohut (1966, 1968, 1971) initially proposed such a nosology as a reflection of the separate developmental lines he postulated for object libido and narcissism—a version of his views that made it absolutely clear that his nosological distinctions are not based on epigenetic considerations.

"areas" of mental life (see D. Rapaport, 1959, pp. 40–42). As I have mentioned elsewhere (1979a, p. 5), my clinical experience has demonstrated that the problems Kohut dichotomizes in his schema invariably coexist: they are, in fact, only alternative ways of perceiving the same phenomena (L. Sadow, personal communication; Moraitis, in press). Hence I believe that we may legitimately use the developmental lines we have conceived only as indicators (analogous to the scales on our thermometers) about the current state of an individual's functional organization. And as I have tried to demonstrate elsewhere (Gedo and Goldberg, 1973), progression and regression in functional organization invariably involve all of the lines of development concurrently.

To approach this matter from another perspective, the particular psychological issues around which a specific psychopathological constellation seems to be organized are determined by the configuration of the actual life circumstances the individual is confronting; in this sense, the psychological issues themselves are epiphenomena. The crucial considerations for personality diagnosis concern the range of potential behaviors available to the person in response to the varied contingencies of life. If psychological development has been arrested in the course of childhood, this range may in fact be limited to the more archaic segment of the expectable human repertory—hence Kernberg's contention about the universality of oedipal behaviors cannot be reconciled with the epigenetic view of development that has gained general acceptance in psychoanalysis. To put the matter differently, although persons may have their development interrupted for various reasons before they attain the oedipal phase, the resultant psychopathology will not be confined to the so-called "narcissistic" realm, but will involve all aspects of behavior, including those pertaining to object love, that were available to the individual at the stage at which development had been arrested. And conversely, in most instances, archaic pathology will not produce arrest in development, so that individuals with the whole gamut of unresolved problems originating in the "pregenital" era will generally experience the usual oedipal vicissitudes. To use Kohut's terminology, Tragic Man is beset with superego conflicts and Guilty Man bears his share of tragedy.

To repeat, an adequate psychoanalytic nosology must simultaneously take into account the fact that human behavior always expresses the totality of the manifold functions we generally divide, for didactic purposes, into a series of developmental lines, and it must permit us to keep track of the multiple, complexly interrelated legacies of the unresolved problems stemming from the succession of developmental phases. To accomplish all this, it has proved helpful to utilize a hierarchical schema, such as the one Goldberg and I proposed in *Models of the Mind* (1973), and that I elaborated in *Beyond Interpretation* (1979a). In other words, we must avoid reducing the complexities of human adaptation into two or three syndromes such as "borderline states," "narcissistic disturbances," or "neurotic" conditions.

From the vantage point of the theory of psychoanalytic therapy, such a hierarchical view requires us to delay closure with regard to personality diagnosis, i.e., to adhere at all times to a policy of open-minded agnosticism about the relative significance for adult adaptation of the derivatives of various childhood vicissitudes characteristic of differing developmental phases. With consistent application of this approach, or, if you will, of Freud's inductive investigative method (cf. Sadow et al., 1968), we may learn about the variety of complex ways in which disparate residues of the past may be interrelated. In the process, we should discover the empirical evidence that will permit us to make valid choices among the competing clinical hypotheses now current on the psychoanalytic scene.

We have not as yet accumulated the extensive observational data needed to construct a rational psychoanalytic nosology based on such inductive methods. At this time, I shall therefore confine myself to offering one illustration of the results I have already obtained—a case report that may illuminate the specific connection at various phases of the epigenetic hierarchy between developmental lines generally regarded as independent of each other. Because of the importance of the controversy around the issue of "narcissistic" pathology, I have chosen to focus on an example in which the distinction between Guilty Man and Tragic Man turned out to be meaningless.

Case 15

The patient was referred to me by a colleague in another city who was a friend of his family and had served as his adviser and surrogate parent while he was in college. He contacted me a few months before starting medical school in Chicago to arrange for an analysis at the earliest opportunity. Although he indicated that he had personal problems of sufficient magnitude to have required psychotherapeutic assistance for subjective discomforts in the recent past, he also made it clear that he was interested in analytic treatment in order to prepare himself to become a psychoanalyst. He was embarking on his medical training as a preliminary step in that endeavor, with little enthusiasm about the nonpsychological aspects of this educational experience. His expenses, including my analytic fees, were to be paid out of the ample allowance granted by his maternal grandfather, the patriarchal head of a considerable commercial empire. We agreed to undertake analysis on a five-session-per-week basis as soon as he got settled in school in the fall.

He made the necessary arrangements quite promptly, an effort motivated by his great distress about a number of disturbing events. Among these, the gravest may have been the fact that his only sibling, a brother two years his junior, had begun to show unmistakable signs of a schizophrenic psychosis. As we gradually learned in the course of the treatment, there was in fact nothing new in the emergence of the brother's disturbed behavior—it had merely become more unacceptable socially as the young man had to face the demands of leaving home. In fact, it was the patient's success in accomplishing that task which appeared to have stimulated the younger brother into activities that revealed his thinking disorder in a manner the family could no longer deny. The responsibility for maintaining the disavowal of this pathology had formerly fallen largely on the patient; until he left for college, the brothers had in some ways behaved like twins. Not only did their mutual identification and imitation seem to improve the younger boy's performance; it also led the patient to acquire some startlingly primitive patterns of thinking—silly concretizations rationalized as humor, the idiosyncratic, hostile use of words as deliberate provocations, and the construction of neologisms that he regarded as creative achievements.

At first, the patient seemed very concerned about the eventual fate of his brother, but it soon turned out that his anxiety was connected more with the fantasy that he might be able to rescue the latter (or that he might already have *failed* to accomplish this!) than it was with the brother's welfare. He scarcely thought about his brother's progressive deterioration in later years, except insofar as he felt put on the spot when the family looked to him for expertise in the management of their difficult invalid. Actually, he was rather annoyed by the inconvenience these matters caused him, especially in relation to his mother. The burden of the schizophrenic son fell almost entirely on her, and she was continually outraged, delinquent, and filled with self-pity about this. She tried to enmesh the patient in her narcissistic concerns, and he experienced some temptation to rush into the breach to comfort her. By and large, he did manage to limit his involvement in a realistic way, however, as he was quite aware that his mother was insatiable.

The parents had recently concluded an acrimonious divorce, so that neither had been on best behavior for some time. The father had bankrupted his family business but continued to live luxuriously with his Cuban mistress, a girl scarcely older than the patient. His shady dealings seemed to confirm the steadfast judgment of the patient's maternal grandfather that he was unreliable and dishonest, an opinion the patient had learned from his mother as a young child. Recent events had merely confirmed the patient in his long-standing attitude of distant reserve and anxious wariness about his father. Subsequently, we had occasion to observe that much of the latter's misbehavior must have been a rageful reaction to the frustrations of his marriage. He demonstrated considerable good will toward his children after creating a new life for himself within the Cuban exile community, although he remained somewhat infantile, suspicious, and self-centered, especially in relation to his young second wife after she had a baby. Toward the patient, however, he was generally friendly if treated with a modicum of consideration. The mother, on the other hand, always remained maximally difficult, a spoiled rich man's daughter who felt entitled to a life without frustration and arrogantly asserted her innate superiority. She was particularly vain about her appearance and reacted to entering middle age with poorly controlled rage. Her progressive deterioration into depression and alcoholism finally convinced even her family of origin that she could not be trusted with adult responsibilities. Her downhill course was halted when she finally escaped her father's tyrannical control after his death, although he left her only the income from a moderate-sized trust. Until well into analysis, the patient had accepted her rebellious view of his grandfather as a potential enemy.

As one might expect, such a woman had never taken charge of her household or of the raising of her children. When the patient was in his infancy, she had been assisted by her own mother, a person remembered as both gentle and competent. This grandmother died rather suddenly during the mother's second pregnancy. Sometime before the birth of the patient's younger brother, a middle-aged woman was recruited from Italy to take care of the children. This nursemaid stayed with the family until her retirement about 15 years later, except for a period of about one year (at the time the patient was 11), when she went back to Italy because she felt exploited by her employers. She subsequently relented and returned for awhile because the younger boy had begun to unravel in her absence, but as he gradually turned against her in adolescence, she left for good. The patient did, however, keep in touch with her by correspondence.

As a result of the availability of the reliable nursemaid, the patient's upbringing was reasonably orderly and, in terms of externals, without notable incidents. Predictably, the younger boy became more attached to the nursemaid and was therefore spitefully rejected by the mother, who then demonstrated ostentatious preference for the patient. As he remembered it, she was in the habit of staying in bed until lunchtime; the patient was brought to her every morning and spent several hours eating and playing with her—an existence à la Watteau, as W. S. Gilbert put it. He also recalled his malicious gloating about the fact that his brother did not share in these privileges and their attendant gratifications. On the other hand, the patient had been furious about the nursemaid's efforts to compensate the younger child for this discrimination. Predictably, the mother invariably disappeared in the afternoon, and the shoe was then on the other foot, with the patient experiencing profound jealousy and rage about his brother's preferred position with the nursemaid. He spent much of his time teasing and torturing his brother, simultaneously provoking the nursemaid through this sadistic misbehavior. She attempted to exert some control over him, but these efforts were repeatedly undermined by the explicit attitude of the mother that servants were hired to put up with such inconveniences.

Aside from feelings of boredom and aimlessness on Sundays, when neither the mother nor the regular nursemaid was available to the children, the patient's only sign of disturbance in childhood was a water phobia that led to great difficulties in keeping up with expectable peer activities. His equilibrium was severely upset, however, when the nursemaid absented herself at the time he was 11, although the boy was not aware of the connection between his distress and her departure. She left while the patient was away at a summer camp; although he had adjusted reasonably well in previous years (except for water sports), he now experienced overwhelming homesickness. He felt no better after getting home, and soon afterward he began to be preoccupied with some of his physiological processes. At their worst, these hypochondriacal obsessions took the form of fears that he might stop breathing; more often, he was merely worried that he might be unable to think of anything beyond the status of his respiratory apparatus. These symptoms persisted, with greater or lesser intensity, depending on the availability and adequacy of caretakers, until he started analysis.

Nonetheless, he drifted away from the nursemaid after this initial lapse in her devotion. During his early high school years, he attached himself to some of his teachers, with fantasies of having attained a special status with them that would have connoted some extraordinary merit on his part. In one instance, that of his music teacher, there may have been a grain of truth in such a fantasy; this man did single out the boy in a personal way that occasionally verged on homosexual seduction, perhaps not unintended. At the same time, this teacher was rising rapidly in the musical world. By the time we began the analysis, he had become quite famous, and the patient still entertained hopes, now clearly unjustified, that this celebrity loved him.

Despite the overtures of this teacher, the patient had never crossed the line into homosexual activity. On the contrary, he started dating relatively early, selecting only those girls whose appearance satisfied his vanity. He began to have sexual relations in late adolescence, but with great anxiety about his performance. His first steady girlfriend was extremely critical in this regard and often humiliated him by unfavorable comparisons with her former lovers. He was unable either to defend himself or to extricate himself from this intolerable bind until he left for college. Soon after leaving home for the first time, he entered psychotherapy because of an exacerbation of his hypochondriasis. In spite of his friendship with the colleague who later referred him to me, he selected a young female psychiatrist opposed to psychoanalysis and formed a strongly erotized bond with her. With some interruptions, this relationship sustained him through the college years and permitted him to do well enough at his studies to gain admission to medical school. As his separation from the therapist was approaching, the patient once again started a sexual affair; on this occasion, his girlfriend did not object to his physical performance, but she lost interest in him when it became obvious that their career plans would take them to different parts of the country. This rejection was one of the recent events that impelled the patient to begin the analysis as soon as he arrived in Chicago.

As soon as he was settled in the analysis, his frenzied subjective state abated, to be succeeded by one of astonishing smugness and arrogance. It was apparent that this change was contingent on his fantasy, loosely based on the referring physician's account of my qualifications, that he was now connected to a psychoanalytic celebrity, the best of analysts, as befits the most precious of analysands. The intensity of his need for this illusion about having established a mutual admiration society precluded the use of analysis to establish the truth (not to speak of effecting any change!). His communications utterly disregarded the basic rule, although he never overtly admitted his numerous flagrant violations of our agreement. He concentrated instead on exhibitionistic bragging and contemptuous depreciation of everyone else.

As a result of these delinquencies, he gave the misleading impression for a long time that he was currently doing well on all fronts, especially in medical school. It was true that he had ingratiated himself with some of the instructors, but even in this regard his extraordinary, narcissistic demeanor had led to widespread disaffection. In terms of the academic work itself, his rash and arrogant policy of doing as little as he felt he could get by with got him into progressively deeper difficulties. But I learned nothing about these matters for the first two years of my work with him; the truth suddenly emerged when the patient failed in several subjects on the preclinical part of the National Board examination.

The result came as a surprise in itself, but the patient's reaction to it was truly astounding. Initially, he was utterly devastated with humiliation; some of the time, he disavowed this humiliation by falling into paranoid attitudes toward the faculty. But once he recovered from the acute trauma, he firmly decided to drop out of medical school, with a mixture of overt contempt for what the training could offer and an embarrassed acknowledgment that his level of commitment and interest was not adequate to the task. He realized that he did not, in fact, wish to do analytic work, but only wanted to partake in the prestige he attributed to the field—a need that his fantasy of being my outstanding patient seemed to satisfy.

The revelation of his systematic lying and fraudulence through the first several years of the treatment did shake his false sense of certainty about my perceiving him as unique in some favorable manner, although even this small change in his attitude entailed repeated statements on my part about the inevitability of analytic failure if he continued consciously to withhold and distort information. He did become sufficiently frightened about the possibility of being dropped as a patient to start adhering to the method of free association more or less faithfully from then on.

As a consequence, it now became possible to grasp the nature of the archaic transference patterns present from the beginning of the analysis, but formerly covered over by the patient's enactment of an identification with his father's imposturous behavior. Once this source of his insensate approach to the analytic task was interpreted, not only did he become more cooperative, but his uncertainties about his father's actual assets and limitations also disappeared. The *motive* for his lengthy, covert resistance turned out to be embedded in reliving his childhood relationship to the nursemaid in the transference; i.e., his negativism was equivalent to his childish sadism toward those who did not accord him some special status. His associations now became filled with rageful expletives, direct personal insults, obscenities, carping and depreciative attacks on me; often they degenerated into chains of nonsense verbalized in a teasing manner.

The patient did recall how much the nursemaid had suffered under his unceasing misbehavior, however, and he was overcome with deeply felt gratitude and affection for her. Subsequently, he took pains to maintain more regular contact with her, to visit her whenever possible, and to give her, at long last, richly deserved acknowledgment for her patience, devotion, and loyalty. In the transference, however, no such turn to positive feelings took place. Every interruption of the analysis, including ordinary weekends, was experienced as a desertion and rekindled his rage. As had been the case all along, his hypochondriasis recurred whenever he felt abandoned; his thoughts became narrowly focused on his physiological state at these times, and he had no inclination to engage in his customary activities or to seek out other people.

The only alternative available to him at these moments of "narcissistic regression" was frantic masturbation, as often as five times in one day. This act was invariably accompanied by a stereotyped fantasy in which a woman who had eight or 10 children submitted to him sexually. Although the identity of this person shifted around somewhat, most frequently she was an impoverished South American peasant, worn and ugly.

In his actual dealings with women, he avoided sexual contact with any of the strikingly attractive young women he managed to date from the time he began analysis, although he was cognizant of their desirability in the eyes of others. The only affair he conducted for the first several years of the treatment was a brief fling with a vulgar and psychopathic girl, whom he soon rejected because she was by no means as submissive as a peon ought to be. When he was on vacation, he would occasionally enact his fantasy with a prostitute, without experiencing his customary anxiety about potency. And if a woman showed real interest in him, he took sadistic pleasure in remaining totally unaffected by her excitement.

With persistent and systematic interpretation of these transference reactions, he gradually gained insight into and mastery over his archaic need to share the perfection of an idealized other and/or to assert his own grandeur. It was possible to reconstruct the history of his efforts to maintain the illusion of his uniqueness and glory through disavowal of his symbiotic need for a sensible caretaker—in childhood, his absolute dependence on the Italian nanny, whose departure led to the outbreak of his hypochondriasis. We made the assumption that this woman rescued him from some equivalent of this state when she originally took responsibility for him late in the second year of his life. All in all, the analytic work uncovered the syndrome Kohut (1971) once called a "narcissistic personality disturbance"; in his terms, both an idealizing transference and a (secondary) mirror transference developed in a spontaneous manner. The patient was a tragic person, indeed, mired in impossible infantile ambitions and a ludicrously primitive value system.

As we uncovered these repressed and disavowed aspects of the patient's archaic mental life through the analysis, there were impressive changes in his day-to-day adaptation. His relationships with family, friends, and new acquaintances improved markedly; he prepared himself to enter his grandfather's business by taking appropriate courses at a local university and ultimately began to represent that firm in the Chicago area. Concurrently, he realized that his hypochondriacal preoccupations had disappeared as a result of his commitments to people and activities that interested him. From the viewpoint of external observers, he now appeared to be a very promising young man of real sophistication, and his subjective state, for the first time in his life, remained stable and without dysphoria. From the perspective of the analytic process, however, successful resolution of these "narcissistic" problems turned out to be no more than one essential step. Although this requirement seemingly had to be met before other crucial issues in the patient's emotional world could be approached, the material that subsequently came into focus had, in actuality, always formed part of the clinical picture; in that sense, the description I have thus far provided is a selective one—*accurate* in detail, I hope, but perceived as one gestalt only on the basis of one of the conceptual categories made available by psychoanalytic psychology.

The nature of the psychological configurations left out of the foregoing description emerged as a new gestalt within the transference relationship that paralleled the establishment of a stable equilibrium with regard to archaic issues. Put rather briefly, the patient remained emotionally absorbed in his analysis and resistant to any change in his status quo. His clinging to the past was most remarkable in his dealings with women—he experienced a chain of seriocomic misadventures through which he managed to be rejected as a nonsexual being over and over again. At the same time, he was reenacting with these innocents the sadistic harassment to which he had subjected his nursemaid by arousing and then disappointing their expectations for a relationship of mutuality. In his eyes, however, all women were peons to be despised; I was the only person of interest and merit in his subjective universe. The sessions became highly charged sexual encounters for him, filled with fantasies of passive gratification, as his hours in his mother's boudoir had been in his childhood; the erotic aspects of the maternal transference had come into the open. The inevitable frustrations of these infantile wishes and ambitions filled him with rage and humiliation, spitefulness and despair.

Am I suggesting that the archaic "narcissistic" components of the pathology were mere regressive defenses against these hurts, as the clinical theories of the past would have it? Or is this case one in which the formulation of van der Leeuw (1979) is applicable—was the patient's romance with his mother (as repeated in the analytic transference) no more than the expression of a tyrannical desire to manipulate an animate sexual instrument? Both possibilities had to be carefully considered, but the clinical evidence eventually established beyond any doubt that neither was valid in this instance. The actual circumstances were a great deal more complex— and much more interesting!

At the climactic, oedipal phase of the epigenetic sequence, commitment to "narcissistic" attitudes toward other people amounted to an avowal of love for his mother, particularly in view of the latter's encouragement of such an identification with her pretensions as a *grande dame.* Castration anxiety was relatively minimal because the father was only too glad to have the child take over the burden of his insatiable spouse, but the very absence of age-appropriate masculine competition exposed the boy in an inescapable manner to the impossibility of being an adequate sexual partner for an adult woman. His humiliation was mitigated through his identification with his mother's arrogance and through the assumption of a contemptuous attitude toward sexual life in general. His masculine ambitions therefore focused on achieving the status of the awesome maternal grandfather, a naive conception of authority based on the external trappings of wealth or an imperious manner. One of the disturbing factors that upset this attempted adaptation when the patient reached adulthood was the discovery that his grandfather was just as much a ladies' man as his father—the grandfather had a glamorous and devoted mistress, a woman in her thirties whom the patient found disturbingly attractive. The ugly peons in his masturbation fantasies were the products of his efforts to ward off such dangerous thoughts. In the 1970s, castration could still take the form of being disinherited!

In the context of these erotic and competitive wishes and of the anxiety they aroused, the child's general integration continued to depend on the availability of a symbiotic partner. In other words, the "narcissistic" aspects of his behavior certainly did not constitute a regressive response to the conflicts of the oedipal phase; on the contrary, the boy was able to experience the relatively more differentiated oedipal wishes, either in childhood or when they were reawakened within the analytic transference, only if his archaic vulnerability was patched over through external assistance. In fact, his difficulties with women in adult life stemmed more directly from his poorly controlled rage whenever his affection did not evoke immediate reciprocation—"mirroring," as he put it after reading the work of Heinz Kohut. By the same token, the need to maintain his integration through external assistance had been the decisive aspect of his psychological world in terms of the fate of his Oedipus complex, so that it is not possible to understand the oedipal outcome without taking into account the mutual influence of the developmental lines Kohut (1966) appropriately differentiated as those of "object love" and of "narcissism." To use the vocabulary of his more recent work, the greatest tragedy of this patient's life was his inability to establish intimacy with a beloved woman, and the most important source of guilt during his periods of remorse was his awareness of the need to exploit certain relationships in a symbiotic manner.[2]

If I have focused on the complexities of these issues as they appear in the oedipal drama, I do not mean to imply that this is the only phase of development in which conflicts around object love and those concerning personal aims are not separate entities but only different frames of reference utilized by the observer. I have chosen not to encumber my exposition by providing a detailed account of additional phases of the epigenetic sequence for the illustrative case in question. Suffice it to state, in closing, that phallic exhibitionism or anal rebellion can be conceptualized, whenever it is convenient for our immediate purpose, as love or hate for the mother. How can we ever have supposed otherwise?

[2] Terman (in Panel, 1977) has described an analysis in which the oedipal material was consistently interpreted from the perspective of its effects on self-esteem. Aside from the inherent interest of this technical variation, Terman's account is another convincing demonstration of the inevitable interpenetration of object love and narcissistic issues within the oedipal phase of development. However, Terman obscures the significance of his findings by attempting to subsume the patient's erotic wishes under the rubric of Kohut's "mirror transference." It would be more cogent to see the ambitions of the oedipal child as potentially pathogenic if his prior development has not prepared him adequately for the age-appropriate frustrations of those ambitions.

SECTION III

CRITIQUE OF OBJECT RELATIONS THEORIES

In the last three decades, while drive psychology was relegated to a position of secondary importance by post-Freudian ego-psychological theories, clinical discourse in psychoanalysis increasingly focused on the influence of the environment on the development of the personality. To be sure, it had been widely recognized that even the development of the drives is crucially affected by interpersonal transactions during critical periods of childhood (Freud, 1905b; Abraham, 1924). From that realization, it was but a short step to a decisive shift of emphasis on the part of many authors—a change from primary concern with libidinal (or aggressive) aims to concentration on the nature of the relationship to the libidinal object. Modell was one of the first to express misgivings about this spontaneous and unsystematic change within clinical theory. He wrote: "The area of clinical experience that awaits better conceptualization is that of disturbed human object relationships. What is now needed is a model that would better conceptualize the [individual's] relationship to the environment and would encompass progressive and regressive alterations in object relations" (1968, p. 125). ?

In spite of such voices of caution, the object relations approach has gained increasing popularity in recent years. As the intellectual influence of Heinz Hartmann on American psychoanalysis has receded, it has been replaced in many quarters by an interest in the clinical work of a British school of dissidents from traditional theory that includes authors such as Fairbairn (1954) and Winnicott (1958). In this country, the focus on object relations has generally remained within the theoretical framework of ego psychology (cf. Jacobson, 1964) because, in its most expansive version, that framework classifies attributes of the personality such as the capacity to adapt in the social field as "ego functions." George Klein (1968) was the earliest to point out that this constitutes an illegitimate extension of the "ego" concept. In the past decade, there has been a salutary retrenchment in the overuse of the ego, and object relations have continued to be used as a theoretical category without being correlated with the tripartite model (Freud, 1923) in any logical manner. But the advocates of this viewpoint have properly differentiated two meanings of the term "object relations." In the first place, it refers to interpersonal transactions on the stage of social reality (as represented, for instance, in the quotation from Modell in the preceding paragraph). More important, however, is another sense in which the term has been employed, one that invokes an intrapsychic frame of reference. In this second sense, it refers to memories of past transactions with the important figures that we once called "libidinal objects." Kohut (1971) has further clarified that the primary caretakers are not necessarily invested with "object love"—in Freud's terms, the object relationship with them may be exclusively "narcissistic."

Object relations as actualities in the interpersonal field have been used as important indicators of adaptive capacity by virtually every psychoanalytic observer. Anna Freud (1965), for example, chose the developmental line of object relations as the most important functional capacity in the assessment of childhood psychopathology. She called it "a sequence for which the successive stages of libido development. . . merely form the inborn, maturational base" (pp. 64–65). A significant group of recent writers has elevated object relations, understood in the second, intrapsychic sense, to a position of much greater importance within psychoanalytic discourse. Although the theoretical assumptions underlying this tendency are frequently not fully articulated, some of these authors have conceived of "internalized" object relations, formed in early childhood, as *determinants* of later behavior. Both the failure to articulate the assumption that such childhood transactions constitute a source of future motivation and the failure to fit such a hypothesis into existing clinical theory have created considerable confusion in our literature. In Chapter 8, I assess object relations theories from the vantage point of their metapsychological coherence in an effort to repair these omissions.

Although such an assessment of object relations theories of the personality leads to the conclusion that their general acceptance would only aggravate the current disarray of psychoanalytic psychology, this reservation does not imply that it would also be fruitless to approach particular bits of clinical material from the perspective of the developmental line of object relations. (For one such effort, see Gedo and Goldberg [1973, pp. 61–62, 66–69, 76–81].) Like other specific segments of our clinical theory (e.g., the concept of transference or that of intrapsychic conflict), this avenue of exploration should not be employed in isolation; to place exclusive reliance upon it is to run the risk of being led astray by the appearance of all-too-frequent atypical patterns. To give only the most obvious of examples, the repetition of a particular form of interpersonal transaction does not necessarily mean that a similar relationship took place in childhood; it may represent, among many other possibilities, a current identification with the behavior of some idealized personage. As I have stated elsewhere, "The position of functional capacities attained along any single developmental line cannot be utilized by itself as an indicator of psychopathology. Meaningful psychopathological constellations consist, rather, of typical combinations of the development of crucial functions" (Gedo and Goldberg, 1973, p. 154).

In addition to the pitfall of reductionism, the use of object relations theory presents a number of other problems and difficulties, many of which are discussed in Chapter 9.

CHAPTER EIGHT

Theories of Object Relations: A Metapsychological Assessment

In the endless controversy about the relative influence of nature and nurture on the character of man, Freud took the most complex of positions, that of giving equal weight to constitutional factors and to the effects of the environment. Psychoanalytic psychology has taken innate psychobiological dispositions into account in its drive theories (Freud, 1905b, 1920), but Freud's emphasis on the importance of childhood experience for personal destiny did not at first find a systematic place within his psychoanalytic theories. Only with the conceptualization of the structural theory in the 1920s could this factor implicitly find its proper niche as a codeterminant of ego and superego development. At the level of metapsychology, it was articulated as a major assumption of psychoanalysis by Hartmann (1939) in the concept of an "average expectable environment."

In the past generation, environmental influences have increasingly come to be characterized, with some degree of reductionism when compared to Hartmann's

This chapter was previously published in the *Journal of the American Psychoanalytic Association,* 27(1979):361–374, and is reprinted here by permission.

broad definition, in terms of transactions between the child and the significant persons of his milieu. These transactions are simultaneously seen from two complementary standpoints: from that of an external observer, they constitute concrete events on the stage of actuality; from the intrapsychic viewpoint, they involve representations in the system of memories (cf. Sandler and Rosenblatt, 1962). In acknowledgment of the need to embody the influence of early experience with the caretakers as one determinant of development, object relations have found a place in the schema of every serious theoretician of psychoanalytic psychology. Perhaps the only exception can be found in the work of the most conservative of id psychologists, such as Melanie Klein, although in their explicit discussions Kleinian authors such as Segal (1974) stress their agreement in principle with the need to give due weight to the effects of nurture on psychological development. In clinical discourse, however, many Kleinians and other id psychologists, such as some of the structuralists in France, tend to omit from consideration object relations at the level of past events in the interpersonal realm; they seem to view the representational world of transactions between the subject and his objects as if it were exclusively the product of drive derivatives active in the arena of unconscious fantasies.

Unfortunately, our quasi-unanimity about the significance of environmental influences in early childhood has failed to produce a theoretical consensus with regard to the proper place of object relations in our conceptual armamentarium. Among the welter of confusing positions on the issue currently being advocated, I should like to focus my discussion on a limited number of major clusters. It should be emphasized that each of these theoretical alternatives is scientifically tenable in principle and more or less cogent on the clinical level. However, every metapsychological option entails a different set of problems, hitherto largely unresolved, in terms of fitting a particular conception of object relations into the overall framework of psychoanalytic theory without producing internal inconsistencies or failing to account for a segment of the accumulated clinical evidence.

The topic of object relations has of late gained prominence—and created unprecedented confusion—as a result of new departures embodied in the scope of recent object relations theories. To be precise, a number of contributors, probably starting with Winnicott (1960), have conceived of the memories of early object relationships as a primary source of motivation. Some of these authors seem to have been aware of the fact that their hypotheses demanded a radical revision of psychoanalytic metapsychology; others pass over these departures from Freud's theoretical framework without explicit mention of their significance.

Confusion has been compounded by the widespread failure of some innovators to specify whether they look upon "primitive internalized object relations," as they often call them, as the only source of human motivation or merely as an auxiliary explanation to be invoked whenever behaviors are not adequately illuminated by Freudian drive theories. There is, of course, a third alternative, that of viewing the drives as the primary determinants of the configuration of early object relations, which, in turn, can be seen as the subsequent, secondary source of motivation. This third option obliges its exponents to specify the precise *manner* in which the drives influence early object relations. This is a very difficult issue, largely because we cannot bring psychoanalytic clinical evidence to bear upon it. To illustrate the wide differences of opinion in this regard, I should only like to mention that Loewald (1971) has attempted to bridge this theoretical gap by postulating that the drives are not to be understood as biological givens at birth. Instead, he assumes that they are psychic dispositions formed in the course of earliest childhood through transactions within the mother-infant dyad. Loewald has thus forged a theory of motivation that is metapsychologically coherent, but one that reverses the usual conceptions of the connection between drives and object relations.

In contrast, many authors have inadvertently created subtle inconsistencies in these matters. Kohut (1977) has recently made an explicit claim to the effect that scientific disciplines are entitled to go on using several uncoordinated theoretical fragments. Although few would argue with the necessity for theoretical complementarity in the sense proposed by Niels Bohr, I would maintain that this is always a measure of last resort; further, that if we have a choice, a unitary theory is preferable to a patchwork, the components of which bear no discernible relation to each other. In other words, I cannot accept the legitimacy of using several motivational theories simultaneously without a rationale for the manner in which these classes of motivation are related.

As we might predict, some theoreticians *have* tried to resolve this dilemma by espousing one of the available unitary views of motivation—either by rejecting the need for postulating that early object relations are sources of later motivation or by substituting object relations theories for earlier views altogether. The most instructive example of the first of these positions may well be the earlier work of Kohut (1966, 1971), which was an effort to subsume a wide array of primitive behaviors under the explanatory aegis of the libido theory. This piece of theory building is particularly instructive precisely because Kohut has clearly found it necessary to abandon these traditional views, although his 1977 book slurs over the radical change in his metapsychology implicit in espousing a pair of "complementary" theories of motivation. In other words, Kohut has failed to specify the rationale that forced him to scrap his use of drive psychology in this area. I assume, however, that he had found it impossible to provide consistent explanations formulated in terms of the drives for some of the phenomena encountered in the course of analyzing certain archaic personality configurations. Before I try to consider these complex empirical questions, I should like to note that Kohut's complementary theories, if they are taken at face value, assume mutually contradictory positions about the nature/nurture dilemma. In his hypotheses about man in conflict about his drives, Kohut comes close to an exclusively biological orientation; at the same time, in those about Tragic Man, so-called, he clearly disregards the influence of innate predispositions.

Let us return now to the empirical core of this controversy by examining the reasons that have impelled so many thoughtful contributors to elevate object relations from their former role within psychoanalytic psychology, that of serving as one of the most reliable indicators of the overall maturation of the personality (cf. A. Freud, 1965; Gedo and Goldberg, 1973), to a position of decisive significance as one of the sources of human motivation, perhaps even the exclusive one.

As I have tried to show previously (Panel, 1976), the first challenge to the libido theory as a universal explanatory framework came from C. G. Jung as an outgrowth of his experience with psychotic patients. Freud (1914) concurred with the judgment that in the psychoses the object world had been decathected, so that many psychological phenomena in these conditions could not be understood in libidinal terms. Freud developed the concept of narcissistic libido to cover these contingencies. Although he never repudiated that explanation, his revision of drive theory in 1920 actually amounted to the admission that a psychology of sexual love, even one that paid proper attention to love of one's own person, is not a sufficient explanation of the realm of mental life that he identified as lying "beyond the pleasure principle."

Subsequent psychoanalytic experience with primitive personality disturbances has amply confirmed

Freud's wisdom in adopting a more complex theory of motivation, one that takes cognizance of man's destructiveness, particularly when it is self-directed. In terms of metapsychological coherence, Freud's dual-drive theory is still adequate as an inclusive theory of motivation. It has failed to gain general acceptance in its original form because of certain clinical limitations, too familiar to need specification here. From the standpoint of clinical theory, Hartmann's proposal (1948) to postulate primary drives of sexuality and aggression has consequently carried the day. It has been overlooked, however, that the elimination of primary masochism from our conceptual schema leaves us without any explanation for the motivation behind the phenomena of the repetition compulsion; like sexual wishes, aggressive wishes do *not* lie beyond the pleasure principle, even if they have been turned against one's own person.

To be sure, certain authors (e.g., Arlow and Brenner, 1964) do not accept the need to distinguish between subjective wishes and the unconscious phenomena Freud had attributed to the repetition compulsion. Those who see all maladaptive behaviors that are repetitions as the fulfillment of unconscious *wishes* of some kind (generally as wishes for self-punishment) do not, in fact, need to look beyond Hartmann's drive psychology for an adequate motivation theory. Ironically, in this regard many ego psychologists may be viewed in the same light as the school of Melanie Klein, because the latter can also legitimately make do with traditional drive psychology, even if in a different version, as a result of postulating the presence of unconscious fantasy life from earliest infancy.

The majority of clinicians, however, continue to adhere to Freud's distinction between the realm of the pleasure principle and that of the repetition compulsion at the same time as they opt for the dual-drive theory of Hartmann in preference to that of Eros and Thanatos. As I stated before, this popular combination of theoretical views leaves that body of clinical data classifiable under the rubric of the repetition compulsion without motivational underpinnings. In my judgment, the conception of early object relations as an additional source of human motivation was one major tendency to fill this metapsychological void. Perhaps this circumstance may also help us to understand the fact that most theoretical proposals to elevate early object relations into a source of later motivation have made no claim to universality. On the contrary, they have generally continued to espouse some form of drive psychology, sometimes inconsistently oscillating in their explanations between these differing frames of reference. Even the work of major contributors such as Kernberg or Mahler and her collaborators has not been free of confusion in this respect.

There are, of course, considerations that discourage total reliance on an object relations theory of motivation beyond the history I have summarized. Few serious students of Freud would feel comfortable with such a radically environmentalist viewpoint on the nature/nurture question. On a more empirical plane, psychoanalytic clinical evidence gathered through the treatment of individuals whose most important conflicts are centered on the Oedipus complex neither requires nor lends itself optimally to the use of an object relations approach. I have reviewed this issue in some detail in my collaborative work with Goldberg (Gedo and Goldberg, 1973). At any rate, many contributors seem to have experienced no discomfort about the simultaneous use of two theories of motivation, and few efforts have thus far been made to specify how drive theories and object relations theories might be correlated in terms of a consistent psychoanalytic framework. In order to gain scientific respectability, those who use object relations concepts as theories of motivation would clearly have to systematize their hypotheses in this area. Moreover, they would also have to specify their conception of the manner in which early object relations are transformed into sources of later motivation. An effort to define a correlation between drives and object relations was in fact made by Kohut in his earlier work (1971). He there proposed a distinction between object love, i.e., the libidinal cathexis of a person, and object relationships in general, which Kohut then believed to be motivated by narcissistic forces. This attempted explanation has subsequently collapsed as a result of Kohut's recent abandonment of reliance on the libido theory in conceptualizing early object relations.

Paradoxically, we have reached these conceptual difficulties at a time in the history of psychoanalysis characterized by a loss of confidence in Freud's metapsychological assumptions. It would not be appropriate to review in detail the complex epistemological arguments that have eventuated in this development. Suffice it to say that even the defenders of the traditional viewpoint (e.g., Horowitz, 1977) have tended to fall back on a metaphorical interpretation of Freud's energy constructs. Perhaps the most succinct statement of the recent disenchantment has been made by Swanson:

> Psychic energy, libido, and related concepts in Freud's drive-discharge theory are either impossible, useless, or mistaken. If they are defined in a mind-body interactionist framework, they are impossible in the sense that they violate energy-conservation laws of physics. If they are defined in any abstract framework, they are useless in that explanations of behavior so based are trivially and incorrigibly circular. If they are defined instead as biological concepts, the implied notions of energy flow in neural networks are mistaken. . ." [1977, pp. 629–630].

The paradox to which I alluded a moment ago thus presents itself: far from having established more than one theory of motivation, psychoanalytic psychology is in danger of having none at all! Needless to say, the necessity to reconstruct the whole edifice of our theoretical framework has not as yet been widely accepted. Nonetheless, a growing vanguard of contributors has begun to make efforts to that end. Although these initial attempts have in most ways been confusingly different from each other, one particular trend among them heralds a growing consensus about developing a new psychoanalytic theory of motivation.

A number of diverse proposals, including one of my

own (Gedo, 1979a), share this common feature. It has probably been stated most cogently by George Klein (1976) as part of his attempt to articulate the basic discoveries of psychoanalysis about mental life. Among these fundamental propositions, Klein articulates one that has become most relevant for a new theory of motivation unencumbered by untenable energy assumptions: man's biological propensity actively to seek repetition of the patterns of his previous experiences, whatever their qualities may have been. I would add that these patterns include not only the reproduction of the qualities of earlier experience but also the repetition of certain quantitative parameters, such as rates of change. Dahl (1978) has formulated an explicit hypothesis about motivation based on such premises, one that employs the idea of emotions as the subjective aspect of patterned experience. If the qualities of earliest infantile experiences, including some of their quantitative aspects, could be shown to underlie man's personal goals, the influence of the caretakers on later behavior could then be understood in terms of the importance of their activities in codetermining the patterns of these qualities of experience. In other words, a psychoanalytic psychology built around attempts to reproduce patterns of experiential qualities would give proper weight to the importance of nurture without neglecting the importance of constitutional variables.

Because the caretakers have so much influence on early experience, it might be legitimate to include these new hypotheses among theories that stress object relations. Sandler and Sandler (1978) have done exactly that in an assessment of their proposed theory centering on the qualities of early experience. I believe, however, that classifying such concepts in terms of "object relations theories" is somewhat misleading; one decided advantage of stressing the centrality of the quality of patterns of infantile experience is the resulting expansion of focus from the narrower field of infant-caretaker transactions to the totality of the early environment—an expansion Hartmann (1939) urged us to undertake a generation ago. In other words, infantile experiences often acquire some of their characteristic qualities on the basis of somatic vicissitudes, for example, or through the impact of the inanimate milieu, rather than by way of transactions with the object world alone.

In a different context (Gedo, 1979a), I have proposed naming the sum of personal goals stemming from the need to reproduce the patterned qualities of earlier experience the "self-organization." Others have also advocated designating theories based on the active repetition of patterns of earlier experience by reference to a concept of self. George Klein (1976), for instance, centers his hypotheses on the concept of a "self-schema." The earliest of these theories may have been Lichtenstein's conception of a "primary identity" (1961). At any rate, we are probably facing a terminological muddle in these matters because of Kohut's decision to refer to his own work as a "psychology of the self." As I have tried to show, Kohut's ideas have moved from a drive-psychological matrix into an object relations framework, and he touches upon "the self" only in terms of the subjective sense of personhood. Nonetheless, all those who advocate "self" concepts may mistakenly be thought to share Kohut's premises.

Terminological problems aside, I believe we should continue to make distinctions among different types of psychoanalytic theories. On the one hand, psychoanalysis can view human motivation in terms of the duality between the realm of subjective wishes and that of the repetition compulsion, the dichotomy enunciated by Freud in 1920. We can either conceptualize that dichotomy as Freud did in his dual-instinct theory or in the manner that has become popular in the past decade, i.e., in accordance with "complementary" drive and object relations theories. The other alternative we have at our disposal is a radical reformulation, based on a fundamental change in our conception of the repetition compulsion.

The ground for such a change has been prepared for some time. As long ago as 1961, Jules Weiss was able to show (in an unpublished paper) that Freud had been in error when he conceived of repetitive phenomena in the context of instances where they cause severe maladaptation. As Weiss pointed out, repetition is in fact characteristic of the negentropy of living systems. In other words, *all* behavior is necessarily in part under the aegis of the repetition compulsion, and the quality of adaptation resulting from any given bit of behavior can only be judged in terms of the observer's subjective values. Consequently, it is not legitimate to regard seemingly inconvenient instances of repetition as different in principle from pleasurable or profitable ones—sexual gratification, for instance. Psychoanalytic theories based on these considerations are, in my judgment, the ones organized around a meaningful concept of self. And it is only on the basis of such an understanding of the organization of personal behavior that we shall gain the ability to develop cogent psychoanalytic theories about the role of *objects* in the intrapsychic world.[1]

To recapitulate: the chronic confusion about the role of object relations theories in psychoanalysis has arisen mainly because we possess two distinct types of theories involving these concepts. The first kind was introduced by Freud in 1905, and it is to be understood as a limited aspect of the examination of psychic life dealing with the consequences of instinctual needs in terms of the people involved in gratifying these. Such theories have been elaborated, especially in the developmental dimension, ever since; every serious psychoanalytic theoretician has given due weight to the importance of past transactions with significant persons for current behavior.

A second type of object relations theory conceptualizes past transactions with people as the general source of human motivation. Theories of this kind belong to the realm of metapsychology and take an extreme environmentalist position in the nature/nurture controversy. Although they have generally failed to face the fact that such theories are not compatible with Freud's conception of the drives as the universal motivating forces of human behavior, recent advocates of object relations theories in this second sense build much or all of clinical theory on

[1] The ideas presented in this paragraph are elaborated more fully in *Beyond Interpretation* (Gedo, 1979a, Chapters 11 and 15).

the foundation of early childhood interpersonal transactions. Much confusion stems from inconsistent oscillation on the part of many authors between such hypotheses and traditional drive concepts. However, we also continue to have real traditionalists within psychoanalysis; this group tends to disregard those clinical phenomena for which the new breed of object relations theorists finds it necessary to formulate new theoretical constructs.

In my judgment, object relations theories of the more limited type are essential tools for the illumination of certain modes of archaic mental functioning (see Gedo and Goldberg, 1973, pp. 53–69). I do not believe that the more ambitious kind of object relations theories can serve as adequate explanations for the full range of human behavior. This limitation has been implicitly recognized by those who plead for the simultaneous use of two theories of motivation. But a dual theory of that kind is tenable only if we accept some bridging concept to tie together its component parts in a coherent manner. Freud introduced the death instinct as such a bridging concept. Those who do not accept this idea introduce internal inconsistency into their work in positing that phenomena from beyond the pleasure principle stem from early object relations which are, in turn, structured in accordance with drive vicissitudes—and yet do not fulfill any wishes!

Another theoretical option has begun to be adumbrated in the recent literature. This alternative would develop a theory of motivation founded on the patterns of earliest experience and the biological necessity for their repetition in the active mode. These evolving hypotheses, which seem to offer the best opportunities for the future of psychoanalytic psychology, might best be designated hypotheses centering on the self-organization.

CHAPTER NINE

Transference, Fantasy, and Object Relations

Psychoanalysis as a therapeutic procedure came into being in the 1890s as Freud gradually discovered that human behavior was largely determined by motive forces unknown to the "agent" whose life they shape. Such sources of motivation, to use a contemporary metaphor, seem to originate in the black holes of space. In his first extended report on his experiments in treating hysterics through a "talking cure" (Freud, 1895a), Freud ended the exposition by noting that similar forces made themselves felt in the therapeutic situation, once again diverting the patients from rational courses of action. In this manner, Freud came face to face with the phenomenon of transference, a vector amenable to direct observation in the treatment setting. Because transference is subject to such immediate study, it is not only the most troublesome aspect of the therapeutic transaction but also the one most revealing of unconscious motives. Another way to conceptualize the effects of such unconscious forces was to view them as endopsychic resistances to the process of investigating the patient's inner life. Freud consistently defined psychoanalysis as the treatment in which adequate attention is given to transference and resistance.

In parallel to these discoveries about the laws of psychological treatment, Freud was led to qualify his original etiological formlation that "hysterics suffer. . . from reminiscences" (Breuer and Freud, 1893, p. 7). This aphorism summarized the finding that numerous symptoms had symbolic meanings, but had lost their functions as compromise formulations, simultaneously expressing and disguising those meanings, when decoded into discursive language. Freud had found that these obscure symbolic communications represented memories of significant events in the past, frequently from a distant era of childhood. For a number of years before the turn of the century, he had the impression that memories of active sexual experiences at an early age were the crucial etiological variables in the genesis of psychopathology, only to realize that, in most instances, the "forgotten" material he recovered in treatment did not concern actual historical events but repressed systems of fantasy both past and present (see Sadow et al., 1968). It was but a short step from this insight to its corollary, the conclusion that the most fruitful focus for psychoanalytic inquiry is the elucidation of the nature of this intrapsychic world.

As a collective scientific enterprise, psychoanalysis adopted the exploration of that world as its program for priority action for half a century. The impact of this choice was so pervasive that individuals whose adaptive style did not fit the autoplastic mold characteristic of the neuroses, in the narrowest sense of the term, were thought to suffer from defects of structuralization and attempts to analyze them were deemed risky. In practice, of course, an increasing number of clinicians tried to broaden the scope of psychoanalytic treatment by using it to deal with a wide variety of character disturbances, including those with predominantly alloplastic adaptive styles (cf. Panel, 1954). These frontiers were gradually crossed in the years following the conceptualization of the structural theory (Freud, 1923), and the expansion found its rationale in the paradigm that came to be known as "ego psychology." Perhaps the decisive step in this advance was Hartmann's (1939) focus on adaptation as mediated by the specifics of ego development—issues far removed from the realm of unconscious fantasy life.

Increasing clinical experience with patients who did not suffer the slings and arrows of outrageous fortune in the mind alone but tended to take arms against a sea of troubles in the interpersonal arena of social reality has shifted the focus of analytic scrutiny to the actualities of patients' relationships with other people. In my judgment, there can be no question about the salutary effects on analytic practice of this new emphasis on object relations. To mention only one of the most transparent of the many improvements in technique it has brought about, analysands are much quicker to renounce damaging enactments in social life when they gain insight into the implications of such enactments as misuse of other people than they were when informed of the (perfectly valid) connections between their activities and infantile sexuality. These considerations have proved to be particularly important in treating individuals whose personality organizations have not obtained the degree of structuralization portrayed in the tripartite model of the mind (see Gedo and Goldberg, 1973, pp. 55–69). Instead of presenting us with conflicts between unacceptable wishes and an internalized morality (or, at the very least, some appreciation of the undesirable consequences of realizing their wishes), people of this type respond to the analytic situation with open (and often unconflicted) demands for direct assistance or gratification. Contingencies of this kind can scarcely be conceptualized by means of distinctions among the mental agencies Freud posited in 1923—a fact to which Freud himself gave notice when, shortly thereafter, he placed the definitive differentiation of ego from id around the time of the resolution of the Oedipus complex (Freud, 1926, p. 164).

In other words, as analysts gained experience with patients whose personality organizations were in a relatively less differentiated mode than those of the prototypical individuals Freud presented in connection with the structural theory (1926, pp. 101–108), they were confronted with a significant lacuna in clinical theory. Because of the obvious prominence of interpersonal issues in the problems of living for which these people sought assistance, many innovative theoreticians centered the new concepts they introduced to deal with such clinical contingencies on the framework of object relations (e.g., Fairbairn, 1954; Winnicott, 1958; A. Freud, 1965). Because this vantage point, in turn, did not offer an advantageous perspective for the study of the intrapsychic world, the most sophisticated object relations theories, such as that of Jacobson (1964), postulate that actual transactions with other people reflect schemata of object relationships laid down—or "internalized"—early in childhood. From this standpoint, object relations theory ceases to focus on overt behaviors in adult life; it attempts, instead, to formulate the nature of the individual's basic conception of his roles vis-à-vis others. Such an understanding of the range of a person's object relationships provides a very useful indicator of the ways he functions in some of the areas of existence most essential for adaptation (see Gedo and Goldberg, 1973, pp. 78–79). In the past decade, some of the more challenging clinical proposals, including those of Kernberg (1975), Mahler and her collaborators (1975), and Kohut (1977), have used object relations theory as an organizing framework.

I have discussed the limitations of the object relations approach as a general psychology of motivation in the preceding chapter. Here, I want to examine the implications of this point of view when its use is confined to modes of psychological organization for which it is *appropriate,* i.e., conditions in which we are unable to distinguish ego, id, or superego aspects. Specifically, I wish to scrutinize one of the basic assumptions of object relations theory: the hypothesis that object relations in adult life (and, *a fortiori,* those observed *as* the analytic transference) are reflections of schemata structured in early childhood that necessarily channel and limit the individual's capacity to relate to others.

One common pitfall of the object relations viewpoint is the tendency to see the correlation between adult interpersonal performances and the actualities of childhood events as real homologies. As Leo Sadow (1979) has pointed out, in translating archaic transference configurations directly into putative memories, contemporary writers are reverting to the error Freud overcame when he realized that the child's capacity to create fantasies forms a prism that deflects the effects of historical *events* in quite unpredictable ways. Freud (1899) termed the results of this process "screen memories." By analogy, we might say that the relationship within the transference constitutes a screen that may or may not form an accurate reflection of an actuality in the past. As Boesky (1980) has correctly noted, however, theorists of object relations have made certain allowances for the distorting influence of the child's perceptual-cognitive processing on the ultimate configuration of his self- and object representations. Kernberg (1975) has stressed the role of defensive operations in this regard, particularly that of the need to project aggression onto the object. Even if we take these voices of caution into account, however, it seems that object relations theory is bound to place less emphasis on the capacity of children to determine the manner in which their early experiences will be encoded in memory than our cumulative analytic work of 90 years should suggest. A brief clinical illustration may help to substantiate this opinion.

Case 3: A Further Discussion

I have already recounted my lengthy contact with a suicidal patient, initially seen in several segments of psychotherapy and eventually in a successful analysis (see Chapter 1). In adult life, this woman tended to form relationships in which she took a protective role toward the disadvantaged, often engaging in combative behavior with their oppressors at the same time. These patterns were already in evidence when she started school, particularly in her fierce struggles on behalf of her baby brother, and culminated during her adolescence, when she defied her father in order to safeguard her brother's interests. It took many years of treatment to trace this issue back to her more remote past, but it did become possible eventually to connect it to the child's identification with a beloved step-grandmother who died when she was about four. As far as we could determine, this particular thread had no further precedents; the patient's actual relationship with her mother had been of a very different kind, although she was unable to give an accurate account of that history in the earlier phases of her analysis. (My statement reflects the conclusions we ultimately reached through reconstructions based on the unfolding of the transference.)

These very early bonds seemed to have more influence on a second mode of relating to people in adult life, a savagely masochistic pattern full of self-abasement and illusions about the meritorious qualities of the object. This pattern apparently began with a defensive pseudoidealization of the mother after the loss of her grandfather, who moved to another city not too many years after the death of his wife. Each pseudoidealization of a new object might last for several years; when the inevitable disillusionment supervened, the patient's self-esteem collapsed until she found someone else she could idealize. Her serious suicide attempt in her mid-twenties followed a traumatic disappointment in a lover. This event echoed her realization in adolescence that her father was willing to let her become a prostitute. Her husband's collusion in her affairs had a similar flavor of sexual exploitation, but she had become aware of *his* inadequacies some time before she turned to other men. Similarly, her renewed disappointment with her father in adolescence had followed the realization when she was about 11 that her mother was grossly inadequate. Treatment safeguarded her against recurrence of the depression as long as the idealizing transference went unchallenged; in the midst of the regression induced by the analytic process, depression returned as a transference phenomenon in its own right, and her relationship with me then revealed the childhood antecedents of the defensive idealization.

The object relationship that emerged resembled the adult pattern only in its savagery. This finding parallels Freud's (1900) conclusion that the affective quality of dreams always echoes real emotions about the latent material. The fact that we were confronted with very archaic modes of functioning was evident from the confusing and confused changes in who was victim and who was aggressor in the barrage of hostility the patient emitted. In other words, this transference reaction presumably revived conditions in the era before the secure establishment of the differentiation between the child's own volition and that of her mother. At the manifest level, she would attack me as a tyrant or assail herself for worthlessness, always on more or less tenable grounds involving some current issue. But these matters invariably stood for issues of life-and-death intensity between implacable antagonists. Her negativism was absolute, as her manifest position shifted to an opposition to whatever she thought to be mine. Equally abruptly, roles could be reversed altogether; she then became the unreasonable and tyrannical scold who corrected me, her errant child.

This clinical encounter is not adequately described in terms of the projection of unacceptable components of the self onto the representation of the object. Such an explanation does account for part of the picture, but the situation was a great deal more complex. Interpersonal transactions were registered with precision only with regard to their affective qualities, and these were recreated in the transference in endless permutations. As for the question of who was doing what to whom, and why it was being done—there were a number of alternative schemata pertaining to these issues, generally of a mutually contradictory sort. The manifest clinical outcome was one of confusion. It is very doubtful that *any* of these schemata represented an accurate memory of actual events. What had to be emphasized in our reconstruction of the early childhood transactions was the chronic warfare between mother and child about every aspect of perceiving and processing the world—a battle for her very soul! The patient felt worthless—to be most precise, *nonexistent*—as soon as she stopped fighting. But these struggles were fundamentally different from those she later waged on behalf of others, which were invariably just, reasonable, and goal-directed. When she fought for herself, *any* cause would do—even attacking me for defending such a worthless individual as herself!

As a result of a series of later traumata and losses—the flight of her father from his unbearable marriage during the patient's oedipal years, the death of the one humanly protective figure in the family, etc.—the child's successful struggle to establish her autonomy vis-à-vis her psychotic mother became for her a source of guilt and had to be repressed or at least disavowed. A "false self" of masochistic compliance was erected, which masked this woman's iron determination and lonely courage even from herself. Like Galileo, she appeared to have recanted before the Inquisition, but unconsciously her cosmological convictions never changed. It is true that her adult relationships duplicated many important features of her object relations in childhood, but as a result of the massive defenses erected against the true self—its veritable relegation to the status of the id—these persisting childhood patterns were themselves epiphenomenal. Even her depression and pervasive sense of worthlessnes were *consequences* of this successful defensive shift. Her deepest and most "authentic" feelings only came to the fore when she was able, without guilt, to wage wars for freedom and justice for the sake of others—and these battles generally lacked personal involvement with her opponents. Of course, this woman's personal destiny *had* been determined by the qualities of her early experience (cf. Chapter 8 and Gedo, 1979a), and this emotional flavor was repeated endlessly throughout her life. But her adult object relationships re-created *only* these experiential qualities, whereas their masochistic details repeated not the early childhood transactions uncovered in the analysis as transferences, but a complex set of fantasies elaborated in early latency in order to mask them.

To look at these matters from a slightly different perspective, we may inquire about the role of "early object relations" in structuring personality from the standpoint of analytic observations such as those contained in the foregoing case illustration. In the broadest sense, it is undeniable that a struggle against engulfment in the delusional world of a parent is a decisive influence on psychological development. Because such a struggle involves transactions with a *person,* I suppose it is more or less legitimate to conceptualize it as a vicissitude of object relations. In my view, however, such an extension of the concept renders the idea of object relations almost meaningless—it would not be much more arbitrary to assign an etiological role to war and pestilence because these agents inflict so much suffering on mankind. As Freud (1895b) clearly stated, numerous nonspecific, "stock" factors invariably play a part in the production of every syndrome, and the only ones that can be assigned an etiological role are those which are *never* absent.

Caretakers provide every child with a milieu that stimulates and challenges the child to adopt a set of adaptive responses. Although I would not go so far as to claim that parental pressure like that of the psychotic mother in the illustrative case is expectable in an "average environment," in Hartmann's (1939) sense of the term, I do believe that it is extremely common, and that the unusual circumstance in this instance was the child's ability to rise to the challenge and avoid being enmeshed in a folie-à-deux. I may be on somewhat shakier ground in my conviction that she was enabled to avoid this development by her very superior cognitive equipment, rather than through the assistance provided by alternative caretakers. In either case, the quality of her early experience was ultimately determined by her own responses to her mother's delusions. With Galileo, she *could not* abandon her own beliefs. As he said, *eppur si muove*! Or, to extend my metaphor: it is not the Inquisition that creates heretics but the irrepressible imagination of man.

It is evident, nonetheless, that those qualities of early experience which are continually re-created by the force in human psychological organization Freud (1920) named the "repetition compulsion" are codetermined by the activities of the primary caretakers. Hence it is generally important to learn as much as possible about those activities because such information facilitates our reconstructive task, i.e., the precise description of the crucial "inner" experiences of early childhood. In this regard, patients' recollections and conjectures are notoriously unreliable. In the case I have just described, for example, the earliest memories concerned a phase of childhood that postdated the relevant events, but the patient could not imagine that her infancy might have been any different. Thus she assumed that her mother had been cold, uncaring, and unempathic. It came as a shocking surprise to her that transference developments pointed in the opposite direction, i.e., to the reconstruction that her mother had responded with these rejecting behaviors *after* the child began to resist her influence. To borrow the terminology of Kohut (1971), this mother had not deprived her daughter of the admiring affirmation she wanted; on the contrary, she disillusioned her because, unlike the magic mirror of the fairy tale, she overestimated the child in a fatuous manner.

Having stated all this, we must once again face the fact that "external" reality shapes the organization of personality only insofar as it is encoded in the child's memory system; neither the representation of his own person nor that of the principal early objects is likely to be without major defensive distortions or misperceptions based on the child's immaturity. Hence the object relations schemata laid down in early life are, in principle, primitive fantasy systems. In this respect, my conclusions may sound similar to the views of Melanie

Klein (see Segal, 1974; Segal and Britton, 1981), but I am, in fact, considering developments in the second half of the second year of life and not in the newborn. Moreover, I have absolutely no preconceptions about the nature of the fantasy systems toddlers may be capable of erecting, and in this respect as well I reject the *a priori* assumptions of the Kleinian school.

To what degree, then, do these primitive fantasies limit the range of potential behaviors in adult life? The question is difficult to answer, in part because these archaic memories are almost invariably unavailable to consciousness prior to their emergence as transferences, usually in the form of enactments. In the illustrative case, they did not arise as interpretable material through several lengthy periods of psychotherapy; as I tried to show in Chapter 1, it was the institution of a standard analytic situation of five sessions per week that overcame the lifelong resistance against re-experiencing the terrifying delusional ideas this patient, as a toddler, had mistakenly formed about her mother. In other words, our thinking about the effects of primitive fantasies must encompass not only surface phenomena but, more importantly, the earliest and most deeply buried layers of fantasy as well.

To turn to the clinical data once more, to what degree were the patient's relationships in adult life based on the prototype of the panicky mistrust of her mother uncovered in the analysis? In my judgment, there were no discernible connections between her adult object relationships and these fantasies. It will be recalled that her adult relationships fell into two major categories: with the disadvantaged, she took the part of a protective caretaker (modeled on a grandparent), and with certain pseudoidealized figures, she formed a "symbiosis" with a masochistic flavor that repeated certain features of her transactions with her mother in latency. From one point of view, it might be said that these interpersonal patterns constituted defensive maneuvers to ward off the dangerous consequences of the earlier relationship with the mother. In my opinion, such a conclusion is quite valid, provided we remember that the defense is made necessary by the potential recurrence of anxiety (Freud, 1926) and not by any specific ideation. The situation is exactly analogous to that of anxiety dreams: the distortion accomplished by the dreamwork does not prevent the occurrence of displeasure; it merely creates false connections between the affect and the manifest content of the dream. To restate the matter, both patterns of relating to people in adult life served, in this case, to ward off the anxiety connected to feelings of helplessness. The defense went into operation, moreover, whether the helplessness was caused by being dependent on a tyrant (as was the case in early childhood) or by any other factor, such as the illnesses in the immediate family that she had to cope with as an adult.

It might be preferable to think of the patient's interpersonal relationships from a more adaptive frame of reference as defensive only when defense was needed; most of the time this was not the case, and these behavior patterns served a variety of other aims, many of which, in Hartmann's terms, had become autonomous. I believe this finding to be decisive in refuting the hypothesis that the schemata of early object relationships determine the possibilities for human transactions in adult life. The latter are varied, heterogeneous, and may stem from a whole gamut of earlier or later vicissitudes. It would seem that only the experiential-affective qualities of archaic experiences remain permanently active as motivators of behavior; the fantasies connected with them are epiphenomenal and have no greater significance than the manifest content of dreams. It should be recalled that the patient in question only recovered the primitive fantasies connected with her chronic affective state at the height of the transference in her analysis; previously, these ideas had not influenced her behavior with other people. Moreover, she did not simply repeat one childhood transaction in the transference; her enduring negativism was readily replaced by efforts either to impose her point of view on me or to assault herself as worthless (because she was such a stubborn, negativistic creature). What really counted was the savagery of the struggle.

I should like to underscore this point by considering in greater detail the source of the patient's "symbiotic" needs in adult life. In the transference, these were for some time so absolute that she felt as if she had been hypnotized. However, she could only use idealized figures in this manner; whenever one of the latter disillusioned her, she became profoundly depressed, occasionally even suicidal. Can we conclude that her archaic object relations schema involved fantasied fusion with an omniscient mother (what Kohut [1977] has lately been defining as a "merger transference")? The evidence seems to indicate otherwise: the early relationships relived in the transference went back to the stage before secure differentiation of herself from objects, yet in these states she did not cease asserting her autonomy, whatever the cost in terms of the needs met by her symbiotic partners in *less* primitive modes of her psychic life.

These observations suggest that the symbiotic tendencies evoked by treatment had no mental representation whatsoever; I am even more certain that they did not constitute unconscious *wishes* of any kind. Insofar as the patient had a symbiotic need, she knew nothing whatever about it—it was an inference made by an observer employing natural science methods of observation, not through interpretations of the meanings of the patient's associations. This view is further supported by the fact that the symbiosis was resolved spontaneously (i.e., without explicit discussion of its *meaning*) just as soon as the patient had learned, in the treatment or in any other setting, everything she needed to know to function effectively on her own.

Clearly, one prerequisite for this late acquisition of basic skills in living was mastery of the patient's inability to learn from maternal figures because of the dread of helplessness when exposed to their arbitrariness and tyranny. Yet, it should be stressed that, in this regard, the anxiety transcended the realm of interpersonal transactions. Nor was the source of the fear confined to the single issue, however crucial, of the mother's propensity to infringe on the child's psychological integrity. To mention only one of the other factors involved, it also constituted an identification with the mother's intolerance of her own emotions, the occurrence of which she looked upon as untoward events.

When the analysis succeeded in helping the patient to master the dread of her own affects, her capacity to learn was dramatically improved—without any immediate shift in her object relations. When she was enabled, in addition, to learn through identification (as a result of overcoming the need to protect her autonomy as much as possible through negativism), she rapidly acquired an array of interpersonal skills she did not previously possess. I think of individuals such as this patient as virtuosi of calculus who cannot add two and two together. This is not the place to document how people with "symbiotic needs" overcome their archaic helplessness when they correct the defects of their earliest training in becoming human; suffice it to say that the repair of their cognitive deficits enables them, for the first time, to do well enough when left to their own devices to dispense with symbiotic partners without suffering calamitous consequences.

I have undertaken this short discussion of the issue of symbiotic needs (also called the need for a "selfobject" in Kohut's terminology) in order to show that the consequences of developmental disturbances on adult object relationships are not necessarily based on the "internalization" of the child's *perception* of his transactions with early childhood caretakers; these effects will make themselves felt automatically without the registration of the specifics of those early events. This circumstance may explain the frequent finding, otherwise so difficult to understand, that patients often form symbiotic bonds in the analytic situation who have never done so in their adult social relationships. In other words, these individuals do not become absolutely dependent on caretakers who satisfactorily complement their own defective psychological skills because they have a wish (or "drive") to do so. When presented with conventional social relations, they simply respond in kind without falling into an archaic position. I am of course well aware that this dichotomy is by no means invariable; many people do try to force their social companions into symbiotic roles. But for our present purposes, the instructive instances are the ones in which the symbiotic bond with the analyst is an unprecedented occurrence.

We have been accustomed to think of these surprising developments as fulfillments of archaic needs that have never been met before—I believe this was the case in the treatment discussed in this chapter. The patient did not welcome the establishment of her transference "bondage"; on the contrary, she found her dependence to be disturbing and shameful. The adult behavior did not represent the recurrence of an infantile schema of appropriate relations with the caretaker; obviously, the schema actually established was highly inappropriate and totally different from those aspects of the therapeutic relationship I am highlighting here. As I stated before, the child had brief opportunities to experience glimpses of such a reliable relationship with her step-grandmother and, later, had falsely credited a number of people, including her mother, with offering her the same thing. But in none of those instances had she actually formed a symbiotic bond, suffered separation anxiety, or felt threatened by engulfment. The therapeutic symbiosis was truly without precedent, because she had mistrusted that type of human closeness since the dawn of her consciousness. Yet the mistrust was itself unconscious and not discernible in her adult behavior, i.e., she was not fearful about normal social relations, only of experiencing an archaic bond with someone unreliable.

I have now tried to articulate two major objections to the hypothesis that early object relationships are encoded in mental representations that form templates for adult behavior. First, I have shown that the representations of archaic relationships merely constitute screen memories—significant, but not to be relied on as explanatory constructs without decoding their latent meanings. Second, I have argued that certain primitive aspects of the therapeutic relationship may not constitute repetitions of childhood events; these unprecedented archaic bonds come about if unmet psychobiological needs lacking in mental representation are fortuitously (or planfully) fulfilled in the analysis.

Because of these major exceptions, "object relations theory" in the form in which I have presented it in this chapter cannot serve as a cogent developmental framework for understanding primitive character disturbances. The effort to conceptualize such pathology on the basis of vicissitudes in the earliest phases of development will have to focus more sharply on the child's subjective experience on the one hand, and on the vicissitudes of his various psychobiological needs on the other.

SECTION IV

APPLICATIONS OF THE HIERARCHICAL MODEL

Having stated my objections in the last two sections to various proposals for the expansion and modification of the psychoanalytic paradigm, it is fitting that I devote the remainder of this volume to an exposition of the alternatives I advocate. Clearly, I am in agreement with the need for change. As I have repeated, perhaps all too often throughout the foregoing chapters, I have tried to promote such a reconsideration in two previous books, *Models of the Mind* (1973), written in collaboration with Arnold Goldberg, and *Beyond Interpretation* (1979a).

In this section, I shall not repeat the intellectual content of those works. Instead, I shall try to apply the hierarchical view of psychic life I have proposed to specific clinical problems: the appropriate use of dreams in the analysis of regressed and other primitive mental states (Chapter 10), the differing channels and the subtleties of communication necessitated by the shifting modes of the analysand's psychic organization (Chapter 11), the hierarchical view of psychopathology in relation to the study of particular symptomatic behaviors (Chapter 12) and to that of arrested development (Chapter 13), and the understanding of the Oedipus complex entailed by this viewpoint (Chapter 14).

For the reader unfamiliar with my previous efforts, it may be desirable to provide at least an outline map of their treacherous terrain. In the 1973 book, Goldberg and I made an attempt to correlate the major clinical theories of psychoanalysis along a developmental axis. We used versions of each theory embodied in their graphic analogues, the so-called "models of the mind."

We examined the way each model represents the status of specific mental functions, such as typical defensive operations, typical situations of danger, reality testing, or object relations. Because these mental activities are consistently portrayed differently in each model, we came to the conclusion that the latter describe a series of entirely distinct modes of psychological organization. The characteristics of mental life summarized in highly abstract form in Freud's topographic and reflex arc models of 1895–1900, in his structural model of 1923, and, more recently, in conceptualizations focused on object relations are therefore referable to distinct phases of childhood. We concluded, in short, that the disparate clinical theories in common psychoanalytic usage should not be regarded as competing conceptualizations but as valid fragments of a larger whole.

We then tried to fit these existing concepts together into an appropriate sequence corresponding to a series of five phases of development. We attempted to specify the nature of the transitions from one phase to the next in accord with general systems theory. We believed that the schema we developed in this manner was in complete accord with clinical experience. As modes of organization succeed each other, older aspects of the adaptive repertory are not lost when they are superseded by the new; on the contrary, as new possibilities are added in the course of maturation, the individual is able to use each of his modes of operation in a selective and flexible manner. It is the resort to earlier modes of functioning after the acquisition of newer alternatives that we call regression.

The overall schema we elaborated for the entire range of phases of development and repertory of modes of functioning constitutes a "hierarchical model" of mental life. A revised version of this model is reproduced as Figure 1.

Some additional words of explanation may be in order to facilitate use of this diagram. The horizontal axis represents the passage of time; successive developmental phases are therefore represented on this axis from left to right, and they are separated from each other by vertical lines that stand for the stable achievement of certain capacities crucial for the reorganization of behavior into a new mode. Starting at these nodal points, successive modes are superimposed on previous ones in the vertical dimension. In this manner, the model assumes the form of a grid; each module within this grid contains a verbal description of certain aspects of functioning in that mode. Obviously, Figure 1 contains only a limited number of the relevant issues that should ideally be included in the description of each mode. Some of the most crucial questions left out in this version but considered in alternative ones are the principal psychological problems typical for each mode, the modalities of therapeutic intervention appropriate for each of these, and the subordinate (i.e., preexisting) psychoanalytic clinical theory most relevant for its elucidation.

In *Beyond Interpretation* (1979a), I amplified this complex approach to the study of behavior through a further revision of psychoanalytic theory. My primary intention in this work was to increase the relevance of analytic

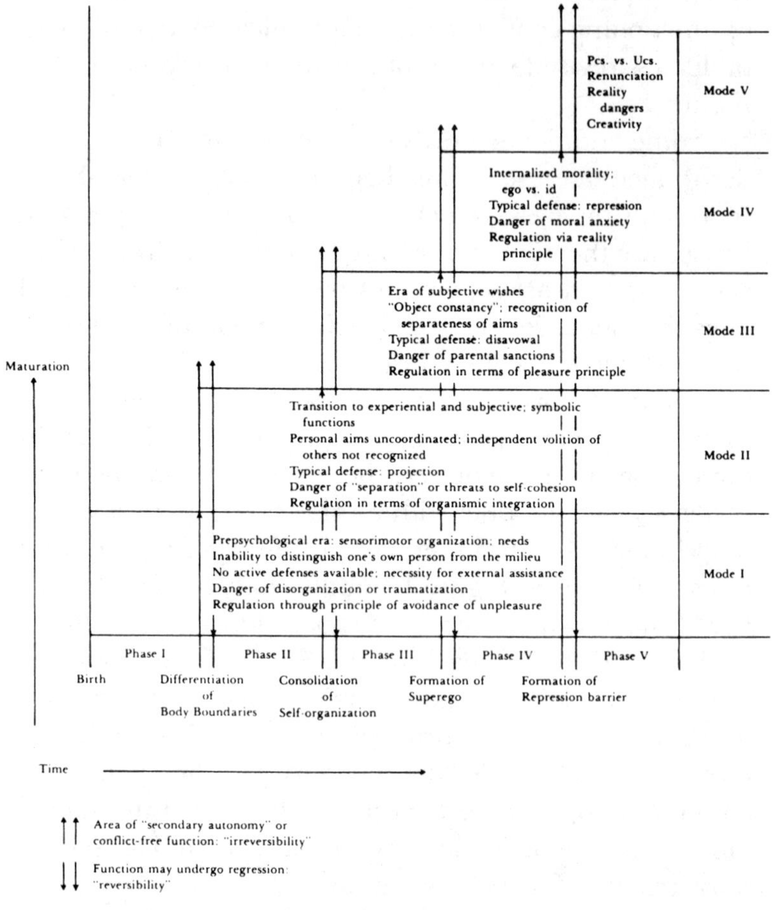

FIGURE 1

THE HIERARCHICAL MODEL: FUNCTIONAL ORGANIZATION IN THE VARIOUS MODES—REVISED (from Gedo, 1979a)

constructs for the data of clinical observation. At the same time, I tried to eliminate those features of Freudian metapsychology that are now regarded as epistemologically untenable. The central concept of my proposed system is that of human personality as a hierarchy of personal aims. These goals consist of the biological needs essential throughout life and of conscious and unconscious subjective wishes. Wishes may stem from basic needs or from the child's acquired ambitions and ideals. The entire hierarchy of aims constitutes a relatively stable structure, a primary identity that undergoes later transformations only insofar as the individual acquires new systems of values. I prefer to call this basic core of the personality the "self-organization."

This patterned structure determines the individual's potentials for action; it is thus the organizer of subsequent psychic life. Behavior can only consist of the active repetition of these basic motivational components, at best in new combinations. As a theory of human motivation, this proposal replaces the classical conception of motivation as a combination of instinctual drives, ego interests, and superego pressures by one that postulates a single source of volitional behavior, ipso facto laden with affect. This source is the principle of active repetition of earlier experience, whatever its quality may have been. The earliest experiences of life are, to a large extent, codetermined by external influences, and this is the avenue through which the impact of nurture is built into the schema.

This epigenetic view of self-organization is ultimately

derived from Freud's original conception of the repetition compulsion as a principle regulating behavior prior to the establishment of the pleasure principle. In other words, I would extend the area governed by the repetition compulsion to the entire range of human action; other principles of behavior regulation are not alternatives to it but only complementary determinants.

I have fitted this new hypothesis into the hierarchical schema of *Models of the Mind.* The most important correlations between the two approaches match the sensorimotor action patterns of infancy with Mode I, the integration of discrete, uncoordinated aims into a cohesive set of goals with Mode II, the capacity to seek subjective satisfactions on the basis of purposeful choices under the sway of the pleasure principle with Mode III, the capacity to tolerate intrapsychic conflicts without disorganization with Mode IV, and the ability to achieve inner harmony with Mode V.

CHAPTER TEN

Dreams and Primitive Modes of Psychic Organization

Among Freud's manifold accomplishments in creating psychoanalysis, only two have stood the test of time without need for modification. The standardization of the psychoanalytic situation as the characteristic observational tool of depth psychology was the more fundamental of these contributions. The other aspect of Freud's work that has required no change was a greater intellectual feat—his discovery of the method of dream interpretation based on decipherment of the language of the primary process.

Psychoanalysis as a method of treatment has been applied with increasing effectiveness in a steadily expanding range of psychopathological conditions. Although some investigators advocate departures from the classical analytic technique in what they consider to be "borderline conditions" (see Kernberg, 1975, 1976),

This chapter was previously published in *The Dream in Clinical Practice*, edited by Joseph Natterson (New York: Jason Aronson, 1980), and is reprinted here by permission.

many others—including myself—have attempted to use the classical technique to treat all personality disorders with the exception of the psychoses (e.g., Settlage, 1977). In the context of this more radical approach to the psychoanalytic management of archaic transferences, systematic dream interpretation retains its traditional role as the royal road into the realm of unconscious mental life.

If the topic of dreams in the treatment of severe personality disorders nonetheless merits fresh consideration, such an effort is justified by the overall evolution of the psychoanalytic theory of mental life rather than by changes in our actual approach to the translation of the meaning of any particular dream into discursive language. More specifically, as I have repeatedly stated, recent emphasis on the developmental perspective in the clinical theories of psychoanalysis (see A. Freud, 1965; Gedo and Goldberg, 1973) has made it possible to refine our theories of therapeutic technique. This evolution has moved in the direction of conceptualizing separate modalities of treatment for each of those distinct aspects of an individual's psychopathology that result from the vicissitudes of a different phase of early development. One classification of appropriate treatment modalities was proposed in my collaborative work with Arnold Goldberg, *Models of the Mind* (see especially Chapter 11). In order to provide a framework for further discussion, I shall briefly summarize that schema here. It should be kept in mind through this account that the technique of interpreting one specific dream remains the same, whatever overall therapeutic strategy is being pursued. Moreover, it must be stressed that every analytic patient will sooner or later present behaviors referable to the poorly resolved sequelae of each phase of development. Hence every analytic procedure must consist of the application of all possible modalities of treatment in various combinations. This point of view may seem novel, but in fact it simply articulates the logical consequences of an epigenetic theory of psychological development.

In accord with this hierarchical schema, it is appropriate to use interpretations about intrapsychic conflicts and their childhood genesis when dealing with material organized in the psychological mode characteristic of the oedipal phase of development. In other words, for the "transference neuroses" proper, it is optimal to use the model technique of psychoanalysis. The free associations produced by all analytic patients, however, contain material not only in this mode but also in more mature and more primitive ones. The mode that reflects post-oedipal phases of mental organization permits the analysand to apprehend his internal life through introspection, i.e., without the interpretation of defensive operations. In such circumstances, the role of the analyst is optimally confined to lending his presence to the procedure as an empathic witness. In more archaic modes of psychic organization, on the other hand, more active modalities of intervention are required, in line with the relative lack of autonomy in self-regulation prevalent in those states. Borrowing a phrase from Winnicott, Modell (1976) has summarized the proposals about the optimal therapeutic handling of these regressed states we put forward in *Models of the Mind* as the provision of a "holding environment." Goldberg and I specified a series of psychological issues that must be dealt with in these regressed conditions, of which the principal ones involve tension regulation, the establishment of a single and coherent hierarchy of aims, and the correction of unrealistic illusions, either about oneself or the persons around one. In circumstances of stimulus overload, the appropriate therapeutic modality is that of "pacification"; when the cohesion of the self has become compromised, the analyst must address himself to its reunification; for the illusory thinking characteristic of pregenital disturbances, efforts at optimal disillusionment are indicated (see also Gedo, 1979a, Chapter 2).

It should be emphasized that the need to employ any or all of these aspects of a "holding environment" in a particular psychoanalytic procedure has no implications, in and of itself, with regard to diagnosis. Nosological categories based on psychoanalytic principles cannot be established through focusing on such cross-sectional samples of behavior; diagnosis must take into account long-term progressive and regressive sequences, particularly as they occur in the transference relationship within the analytic situation. In other words, regressions to the various modes of psychic functioning that may temporarily require the provision of a holding environment will occur in the course of specific transference developments no matter what the ultimate overall personality diagnosis may turn out to be. On the other hand, this point of view also entails the conclusion that the only conditions in which the central and predominant issue of the analytic process continues to be the quality of the setting as a holding environment are those involving derivatives or sequelae of difficulties of the earliest years of life (what was formerly designated the pregenital era).

What are the implications of this hierarchical model of psychic life for our view of dreaming? In 1925 Freud added the following comment to his discussion of wish fulfillment in *The Interpretation of Dreams*: "Experience has shown that distorted dreams, which stand in need of interpretation, are already found in children of four or five; and this is in full agreement with our theoretical views on the determining conditions of distortion in dreams" (1900, p. 127, n. 1). Freud also provided a series of illustrative children's dreams in which the wishes represented as fulfilled are quite undisguised; among these, the most memorable was that of his daughter Anna, dreamt at the age of 19 months: "Anna Fweud, stwawbewwies, wild stwawbewwies, omblet, pudden!" (p. 130). Earlier, in 1911, Freud had added some examples of undisguised wish fulfillments in the dreams of adults exposed to circumstances of extreme duress.

However archaic some of the transferences we encounter in the analytic situation may be, adult patients in our consulting rooms are never exposed to external stresses of sufficient magnitude to produce dreams of undisguised wish fulfillment, and they never seem to do so purely on the basis of their psychopathology. Whatever their ultimate diagnoses may turn out to be, that is, patients who can be expected to be analyzable have invariably matured sufficiently to distort the infantile wishes that are represented as fulfilled in their dreams. Even dreams that are thought to be typical expressions of infantile grandiosity, such as those in which the dreamer transcends the laws of gravity (see Kohut, 1971, pp. 4–5), cannot be taken literally. Dreams of flying do not signify that the analysand would like to be able to perform acts of levitation; even when the associations do lead to some kind of infantile grandiose ideation, the ability to fly symbolizes the wish to be omnipotent with regard to some current activity of a more serious import. Candidates at psychoanalytic institutes, for example, often represent their wishes to be able to perform analyses without supervision in this guise—especially so after they have read about the common significance of flying fantasies. I would therefore contest Kohut's assertion that certain "typical" dreams containing overtly grandiose ideation can be understood as direct expressions of the dreamer's "self-state" (see Kohut, 1977, pp. 109–110).

The most profound functional regressions in psychic organization are not characterized by changes in the inner structure of the dreams reported in analysis; there are, in fact, no specific pathognomonic signs of such regressions referable to dreams or dreaming. Quite to the contrary, the very capacity to fall asleep and to dream implies some degree of reintegration, and one indication that regression to the most archaic modes of organization did not persist during the night may well be the report of one or more dreams. To be sure, one cannot find such reassurance in the occurrence of unsuccessful dreams, i.e., nightmares. And yet anxiety severe enough to awaken the dreamer is not necessarily a sign of actual regression to an overstimulated state, especially if it is promptly relieved by the interruption of the dream. The principal point I wish to make here concerns the need to focus on the analysand's current mode of organization in the here and now of the analytic session, instead of allowing oneself to be diverted to his state at some point between sessions. There are, of course, exceptions even to this sound precept, but their enumeration here would take us too far afield from the topic of dreams.

From the vantage point of monitoring the occurrence of severe regressions within the analytic setting proper, it should be kept in mind that such contingencies are almost invariably accompanied by strenuous efforts to recover. At the very moment of trauma, we may witness a period of stunned and empty "absence," but in properly conducted analyses, iatrogenic incidents of that kind should be rare indeed. Much more frequently, the regression is set in motion before the start of the analytic hour, and the patient will attempt to use the analytic relationship to effect his reintegration.

One manner of promoting recovery from trauma is self-soothing through analytic-business-as-usual, and this tack may often involve the recital of one or more dreams. In general, it is less than helpful to interfere with such efforts, although, as we might expect, they seldom eventuate in the successful interpretation of the latent meanings of the dreams reported. In any case, the primary analytic task in such circumstances is not the interpretation of content but the detection of the traumatic state and its management through "pacification."

The analyst may be led to the proper diagnosis by noting, among other phenomena characteristic of traumatic states, shifts from the analysand's customary style of narrating his dreams. Possibly the most common change consists of pressure of speech, often with marked obliviousness about the value of the resultant message as comprehensible communication. Another variation involves changes in pitch and volume. In traumatic circumstances, however, one does not feel that the stream of words or the muttering is being aimed against one in a provocative or sadistic manner. A tactful comment about the impression of frenzy or excitement given by the analysand's manner of speaking may have a powerfully calming effect in these emergencies. We must forego a discussion of the reasons for the pacifying results of such interventions; from the viewpoint of our focus on dreams, it suffices to underscore that it is essential to avoid behaving like a machine programmed to uncover unconscious meanings. The analyst must be an empathic and sentient person, ever alert to the potential need to assist the patient with disturbances in tension regulation.

The potential variety of ways in which dream narratives may betray traumatic states defies classification. I shall therefore content myself with mentioning only one additional pattern that is fairly common. If the frantic style I have just described might be likened to stepping on the accelerator while the car is not in gear, the next pattern might be compared to the sound of an engine that will not quite turn over because of a weak battery. The tone is lifeless and flat; speech is halting and slow. There may be a startling discrepancy between the affectively charged material implicit within the dream content and the detached manner of its presentation.

In these circumstances, as in the states of overexcitement, it would be gravely unempathic to proceed with dream interpretation instead of focusing on the analysand's actual emotional state. The appropriate measures may be somewhat easier to carry out in this variety of reaction to trauma than in excited states because one can address oneself to the fact of the disorder and expect to be understood without first having to reestablish conditions conducive to meaningful communication. Noting the paradoxical affect may suffice to direct the analysand's attention to his hitherto overlooked traumatic episode, and some correlation between the meaning of these events and the regression that followed them may succeed in restoring the patient to his usual mode of integration.

Once reintegration has taken place, it is generally quite illuminating to go on to decipher the latent meanings of the dreams themselves, should the associations make this possible. The foregoing statement may seem like a truism; however, I mean something beyond the self-evident proposition that every fresh look into the depths increases our insight. The nature of the new information we sometimes obtain in these circumstances may be quite specific. The bits and fragments of dream available in such conditions, sometimes called "fractionated dream narratives," may reflect a variety of uncoordinated and irreconcilable personal goals and values. These internal contradictions are generally concealed from view through defensive distortions and, even at the manifest level, may be misleadingly "compromised" through operations which have sometimes been designated as the "synthetic functions" (Nunberg, 1930). In traumatic regressions, these confusing defensive epiphenomena fall away, revealing the chaos of the basic aims of the individual in their naked irrationality. In another context, I have called such subsets of personal goals and values "nuclei of the self" (Gedo and Goldberg, 1973, Chapter 5).

In terms of the dreams reported in regressive states, each nucleus of the self continues to find only distorted representation in the manifest content. Primitive aims are generally disclaimed in the course of later development, and their potential reappearance mobilizes anxiety, shame, or guilt. Hence, as Freud (1900) demonstrated in convincing detail, infantile wishes are transformed by the dreamwork. From the structural viewpoint, even the latent content always contains not only the archaic wish (the "id") but also the countervailing repudiation from more mature sectors of the personality (the "ego").

Hence each discrete dream will be completely conventional in its organization in these regressive states, but dreams in pairs or series may reveal not merely conflict about one or more wishes, but a multiplicity of uncoordinated and mutually exclusive wishes of that kind (cf. Alexander, 1925). A relatively simple example may help to illuminate this issue:

> Following a short interruption of his analysis, a young psychotherapist returned for his next session in a state of panic focused on his bodily integrity. He talked in a feverish and disjointed manner but eventually revealed that he had, in fact, experienced seemingly objective signs of illness. He had, however, taken no steps to obtain medical attention and conceived of the problem, confusedly, as something to be handled within the analysis. He began to calm down after I differentiated the physical signs that had to be evaluated by an internist from his hypochondriacal preoccupations. In the following session, the patient calmly reported a number of dreams of the intervening night.
>
> 1. A big fat rat had come out of the woodwork.
> 2. An alligator was sitting in a tree, happily eating a bunch of Concord grapes.
> 3. The patient boarded a bus which was driven by a very nice person. It was headed toward the West.
>
> Associations to all three dreams were given in a scattered way in the course of the remaining sessions of that week. For the sake of clarity of presentation, I shall systematize these by recounting all of the associations most directly relevant to each dream sequentially.

1. During my absence he had lost his appetite and his weight had diminished precipitously. His children own a gerbil, but they have lost interest in this pet rodent since the family acquired a cat. From his reading of one of my publications, he knew about my special interest in Freud's case histories, including that of the Rat Man. He felt that something very disreputable about him was about to come into the open.
2. The second dream reminds him of Aesop's fable about the fox and the grapes. Except that Concord grapes are not sour—they are blue. He read a story—it was a satire about psychoanalysis—in which a tiny dog opened his enormous jaws and swallowed a much bigger opponent. The dog belonged to a little boy who recounts that it had been called an alligator before his father cut off its tail and painted it white. Perhaps he is thinking of the account in my book about the Wolf Man and his dream of wolves sitting on a tree. But an alligator could only get up on a tree by magic, and grapes do not grow on trees. As a therapist, he does *not* practice magic.
3. The only bus he rides is the one he takes to my office. However, that ride does not involve going West. His wife picked him up in her car after a professional meeting; they drove West from there. They had been chatting, but she gradually lapsed into silence. When he asked her what was the matter, she told him that his conversation bored her. Over the weekend, however, he had received a call from a former patient who is about to move West. She confessed her love for him and was clearly hoping that he would invite her to have an affair. He had to struggle to overcome this temptation.

On the basis of these associations, the latent conflicts in each dream might be summarized in the following terms:

1. The unacceptable infantile wish expressed by the first dream is that of being fed and cared for by the analyst as a favored pet. The reference to Freud places this within the context of the father transference; there have been numerous indications that the patient is extremely uncomfortable about the homosexual implications of these passive wishes. They are therefore disguised through projection (into the rat) and reversal (instead of being a pet, he is an aggressive predator).
2. In the second dream, the archaic wish is for the attainment of omnipotence: the automatic satisfaction of his needs without reliance on anyone else. In this situation, the primary need was for instant relief from feeling blue and from the murderous hostility aroused in him by the interruption of my caretaking functions. The day residue was the seductive offer by his patient—she is the victim he is swallowing like an alligator, precisely because he is *not* anybody's pet. In fantasy, he can magically cure himself (and her!) through sexual acting out. The various threatening affects at issue are successfully warded off in the dream through humor, and the grandiose ideation is disavowed, once again, by externalization (onto the alligator and ultimately the Wolf Man).
3. The last dream represents the most unacceptable of his infantile wishes, his desire for a soothing, ever-attentive maternal presence within the transference. The wish is repudiated through representation by its opposite (he is going away from my office) as well as disavowal of its frustration (everything is pleasant, and any stranger can soothe him).

In spite of the unavoidable imprecision of brief summaries of this kind, they do demonstrate that every infantile wish in the latent dream thoughts was adequately disguised in the manifest content in order to satisfy the requirements of various countermotives. To review, the mutually exclusive early childhood goals represented in this trio of simultaneous dreams were:

1. to be the favored pet of an honored father;
2. to be omnipotently self-sufficient and immune to frustration;
3. to have an ever-helpful maternal surrogate at his service.[1]

Although each of these wishes probably originated at somewhat different developmental stages, clearly they had not *succeeded* each other on one developmental line, so that in adult life they continue to exert an active influence on behavior simultaneously. When this person has been at his best level of integration, however, it has not been possible to discern *any* of these sets of infantile goals in his psychic life. At such times, the patient was generally preoccupied with his adequacy (in the sexual and professional spheres), barely aware of any concern regarding the implications of his need for analytic assistance in this regard. In such a state of integration, even the latent content of his dreams reveals only wishes that

[1] It is not self-evident that the first and third of these wishes are mutually exclusive. Their coexistence does not violate the law of contradictions, as the second wish does in relation to either the first or the third. In other words, these specific wishes were incompatible only in terms of the particular historical circumstances of this person's childhood, i.e., in view of the fact that he could not gain his father's approval as long as he depended on his mother.

are derivatives of a later phase of development, when the infantile goals I have attributed to his dream trio had already been fused into one common final pathway and their basic discordance had been covered over.

The last point may best be illustrated by a dream reported several days later in the same analysis:

> He and his wife were shopping for rings, but they could not decide whether to look at Marshall Field's or at Carson's. His associations reveal that Carson's is a substandard store, while Field's carries adequate merchandise. When he was about to get married, he had allowed his future wife to select their wedding rings. He has just received his first copy of a psychoanalytic journal and was surprised to discover my name among the editors. He has obsessional doubts about everything—is Memorial Day really a public holiday? He feels similar uncertainties about his marriage and his analysis.

To summarize briefly the interpretation of this material, the analysand wishes to recement his relationship to his wife and to the analysis; his ambivalence has been displaced to a trivial aspect of the arrangements, and its origins are attributed to questions about my professional status. I shall not belabor the transparently oedipal cast of this material.

The detection of various nuclei of the self through dream interpretation may occur in the stage of recovery from traumatic regressions, as in the illustration I have just provided; on the other hand, certain individuals (most frequently considered "borderline personalities") are permanently organized in a mode characterized by such lack of integration into one hierarchy of aims. Alternatively, regressive episodes in the course of analyses of better integrated individuals may not eventuate in actual traumatization; in many instances, they involve only loss of the capacity to maintain a single hierarchy of personal goals. At the bottom of regressive swings of this kind, the clinical picture will resemble the one I have presented to illustrate the recovery phase from traumatization. As I have stated earlier, in all of these circumstances, the immediate analytic task is to promote the reestablishment (or the initial construction) of a unified schema of goal-directed behavior. Interventions designed to accomplish this task are the measures designated as "unification" in my previous work, and it is a unified schema of this kind that I propose to call the "self-organization" (see Gedo, 1979a).

How can the analyst utilize dream material to promote unification of the personality? There is, in fact, no special prescription to be followed to this end. The latent meaning of dreams should be used in the same manner as any other information in the service of helping the analysand to establish a workable hierarchy of goals and values. In practice, by reference to dream material, the analyst may focus the patient's attention on the multiplicity of his mutually exclusive wishes and on his failure to make choices among them. The principal technical requirement in these contingencies is to counter the patient's tendency to lose sight of the totality of his personal aims through isolated preoccupation with the dominant wish of the moment. Consistent attention to the need for a global view may be succeeded by explicit awareness on the part of the analysand of the nature of this psychobiological deficit in adaptation and its eventual correction through self-awareness.

The third component of a holding environment defined in *Models of the Mind* (Gedo and Goldberg, 1973) was the modification of those erroneous beliefs about one's person and about the milieu that grossly interfere with adaptation—the process we called "optimal disillusionment." Insofar as patients harbor conscious illusions about the world contrary to the laws of nature, we need no confirmation of that fact through dream interpretation. More often, however, these unrealistic beliefs have been repressed or disavowed, and active analytic intervention is required to demonstrate their continuing significance for the analysand's inner life. Dream material can obviously serve as a principal avenue for insight into these problems—I need only cite the familiar and ubiquitous example of disavowed credence in the phallic woman as it shows up in the latent content of dreams. This illustration may also serve as a reminder that optimal disillusionment does not necessarily involve the analyst in the correction of misinformation; it is often sufficient to throw the light of consciousness on an archaic belief system to bring it into line with public standards.

In a certain sense, it might be legitimate to look upon the fulfillment of infantile wishes characteristic of all dreams as a regression to a mode of mental organization that partakes of illusions. I am inclined to take a different view in this matter, however, beginning with an aspect of dreams that usually does not find explicit representation in the way they are reported. I am referring to an implicit awareness on the part of the dreamer that his experience is "only a dream." It is rather the occasional absence of such a sense of differentiation between dreaming and actual waking experiences that patients tend to report, often by stating that a particular dream had a special quality of seeming "real." We are not concerned here with the latent meaning of such a dream element (see Freud, 1900); I cite this issue only to demonstrate that most of the time dreamers do have an implicit sense of the reality that they are dreaming. Imagining the fulfillment of various wishes in such circumstances, however unrealistic the hope for such outcomes might be, does not mean that the person has regressed into a realm of illusion.

In other words, I think we are only entitled to conclude that an analysand holds erroneous beliefs about the nature of things on the basis of assessing the premises about reality contained in the *latent* meaning of the dream. To return to the illustration of belief in the existence of phallic women, the appearance of a woman with a penis in the manifest imagery of the dream does not prove that the dreamer has illusions about the anatomical distinction between the sexes. It is more than likely that such dream material merely expresses the wish that this painful reality were nonexistent. By contrast, the fetishist will assert his belief in the maternal phallus as a reality in indirect ways that defy immediate comprehension—even in his dreams. A specific illustration from clinical dream interpretation may help to sharpen our focus on the kind of illusory thinking that should be corrected by psychoanalytic treatment.

> The analysand whose trio of dreams I reported in the previous vignette continued to demonstrate unaccountable passivity in relation to his difficult spouse for a long time. After considerable work focused on this issue without any alteration in his behavior, I gave an unmistakable sign of impatience, to which he responded with the following dream:
>
> > He was trailing after the best friend of his adolescence who led him through the back door of a restaurant. The place was filled with rows of folding seats, like the grandstand at a ballpark. He made his way across the space with much difficulty. When he got to the street entrance, he wondered why he had done the whole thing backwards.
>
> He experienced some reluctance to associate to this material. In response to my inquiry, he revealed for the first time that his ball-playing friend of the teenage years had been a clever, manipulative child-of-the-streets who had tried to make his way as a gambler. He then veered off into complaints about his wife, starting with her lack of cooperation about buying the proper foods for his special diet, but going on to matters with no seeming connection to the dream. Eventually, I commented that his approach to the analysis of this dream reminded me of his friend's attitude toward life: it was cavalier and lacking in attention to detail. He agreed with obvious enthusiasm and quickly added further associations. These concerned his unwillingness to comply with what he had learned about getting along with his wife through the analytic

> work. He had refused to share her bed for several nights; he had slept on a folding cot instead. The folding seats of the dream also reminded him of a movie theater; he had recently seen a science fiction film in which a man with magical powers was engaged in rescuing a regal woman.

The latent meaning of this dream might be stated as the expression of the wish to rescue his sick wife without having to suffer the consequences of devoting himself to such an impossible effort. But the illusion on which this hope was based was hidden, projected onto a dream screen that was not even reported explicitly in the manifest content. The patient's belief in magic was disavowed; in fact, however, it was the controlling factor in determining his behavior in actuality. Hence the image of following in the footsteps of a gambler signified the patient's adherence to the same system of magical beliefs that underlies a reliance on "chance." This meaning was not evident from the initial account of the dream, of course; the analysand's adolescent companions had in the past figured in his associations in the context of fantasies of liberating himself from his family responsibilities, as he had fled from his parents earlier. Interpretation of the dream as an expression of persistent unconscious efforts to improve his relationship with his wife by means of magic produced a feeling of helplessness and depression in the patient. Disillusionment thus took place automatically, and in this case did not prove to be traumatic.

I have now provided examples of the most important

types of intervention required to make the psychoanalytic treatment setting into an adequate holding environment. To repeat, although such measures are occasionally necessary in specific circumstances in every analysis, in the treatment of persons with disturbances centered on pregenital developmental vicissitudes the issues of tension regulation, the correlation of personal goals, and the relinquishment of illusions are invariably crucial to the therapeutic task. I have tried to give clinical illustrations of the manner in which dreams can be used in the service of pacification in overstimulated states, the unification of a hierarchy of goals in states of fragmentation, and optimal disillusionment when patients hold erroneous beliefs about the nature of things. I have chosen examples from the analysis of a single patient in order to attempt to show how the analyst should shift his focus from one area of difficulty to another and how he must vary his tactics among the available therapeutic modalities.

The process of reaching an understanding of the latent meaning of particular dreams was established by Freud before 1900 and has required no revisions. However, the analyst's use of these latent meanings should be guided by his determination of the specific mode of psychic organization implicit in the material presented at a given session. Concentration on the intrapsychic conflict represented in the dream is most appropriate when there is no problem regarding autonomous self-regulation. In more primitive modes of organization, the analyst should use his grasp of the total context, including the latent meaning of dreams, to supplement the patient's limited capacities to regulate tension, to correlate personal goals, and to renounce illusions.

CHAPTER ELEVEN

The Analyst's Affectivity and the Management of the Transference

> The professor interrupted rarely; when he did so, he mostly used metaphors and allegories. Once... Freud leaned over the couch to sing one or two stanzas to me from Mozart's *Don Giovanni*.
>
> —*John Dorsey* (in Grotjahn, 1979)

From the inception of psychoanalysis as a therapeutic procedure, one of the most difficult technical problems confronting its practitioners has been the management of the analyst's affectivity in the treatment setting. In his major effort to outline the principles of psychoanalytic technique, Freud (1911–1915) insisted on an attitude of "neutrality towards the patient" (p. 164) as one aspect of the requirement to conduct the treatment in an abstinent manner. His recommendations to analytic beginners took full cognizance of the difficulty of "keeping the counter-transference in check," but he did not specify what he regarded as the appropriate way of conveying a neutral attitude.

In subsequent years, the concept of neutrality underwent a subtle shift in the direction of eliminating the analyst's affectivity as much as possible—the ideal of analytic conduct was often described in terms of metaphors based on machinery, in recent times on tools of communication such as computers. Although this tendency to dehumanize the analyst undoubtedly distorted the spirit of Freud's initial proposals, we are now in a position to understand these proposals as a necessary antidote to the opposing tendency—the temptation to abandon treatment by means of insight in favor of procedures utilizing unspoken aspects of the therapeutic relationship. Perhaps the most influential advocate of therapeutic modifications of this kind was Ferenczi. Although he was unable to specify the precise circumstances in which these departures from Freud's recommendations might be indicated, in a series of publications through the last decade of his life (which I have reviewed in detail; see Gedo, 1968), Ferenczi did succeed in showing that a purely interpretive approach in psychoanalysis is not uniformly effective.

A sterile polarization of views was eventually averted as a consequence of growing understanding of the fact that analyzability depends in large measure on the adequate development of certain ego functions. This assumption was formulated most clearly by Eissler (1953). He defined the field of applicability of Freud's model techniques as the range of personalities with optimal ego development; for those in whom such a fortunate predisposition does not exist, analysis had to be modified through the use of measures Eissler designated "parameters." One result of this clarification was a perceptible diminution of concern about the danger of committing countertransference errors through being simply human within the psychoanalytic situation. In the years following Eissler's formulation, Stone (1961) and Greenson (1967), to name only the best-known contributors in this area, made major statements correctly placing the neutrality of the psychoanalyst into a context of human affectivity, and their views probably represent the current consensus about the model technique of psychoanalysis.

The past decade has been marked by increasing interest in describing the technical requirements for effective analytic work with personalities suffering from developmental disturbances (see Gedo and Goldberg, 1973, especially Chapter 11). This intellectual challenge has once again raised questions about the appropriate expression of the analyst's affectivity with regard to patients of this type. Perhaps the most radical proposals about these matters have emanated from Heinz Kohut and his collaborators. The latter has attempted to explain the mode of action of psychoanalytic treatment principally on the basis of the analyst's empathy, in contrast to the Freudian emphasis on accurate interpretation (Kohut, 1975a, 1975b). From this viewpoint, empathy is not merely a cognitive tool, but a mode of affective expression as well. In spite of the general reluctance to accept this concept, I think few analysts would disagree with Kohut's recent definition of appropriate neutrality in the analytic situation: "The analyst's behavior vis-à-vis his patient should be the expected average one—i.e., the behavior of a psychologically perceptive person vis-à-vis someone who is suffering and has entrusted himself to him for help" (1977, p. 253). Despite this temperate formulation, however, certain representatives of Kohut's viewpoint (e.g., Wolf, 1976) have described the ambience of traditional psychoanalyses as cold and critical and advocated its replacement by a warmly accepting atmosphere that few clinicians, I believe, could create without going out of their way. It would be reasonable to ask whether this kind of environment conforms with Kohut's own understanding of the expectable average response to the productions of analysands who develop archaic transferences.

Actually, generalized prescriptive statements about an allegedly optimal analytic ambience that one should strive to provide have no practical value, because the analyst cannot exercise any conscious choice over his underlying emotional responses to his patient. In other words, the technical issue that deserves discussion is confined to the manner in which these responses should be monitored, channeled, or communicated to the analysand. This issue becomes paramount in those analyses that are characterized by archaic transferences, i.e., whenever it is the quality of the analytic setting as a "holding environment" (Modell, 1976; Gedo, 1979a) that constitutes the crucial therapeutic variable. Moreover, it is in these cases specifically that the irrational activities of the analysand are most likely to evoke intense affective reactions in the analyst, placing unusual stress on him with regard to managing the expression of his responses.

It may be fruitful to approach the problem from another direction altogether, by asking whether there are clinical contingencies that *require* emotion-laden interventions by the analyst. I suspect that every experienced clinician has, in fact, frequently encountered situations of this kind, although many of them, with misplaced modesty, might describe their successful management of these as signs of countertransference difficulties. In a wide range of circumstances, analytic patients do not seem to respond to communications in the form of flat declarative statements but can make constructive use of the same information if it is conveyed to them in a tone of urgency. To illustrate, I shall present clinical data from one of several analyses in which this proved to be the case.

Case 16

A college professor in his mid-thirties sought assistance because of severe marital strain, brought about by his withdrawal of continuous attention from his wife in favor of devoting himself to completing a long-delayed dissertation. They had been married for a dozen years and had had two children while he attended a series of graduate schools and held teaching positions that did not fully utilize his scholarly talents. He had used up most of a substantial inheritance in maintaining a high living standard for the family, and he had been quite self-sacrificing in meeting the burdensome demands of his emotionally fragile spouse. He entered this marriage shortly after concluding a year of successful once-a-week psychotherapy with me; in retrospect, his supportive attitude toward his needy wife seemed like a massive identification with the treatment method I had employed with him when he had been in an ominous emotional crisis as a senior in college.

He accepted my recommendation for psychoanalysis and rapidly established an archaic transference, apparently based on the dramatic success of our previous psychotherapeutic contact—he felt that I was a totally reliable person with a magic capacity to restore him to health. In this context, he viewed the process of free association as a ritualistic requirement, the price he had to pay in order to receive my beneficent magic. For the most part, this unconscious fantasy impelled him to work cooperatively; whenever he felt neglected, however, it led him into spiteful, albeit still unconscious, provocations involving his manner of communicating his experience. This negativism took a number of alternative forms. Perhaps the simplest of these, but one that may serve to illustrate them all, consisted of a loss of the capacity to judge whether his language was comprehensible to others.

Sometimes he was able to clarify his intended meaning if told that I could not follow his words; on other occasions, his attempts to restate his message were even more obscure than the initial formulation. Simultaneously, he would often be unable to comprehend the purport of my efforts to clear up the confusion. Such incidents could result in as many as five or six interchanges of escalating misunderstanding, and he showed no capacity to stop this pattern—not even to grasp that we were talking at cross-purposes. These crises could not simply be waited out, because he became more and more confusing and confused if left to his own devices. Such an eventuality would subsequently make him feel even more neglected—with some justification—and result in an intensifying vicious circle characterized by a traumatic state.

In time, I began to entertain the idea that some of these episodes may have signified the enactment of an unconscious fantasy of symbiotic fusion—what Kohut (1971) terms a "merger transference." But the patient's pained and furious awareness of *not* being understood would eventually disabuse me of this notion whenever it did not apply. When miscommunication did occur as a result of the patient's automatic assumption that I was privy to his inner experiences, a simple statement of my lack of understanding would usually suffice to reestablish contact. Moreover, I soon learned to rely on my affective responses to these vicissitudes as the primary guideposts to their significance: when the patient felt at one with me, I did not feel provoked by his incomprehensible language, but I generally felt irritated when his regressive behavior had a spiteful motive. And in actuality, miscommunication took place much more frequently when he was enraged than in harmonious circumstances.

Having convinced myself of the necessity for effective intervention, I generally tried simple measures, such as objective reviews of the transaction that had created the loss of contact and inquiries about its possible significance. To my chagrin, such "neutral" devices seldom interrupted the patient's provocations—he seemed just as unable to grasp the intended meaning of these communications as of the preceding interchange. The situation would then become increasingly frustrating for both participants, and the patient generally misinterpreted the time I needed to regain my equilibrium as a punitive withdrawal, a deliberate cold shoulder. In contrast, we discovered that he was able rapidly to grasp the provocative purport of his own pattern of behavior if I did not bother to conceal my irritation in the course of such interventions. In other words, his capacity to understand my communications seemed to depend on congruence between their verbal content and their affective tone.

With increasing experience, I was enabled to rely on the signaling function of my affective responses to catch such transactions *in statu nascendi.* In these circumstances, of course, I generally managed to forestall my former frustration, so that I found myself speaking not so much angrily as in tones of urgency. In other words, I had gained the capacity to give the patient early signals of danger, thus mitigating the temporary ego deficit of his inability to foresee the proximate consequences of his actions.

As we might expect with a patient in an archaic transference, such an unsolicited intrusion into his psychic life produced its own complications. It proved to be relatively easy, however, to deal with these by modulating the affective tone of subsequent communications: a strident "command" to stop his dangerous behavior might be followed by a quiet reminder that this emergency warning was not intended to infringe on his autonomy but was only provided as information. Once again, he appeared to respond most rationally if the message was conveyed not in words alone, and he was able to understand the meaning of the paraverbal aspects of my communications most precisely if I could provide him with a whole series of alternating affective tones, thus demonstrating that the emotions I expressed were under good control.[1]

Needless to say, the early childhood events that led to the repetitive reenactment of such a transaction were not known to us at first. The patient's knowledge of his own past history was both fragmentary and impregnated with myth (cf. Kris, 1956). When he first consulted me, a bewildered, loosely organized, childlike figure, he had emphasized the loneliness of his past. His father had been killed in an accident before he was two years old; until his mother remarried, he was cared for by grandparents. The stepfather, a successful professional person, had remained a shadowy figure for him. The patient was the only child of his parents, but his mother's second union produced two half-siblings, a girl and a boy who

[1] The future evolution of the microtechnique of psychoanalysis may well lie in the direction of elaborating some analogue to musical notation. The content of our messages correspond to melody, their timing to rhythm, affective expression to intensity, and cognitive style to tone color.

were more than 10 years his junior. The mother was a very beautiful and seductive woman; she had always expected the patient to remain available for her comfort and to serve as her confidant. Even in late adolescence, he was made privy to the sordid details of her infidelities. The boy had been overtly angry and rebellious as far back as he could remember, in spite of a great deal of violent pseudodiscipline administered by the family. In school, he alternated between brilliant scholastic or athletic accomplishments and unaccountable failures. He had always felt on the edge of losing control over himself. Because of his sadistic fantasies, for example, he had only felt safe about sexual excitement if he tied himself up with ropes—until his psychotherapy helped him to differentiate between the inner world and that of social reality.

When the analysis began, his former attitudes could be discerned in relation to his job and to his children. His hostility was now reserved for the administration of the college where he taught; he had a leading position on the faculty body that was conducting a bitter campaign to reform the institution. Although this struggle impressed me as rash and essentially hopeless, there was no question about the fact that the faculty grievances were reality-based. The private meaning of this defiant battle was fairly evident from the excessive solicitude the patient showed toward his children. His efforts to be a good father were often ineffectual, however, because of his propensity to deal with every contingency through an attitude of pseudotherapeutic benevolence, instead of espousing the requisite parental responses directed to upholding rationality and moral values. In sum, the patient was still engaged in his fierce struggle to punish and reform the unreliable caretakers who had imposed frustrations and deprivations on him or on those with whom he was identified.

In the course of a surprisingly successful analysis (of approximately 700 sessions spread over an interval of three-and-one-half years), it became possible to reconstruct the history of the actual transactions that had structured the patient's personality. The validity of these hypotheses was subsequently confirmed by surviving witnesses and by unusually detailed written records about his early development. Here I shall confine my discussion to those aspects of the childhood past that seem relevant for understanding the role of verbal communication in his recurrent negativism and spitefulness.

It should be noted that such incidents constituted only one segment of the endless repetition of various kinds of wild, angry, rebellious behavior that he evidenced in the analysis, as he had during childhood and adolescence. This anally tinged destructiveness alternated with periods when he was charming and cooperative and generally succeeded in arousing high expectations in anyone who cared about him. He would then compulsively return to disorganized, self-smearing activities, taking sadistic pleasure in the disappointment he felt he was causing.

We were able to reconstruct that the need to disappoint others was in the service of mastering intolerable past disappointments of his own through reversal. These childhood disappointments at first seemed related to his mother's disruptive misbehavior after her remarriage. The most damaging of these incidents had been her revelation, at a time of increasing intimacy between the boy and his stepfather, that the latter allegedly insisted that she provide him with children "of his own." The patient's capacity rapidly to form an idealizing transference in both therapeutic endeavors with me was actually based on his childhood response to the advent of his stepfather. Far from having been a shadowy figure through much of the patient's upbringing, this decent and loving man had been a source of reliable support. The development of a strong homosexual transference provided evidence for the relatively conflict-free gratification of the child's passive longings for a father's care that this man had provided. The mother's poisonous report, probably motivated by her jealousy of her son's good relationship with her husband, had succeeded in driving a wedge between them and confirmed the boy in his patterned response of needing to disappoint lest he be disappointed.

It was clear, however, that this pattern did not originate in middle childhood. In spite of the stepfather's best efforts, the patient had been a maximally difficult and ungratifying child all along, and he had tried to provoke his caretakers, albeit in a manner less subtle and less self-damaging than was later to be the case, as far back as anyone could remember.

Later in the analysis, it became possible to correlate these behaviors with the principal events in the patient's life before the age of three. When his natural father was killed in an episode of drunken driving, his mother was quite willing to send the child to her late husband's parents, ostensibly to console them in their bereavement. The paternal grandmother had sunk into a chronic depressive state, however, probably in reaction to the loss of her only son, and the toddler's actual care was entrusted to a series of domestics. From the grandfather's surviving diaries, we obtained documentary confirmation of the child's subsequent regression, including his loss of mastery over the functions of elimination. We assumed that a parallel loss had taken place in his recently acquired capacity to use language for the communication of his thoughts.

Properly concerned about these alarming developments, the grandfather took over primary responsibility for overseeing the patient's care. A well-organized, compulsive character, he retrained the child through an effective regime of intrusive external control. By the time his mother reclaimed the patient and took him to the home of her own parents, he had apparently regained a reasonably tenable and age-appropriate level of adaptation. At that point, deprived of the continuous surveillance of his grandfather and thrust among strangers—mother herself was too preoccupied with her impending remarriage to pay attention—the three-year-old became both rageful and disorganized. Savage punishments were administered in response, probably by his maternal grandmother: he was apparently tied to his crib on several occasions during this period, and his unending tantrums often culminated with his losing consciousness.

The spiteful abandonment of the communicative functions of language within the transference appeared to constitute the repetitive reenactment of the tantrums of the childhood period following separation from the grandfather and the ordered existence he had created. Although decisive evidence for this conclusion could not be found, it seems likely that the much rarer incidents of traumatic confusion, also characterized by interference with the language functions, may have echoed the consequences of the original separation from the primary caretakers, in the second year of life. At any rate, in the rigid therapeutic efforts of the paternal grandfather we can discern the infantile prototype for the patient's experience of the analysis, in particular for the equation of the process of free association with compulsive external controls.

I believe the clinical data I have presented demonstrate that emotion-laden interventions on the part of the analyst are, indeed, indicated in certain specific circumstances. Furthermore, investigation of the patient's special needs that give rise to such a necessity may lead directly to some of the most crucial genetic determinants of his psychopathology. Conversely, eventual understanding of the early childhood experiences that interfered with the maturation of the analysand's capacity fully to grasp certain kinds of communications should help the analyst to adapt his language to the special needs of that patient.

As soon as we state the issue in these terms, we gain a fresh perspective on the broader technical problem of the analyst's affectivity and its expression. To be precise, that question can now be posed more fruitfully in terms of the need to determine the optimal range of affective intensity in a given clinical situation. The communication of *appropriate* affect cannot in principle be condemned out of hand. How the analyst is to determine whether his affective responses are, in fact, appropriate is an important matter but one that must be left for discussion elsewhere. What I must stress here is a conclusion that is, after all, actually self-evident: all human speech is inevitably impregnated with affect. The ideal of communicating without emotion is both unattainable and fundamentally misguided. In view of its genesis in the preverbal communication of infancy, human dialogue can never be like an exchange of teletype messages. As one young woman told me, late in the course of an uncommonly felicitous and moving analytic experience, the sessions should be like the performance of an *a capella* choir—one blending the sweet voices of women!

If we accept this point of view, the technical issue cannot be relegated to the special province of treating individuals who have difficulties with the language functions. The task of achieving optimal harmony in communication is one of the analyst's most difficult burdens in every treatment effort, and the question of affective expression is central to that task. We must give up the simplistic, if comforting, notion that the proper management of our affectivity requires nothing more than its concealment in the analytic setting. At this time, it would be grossly premature for me to attempt to suggest systematic guidelines in the complex and unexplored area of modulating affectivity. In order to give some indication of the kind of possibilities I have in mind, however, I should like to conclude by providing an illustration drawn from the analysis of the patient I have already discussed in this chapter. Here, I wish to focus on his performance as an analysand when he was at his creative best and required responses commensurate with this high level of integration.

Case 16: A Further Discussion

During the last year and a half of treatment, some of the episodes in which the patient experienced difficulty in expressing himself turned out to be intervals of wordless thought. As he gained confidence in his capacity to observe his own behavior, he gradually became aware that these spells actually consisted of thinking in terms of musical themes. With minimal encouragement, consisting of extending the definition of free association to include nonverbal vocalization, the patient was able to communicate these thoughts by humming or whistling the tunes. To my surprise, these very seldom happened to be quotations from vocal music, i.e., they were not indirect allusions to verbal messages (cf. Hannett, 1964). More often, they were extracts from abstract compositions that had, at various times in his life, assumed great importance for this man. In an impressive number of these instances, he was then able to associate to the musical thought and arrive at fruitful insights by pursuing its meaning. Although, in most cases, this concerned some complex emotional state that the patient had never acquired the capacity to describe in words, at other times the music had a variety of other meanings, much as verbal quotations can have in dreams.

I cannot digress to describe the details of the patient's sophisticated, secondary-process use of this nonverbal system of symbols.[2] It is relevant to note, however, that he had started to study music as a child and had maintained a serious commitment to this enterprise throughout his life. In spite of the fact that this effort underwent the same vicissitudes as everything else he undertook, he had not allowed his periodic acts of self-sabotage to deter him from resuming his instrumental and theoretical lessons and from maintaining his extensive musical immersion as a listener. It is only a slight exaggeration to say that I found myself in a situation analogous to that of doing analytic work with someone with an imperfect

[2] I can offer an example of suitable simplicity from the analysis of a person less sophisticated musically, who unexpectedly became haunted one day with the principal theme of the second movement of Beethoven's Seventh Symphony. His associations revealed that he was preoccupied with the insistently ominous quality of this passage; this "message" was related to certain interventions on my part attempting to call to his attention the rashness of some of his patterns of behavior. Ultimately, we realized that his preoccupation fulfilled a function analogous to that of a manifest dream: it expressed the wish for a joyous and triumphant resolution of his dilemma, like the mood he experienced in response to the last two movements of the symphony.

knowledge of English whose native tongue is largely unfamiliar to me. In other words, effective communication about complex emotional states could not take place in my customary manner—it had to be adapted to that of the patient. But I must emphasize that his way, however unusual, was just as adequate as any other.

Systematic attention to the historical roots of this unusual feature of the patient's manner of functioning led us to certain important aspects of his childhood that had never before come into focus in the analysis. In summary, the use of music for the communication of emotions represented the most satisfactory aspects of his relationship with his mother. The latter had trained for a career as a concert pianist, but her lack of persistence and self-discipline precluded the achievement of this goal. She continued to practice at home through the early years of her second marriage, however, and the patient's interest in music began while he played quietly in the same room. He recalled with deep emotion his naive and rapturous admiration of the miracles she could produce on her piano. Her choice of music became more and more meaningful to him as he learned to read her affective state, otherwise very difficult to decipher, through the emotional message of the performance.

Needless to say, one way in which the mother transference manifested itself was that the patient paid much closer attention to the style of my analytic performance than to the literal meaning of my words. I am not referring here to gross difficulties in comprehension of the kind I described earlier, but to the patient's tendency to respond to interpretations phrased in the conventional manner with detached intellectualizations. In order to summon up the remembrance of things past with true emotional impact, he needed the external stimulus of an associative link with the atmosphere of those repressed experiences—a link that evoked them as Proust's madeleines called forth *his* flood of memories. Thus my patient experienced intense erotic excitement, duplicating the thrills of his childhood transaction with his mother, when he judged my analytic performance to have been elegant and superior.

In other words, there was never any danger of gratifying this man's infantile wishes by making countertransference errors—anything less than faultless analytic management left him cold, or even overtly disappointed him. On the other hand, successful conduct of the treatment, even if it happened to be completely "abstinent" in Freud's terms, was intensely stimulating to him. Far from being obstacles to insight, however, these experiences in the transference constituted the most persuasive evidence that permitted the patient to achieve understanding of the significant issues in his life.

What, then, did the patient perceive as superior performance on my part? In particular, what did he regard as the optimal management of my affectivity? Perhaps the simplest way to answer these related questions is to observe that he rated me, as he rated musical performances, primarily on the basis of emotional expressiveness. Thus, any prosaic statement of the truth, however well-timed and relevant, left him disappointed and almost unable to attend to its intellectual content. By contrast, he was brilliantly perceptive in comprehending the implications of affect-laden interventions, even if they were indirect and highly allusive.

To illustrate: the patient reached his insight into the erotic implications of his childhood attachment to his mother when, while he was reflecting aloud about *her* seductiveness, I began quietly to whistle, in counterpoint to his words, one of the pieces she had often played for him, Massenet's *Aragonaise.* It should be noted that his realization that the sexual feelings in the transaction with his mother were in fact mutual, and a great deal more intense on his side than on hers, did not occur because the composer encoded such a message into his theme. The music does lend itself to that interpretation, however, *if* the performer experiences the theme as an expression of sexual longing and flirtation. My intention in repeating the familiar tune was to reenact the mother's behavior in a muted version, in a manner that would, at the same time, constitute an ironic comment on her attitude toward her son. This intervention therefore depended on the simultaneous expression of at least two affects: some pleasure about being the recipient of the patient's admiration and some disapproval about narcissistically exploiting him on that account. This was the complex, wordless message he was able to grasp instantaneously by perceiving its affective overtones, and it was only through this channel of communication that he could gradually learn our shared vocabulary about these matters.

I have now given two examples of specific circumstances in which an analysand was unable to profit from standard interpretations but made constructive use of the same information when it was conveyed in an affect-laden manner. I have also tried to provide detailed genetic explanations of the reasons for these special needs of the patient in question. I have selected these particular examples to illustrate that such contingencies may arise in states of deep regression as well as at times of optimal integration, i.e., presumably in any of the modes of organization we may encounter in analytic practice (cf. Gedo and Goldberg, 1973). Although it is not possible to erect a theory of technique on the basis of a limited sample of experience, it *is* legitimate to use such data to challenge accepted assumptions.

I believe this material demonstrates that the effort to keep the analyst's affectivity out of his communications to the patient is misconceived. We should attempt instead to develop criteria about the appropriate timing, dosage, and style of affective expression in the analytic situation, including precise standards to delimit those circumstances in which our traditional self-restraint indeed constitutes the optimum.

CHAPTER TWELVE

A Hierarchical View of Psychopathology: The Problem of Choice of Symptom

Among the clinical problems unresolved within the traditional theoretical framework of psychoanalysis, one of the most significant is that of "choice of symptom." Aside from scattered *aperçus*, such as the concept of "somatic compliance" to account for the specific locus of hysterical conversions (Freud, 1905a), little effort has been made to correlate psychopathology with the overall psychoanalytic view of mental functioning. As long as this schema was organized around the developmental line of the libido (Freud, 1905b; Abraham, 1924), the only meaningful conclusions that could be drawn on this subject concerned the crystallization of certain symptoms or character traits around particular libidinal fixation points—e.g., the stinginess, orderliness, and obstinacy of the "anal character" (Freud, 1908) or the oral phenomena described by Lewin (1946) and Isakower (1938). Valuable as these insights proved to be, they could not lead to a systematic classification of psychopathology because relatively few of the behaviors that need to be included in a nosological schema have a *direct* correlation of that kind with infantile sexual vicissitudes.

Conceptual progress became possible with increasing appreciation of the importance of multiple developmental lines in the assessment of psychological maturation (cf. A. Freud, 1965). One of the most complex of the developmental schemata thus far proposed is the hierarchical model I elaborated in collaboration with Goldberg (Gedo and Goldberg, 1973; see also Gedo, 1979a). Among the innovations we tried to introduce, made possible by the consistent application of the epigenetic viewpoint to psychic life, the most relevant here is the differentiation between two distinct usages of the concept "regression." The more common of these is what we called "functional regression"—selective resort to more primitive modes of functioning whenever the more mature ones would have produced excessive unpleasure. The resultant behaviors (and the counterreactions to them) constitute much of the phenomenology detailed in our nosology. The other type of regression we labeled "structural"; by this term, we referred to more global losses of functional capacity, requiring a return to the simpler hierarchy of modes of adaptation characteristic of previous developmental phases. We tried to illustrate this distinction by reviewing the cases of the Rat Man and the Wolf Man (Freud, 1909, 1918), with special reference to their obsessive-compulsive behaviors. The symptoms of Freud's two patients appeared to be similar in many superficial repects, yet their significance was fundamentally different in each instance because they involved varying modes of organization, referable to different developmental phases —that of the infantile neurosis in the case of the Rat Man, and that of more archaic, so-called "separation" problems in the case of the Wolf Man.

Briefly, the concept that every distinct phase of psychological growth is characterized by a specific mode for the organization of behavior should permit a more refined classification of psychopathology. In this chapter I hope to explore the implications of such a hierarchical conception of development for the problem of the "choice of symptom." In order to focus this inquiry on a manageable segment of this vast terrain, I shall confine the discussion to a pair of syndromes often coupled as alternative manifestations of archaic personality disturbances (e.g., by Kohut and Wolf, 1978): addictive and perverse behaviors. In disagreement with the majority view, I shall attempt to demonstrate that, in fact, these phenomena typically reflect distinct, if contiguous, modes of organization. I shall try to buttress this conclusion by examining a type of behavior that is simultaneously addictive and perverse. I shall attempt to illustrate these issues by means of a single clinical instance; unfortunately, even by concentrating on one case presentation I can scarcely hope to go into sufficient detail to be entirely convincing. Hence the material in this chapter will only give a suggestion of the advantages of approaching the data in the hierarchical manner. Many questions relevant to this approach will be left unresolved.

Case 12: A Further Discussion

The patient (about whom some details have already been reported in Chapter 4) was a graduate student from a wealthy family; she undertook analysis following a confusional episode precipitated by a combination of overwork, influenza, and drug abuse. The mismanagement of her life had reached crisis proportions following a visit with her parents in her native city. During this vacation, she was involved in an accident, and her father had severely disappointed her by callously and sadistically disregarding her need for emergency orthopedic assistance. We shall see that this transaction was, in fact, by no means unusual in her experience, but on this occasion, for the first time, she had to confront the situation pretty much on her own.

Through her adolescence, the patient had been grossly infantilized by her intrusive mother, and she had postponed independence throughout the college years by allying herself with a tyrannical lover who was overprotective in a similar manner. The requirements of his career had only separated her from this man shortly before the climactic events of her breakdown, and she could no longer turn back to her mother who vehemently disapproved of her affair.

In spite of her history of symbiotic attachments, the patient was determined to make it on her own in Chicago; *she* made the arrangements to see me, and she was in the fortunate position of being able to finance the analysis out of her own resources. I shall summarize the relevant historical data as they emerged in the course of a treatment that lasted about four and a half years on a schedule of five sessions per week.

Although her family was part of the social elite in an East Coast metropolis, this young woman was raised in a relatively conventional manner for the first six years of her life. She was the oldest of three children and the only girl; her brothers were two and five years her junior. She was decidedly the mother's favorite, as the latter had been that of her own mother. In this family context, she was indoctrinated with a belief in her biological superiority and the limitlessness of her potentials. She was *enjoined* to be "the exception" (Freud, 1916), and this conception was buttressed not only by her mother and grandmother but also by a devoted nursemaid and an extensive household staff. But this Paradise was lost as soon as she mastered the task of toilet training and acquired speech. When she took on the conformation of a little girl, she became an object of intense interest to her father, with drastic consequences. Although the experiences to which he subjected her were openly erotic (and often led to intense sexual excitement), the overall purport of her father's behavior was that of sadistic harassment.

The most traumatic of these manifold, repetitive enactments was the father's habit of disguising himself in the costume of a gorilla and surprising the child with sudden mock attacks. She was always terrified and confused about the identity of her persecutor; it was some time before she learned to look upon these chases as a "game"—however grim it was—and the scenario generally ended only when she reached a state of traumatization. She reacted to all this with boundless anger, not only at her father, but also at the mother, who was powerless to protect her. Actually, her mother did her best to do so and succeeded in pushing her husband into psychotherapy. This treatment was eventually effective in altering his behavior, unfortunately too late to prevent its major impact on the patient's development. But the therapist's evident influence over the fearsome gorilla so impressed the child that she determined to become a mental health professional who would devote herself to the protection of children, an enterprise she was beginning to pursue at the time the analysis started.

The more immediate consequences in childhood of her father's behavior were principally twofold: on the one hand, the patient evidenced some regressive manifestations; on the other, her forward move into the oedipal arena was decisively shaped by these prior circumstances. The regressive developments concerned her great rage. She fell back into the wordless tantrums through which she had resisted her mother's perhaps premature attempts to toilet-train her: she held her breath until she turned blue and lost consciousness; she retained her stools or became incontinent, etc. On the side of the Oedipus complex, she experienced her father's assaults as the retaliation of a rival for the mother's affection. Because he made her feel quite helpless, she avoided him as much as possible, and she tried to deal with the intense erotic excitement he stimulated by turning these passive experiences into activity. Her identification with the aggressor led her into imperiousness with the household staff, and the seductive components of these transactions were reflected in enmeshing her next younger brother in an incestuous relationship that continued into early adolescence. Even in later years, she felt devastated when he began to date other girls and remained jealous about these rivals until the terminal phase of her analysis.

The experiences of her oedipal years put the patient well on the way to becoming a delinquent personality when an adventitious catastrophe changed her destiny. Shortly after the birth of the youngest child, her mother was stricken with a severe encephalitis. She was hospitalized for several months, and when she returned home, she presented only a pathetic shadow of her former self. In spite of her accumulated resentment about the lengthy "desertion" caused by the mother's illness (not to speak of the jealousy stimulated by the baby's birth), the six-year-old was now overcome with pity and remorse. She made a heroic effort to curb her misbehaviors, and, insofar as other people could determine, she succeeded in becoming a model of upper-class propriety. In recent years, her skill in acting this part had made her a particular favorite of elderly dowagers who still clung to the traditions of *noblesse oblige*.

Much as she tried, however, the child was obviously unable to alter her basic character structure; in addition, her effort was doomed to fail at that point because it was carried out, naturally enough, through an identification with the mother. Although this process did yield an impeccable social façade, it also led to the acquisition of other, less desirable, aspects of the mother's behavior. And at home, without the external support of etiquette, that behavior was now undergoing progressive deterioration, not only because mother had a severe postencephalitic syndrome but, even more crucially, because she and her husband shared the need to disavow her pervasive losses of functional capacity. Her daughter identified with her flightiness, disorganization, irrationality, arbitrariness, self-pity, and arrogance. At the same time, the girl was terribly disillusioned by her mother's character change (even when we started the treatment, she was still ignorant of the physical disability that had set this in motion), and she reacted by trying to give up her excessive reliance on mother, insofar as she did not hurt the latter too much in doing so. But the mother was extremely distressed by any sign that her daughter was growing away from her; among other manifestations of this pain, she turned increasingly to hoarding supplies of food and to the abuse of alcohol.

It will cause no surprise, then, that the secret substitutes for her mother first tried by the child also consisted of oral satisfactions. She stuffed herself with food and became quite obese. Her bulimia was the first and most lasting of her addictions; in late adolescence, however, she discovered that she could mitigate the social consequences of food addiction by self-induced vomiting after each bout of gorging, so that, like the mother of her early years, she grew up to be a very attractive young woman. By the later high school years, she had learned that marijuana soothed her faster and more powerfully than food, and her addiction gradually shifted in the direction of various pharmacological agents. Yet she never did give up the bulimia altogether; instead of indiscriminate gorging, however, she tended to select certain favorite foodstuffs. Gradually, she became aware that her aim had shifted slightly from oral pleasures per se to filling her stomach to the point of distention. Some time after her menarche (an event that occurred relatively late), she was startled to discover that achieving the goal of filling herself sometimes produced a spontaneous orgasm. In other words, her addiction to sweets had turned into a perversion. In later years, particularly in the course of the analytic work, spontaneous orgasm without prior sexual arousal would occur as a result of powerful stimuli that did not directly involve the alimentary tract, often in the course of dreams (cf. P. Tolpin, 1971). However, these experiences continued to have oral meanings for her; she perceived helpful interpretations or favorable tidings as "good feedings."

At any rate, at the time this girl entered her analysis, she was still incapable of managing her life effectively without the assistance of a symbiotic partner. When an acceptable person was available to help her to organize her behavior, her psychological world generally seemed to approximate that of an oedipal child competing with men for the favor of idealized maternal figures. When she was left to her own devices, on the other hand, her actual lack of competence in self-regulation threatened to overwhelm her with dysphoria. In such circumstances, she attempted to master her feelings by actively stuffing herself, thereby inducing either an alimentary orgasm or, at the very least, tension relief followed by self-induced vomiting. Insofar as her perception of the impending emergency transcended the actual presence of dysphoria, i.e., that phase of a crisis when her lack of adequate planning or reasonable decision making once again led her into actual chaos, she tended to short-circuit her mounting anxiety by resorting to one of her drugs—usually by "getting stoned." As the analytic work gradually diminished her distress, these emergencies became less frequent, and ultimately she gained the courage to turn directly to me for assistance instead of relying on pharmacological self-soothing. When she found that she could rely on the analytic situation as a source of tension regulation, her drug addiction was entirely replaced by an addictive attachment to me. Concurrently, she gradually relinquished oral satisfactions, either literal or symbolic, in favor of pursuing more mature sexual aims. But these latter aspects of the analysis, however fascinating, are not germane to the thesis of this chapter. Instead of merely piling up additional clinical details, we should now turn to a consideration of the data from a more conceptual viewpoint.

I have tried to describe a person suffering from a complex character disturbance, with special reference to the genesis of two major symptom clusters, her addictive and perverse behaviors. In the context of her functioning in adult life, both clusters served as emergency adaptive measures against mounting unpleasure whenever she was unable to use human assistance, whether this inability supervened on the basis of internal conflict or external deprivation. For a long time, it was not possible to discern any real difference in the significance of these alternative devices for adapting to potential emergencies in tension regulation. One key to the solution of this puzzle was found through the observation that, whereas the perverse symptom always followed a compensatory effort to overcome dysphoria in an automatic manner, she often *sought* drug intoxication even when she felt quite well. In view of the fact that the results of "getting stoned" were usually rather disruptive (at the very least they interfered with the analytic process and often with her other enterprises as well), it became possible to focus on her motives for continuing to engage in such self-destructive actions. It then became clear that her devil-may-care attitude about drugs was a pathetic effort to disavow the fact that on certain occasions she had no choice whatever but felt desperately dependent on the pharmacological effects of the drug to control her mounting excitement and disorganization. Because self-soothing by means of bulimia was relatively less efficient, she tended to return to that older pattern when her tension states were developing in a more gradual manner, and it was her *success* in forestalling potential traumatic states that set off her spontaneous orgasms. I shall return to the issue of the meanings of the perversion below. Here, it may suffice to note that this reaction was no longer, as it had been earlier, a part of the effort to regulate tension as such; it pertained to a contiguous mode of behavior regulation having to do with the achievement of autonomy and self-mastery.

In this case, then, the patient's choice between two specific clusters of symptoms depended, in the first place, on the particular adaptive functions they subserved. Although symptom development in general presupposes that the symptom assume a particular functional role, it is self-evident that, from the adaptive point of view, a wide variety of alternative symptoms might in principle serve a given patient equally well. Hence identification of the particular function a symptom performs does not, by itself, answer the question of how that given symptom came to be "chosen" in an individual instance. The addictions of this patient were basically used as self-soothing devices, in the manner often described in the analytic literature. Their connection to the earliest phase of development and to an "oral triad" of eating, loss of the sense of personal boundaries, and sleep (cf. Lewin, 1946) is reasonably apparent. It must be noted, however, that, for this patient, these devices did not originate in earliest childhood but only late in the course of a maximally difficult oedipal period. In other words, this child, whose development before the age of six had already been atypical, was forced to regress to an archaic pattern of tension regulation by gradual loss of her mother as a serviceable symbiotic partner; she was unable to use more age-appropriate behaviors to master excitement because her mother had insisted on continuing to intrude into her life as the regulator of her programs of action as long as the child would permit it. At any rate, the specific resort to bulimia as the new regulator of tension was determined by the particular circumstances of her early latency.

In addition to the functional-adaptive viewpoint, then, we need to use the developmental one in order to understand relevant historical meanings that explain the genesis of a symptom. (The hierarchical model I have used since 1973 uses the vertical axis to indicate the functional-adaptive viewpoint, while it depicts the developmental viewpoint along the horizontal one.) To be most precise, full psychoanalytic understanding requires that every behavior be placed within the historical context in which the behavior arose and through which its *specific* configuration was determined. Thus, in the illustrative case I have offered here, the food addiction arose as a result of a traumatic disillusionment with (an unrealistically idealized) mother. This shift marked the onset of latency. On the one hand, it was a way of regulating tension without turning to mother; on the other, it amounted to an unconscious fantasy of incorporating the mother through an identification with the latter's characteristic methods for reducing her own states of overstimulation. Yet the mother's neurological deficit did lead to repeated storms of excited disorganization, and the child also identified with this disastrous aspect of her. To put this in another way, the food addiction formed one part of a more complex syndrome, i.e., a psychobiological deficit in the capacity to organize behavior that preceded the patient's identification with her mother. The ingestion of pacifying substances served as a home remedy to compensate for the consequences of this deficiency. The issue cannot be emphasized too strongly: from the adaptive viewpoint, this symptom is an archaic one, related to one of the earliest psychic modes that persists within the hierarchy of functional possibilities; from the developmental perspective, it is a neurotic compromise formation, constituting one of the derivatives of an intense oedipal love affair with the mother—according to the vocabulary proposed in *Models of the Mind* (Gedo and Goldberg, 1973), this would be an instance of "functional regression."

In adult life, the addiction always represented the sequelae of behaviors which, in their turn, constituted efforts to solve an intrapsychic conflict. This conclusion is buttressed by closer scrutiny of the connection between the addiction and the remainder of the patient's adaptive repertory. We might gain some understanding of these complex interrelationships by considering the significance of the second major cluster of symptoms we shall examine here, that of her perverse behaviors. It will be recalled that these symptoms emerged in the open some time in adolescence as an unexpected by-product of her bulimia. In the course of the analysis, we uncovered the unconscious fantasy that triggered this sexual response, and it seems highly probable that the same ideation underlay it from the inception. The distention of her stomach had the significance of a pregnancy at term, very much as one might predict. In this sense, the perverse experience constituted a triumphant return to identification with the idealized mother at her most glorious, at the time preceding her illness. (By implication, it also meant a boost in the child's sense of personal worth through the fantasy of eliminating her last rival, the brother whose birth was thereby undone.) I may be on somewhat less certain ground in assuming that, in the patient's unconscious, the *pregnant* woman also stood for the *phallic* woman, because I recall no direct evidence for this equation in the associative material. Nonetheless, I think it justifiable to classify the perversion as fetishistic because it was centered on a fantasy of maternal perfection. As for the symbolic equation of perfection with the possession of a phallus, there was copious confirmatory evidence from dreams and associations. I shall return to this theme later in the discussion.

When it came to assume this new role in the patient's psychological world, the bulimia had undergone "change of function" (Hartmann, 1939) in a number of ways. Most obviously, it was no longer an exclusively pacifying activity—although, of course, in the end orgasm did have a soothing effect. But tension reduction was not the patient's primary goal at these times. On the contrary, it came about as a *consequence* of her realization that she no longer had to fear traumatization, i.e., that strictly speaking, the reduction of tension was no longer an immediate necessity. It had now become an incidental by-product of a search for illusory narcissistic aims. (I have discussed the general implications of this kind of perverse activity in some detail in *Beyond Interpretation* [Gedo, 1979a, especially Chapter 7].)

To repeat, instead of representing the regulation of behavior through the direct avoidance of unpleasure, as it had done previously for the patient, stuffing herself now assumed symbolic, wish-fulfilling meanings under the sway of the pleasure principle. Perhaps the most telling of the changes in the function of the symptom was in the area of its significance in terms of the patient's self-concept: as long as she ingested her favored substances mainly to remain sufficient unto herself, she was filled with a sense of megalomanic grandeur that clashed openly with the actualities of her performance; when the bulimia took on infantile sexual meanings, she felt like a small child, worshipfully dependent on an idealized Other. This shift in attitudes became particularly clear when the perverse symptom "joined in the conversation" (Ferenczi, 1912) within the transference.

I realize, of course, that in using Hartmann's term "change of function" to denote an alteration in the significance of a symptom, I am modifying his usage. Hartmann had in mind the transformation of a piece of behavior from serving primarily as a defense to performing nonsymptomatic, adaptive functions. I believe we are justified in broadening his definition, because we are also in a position to conceptualize a whole series of nodal points in development, similar to the one that marks the passage from neurotic compromise formations to behaviors possessing "secondary autonomy" (see Gedo and Goldberg, 1973, pp. 79–81). The transformation of my patient's overeating from an addictive phenomenon to one having primarily perverse aims is an example of a second nodal point of that kind.

My use of the concept differs from that of Hartmann in still another respect: Hartmann thought of the attainment of secondary autonomy as more or less irreversible. In the narrow sense related to Hartmann's conception of psychological energies and their vicissitudes, that idea was logically consistent. The "change of function" with respect to this patient's bulimia remained freely reversible, however, and even when the nature of the symptom was mostly perverse, it never lost its former qualities as an addiction. In other words, the addictive aspects of this behavior were assimilated into its newly acquired sexual ones (to use a concept of Piaget's). Hence I would emphasize that any change in function is more likely to consist of an addition to the list of adaptive potentialities than in some permanent shift involving the loss of any previously available alternative.

From this perspective, we may look upon the patient's acquisition of the capacity for alimentary orgasm as an instance of one of those transformations of adolescence that I have characterized as a revision of the self-organization (Gedo, 1979a, pp. 228–229). It permitted this young woman to satisfy the need to buttress her deficient self-esteem via the channels of a previously established symptom. This gain in adaptive efficiency led to a marked diminution of her efforts to repair her sense of being an incomplete person with a phallic deficiency through symptomatic interpersonal activity. Thus she was able to mitigate her unacceptable identification with the sadistic father sufficiently to be able to form extrafamilial relationships with peers, giving u

her incestuous misuse of her brother. Moreover, she was able to tolerate outwardly normal sexual relations with men, although she did remain frigid in coitus until the elucidation and mastery of her phallic conflicts in the analysis.

Needless to say, the emergence of alimentary orgasm did not constitute the initial occurrence of perverse symptomatology in the patient's experience. Prior to this development, however, the perversion had taken the form of certain masturbatory fantasies, in addition to entering into the sexual activities with her brother. I am not in a position to describe either activity in detail because these behaviors did not recur in any regular way during the treatment, and it never seemed appropriate systematically to investigate these aspects of her history. I assume, however, that they were analogous in their purport to the occasional perverse behaviors that did occur in the course of the analysis—explicit sexual encounters in which the partner was treated not as a human being but as a living tool. For example, she would occasionally get enraged at a man during coitus because he appeared to her to be focusing on his own subjective experiences rather than devoting himself entirely to her pleasure. By implication, she was seeking total control over a magical phallus through which she could meet all of her needs. But it is important to keep in mind that she experienced sexual relations in this way only in unusual circumstances—after sustaining some kind of injury to her self-esteem, particularly in the analytic setting. At other times, she was capable of affectionate mutuality.

Perhaps I have now provided enough material about the perverse aspects of the patient's behavior to review them in terms of their functional-adaptive and developmental implications. I believe the details of the various perverse activities I have described substantiate my initial statement that these behaviors play the role of restoring self-esteem on an emergency basis. This is accomplished not by means of the overt actions involved, such as gorging chocolate, but through the largely unconscious fantasies that accompany them. These fantasies invariably expressed the wish for omnipotent control over a set of crucial transactions with the milieu (cf. Bak, 1974; Greenacre, 1969). More specifically, these transactions always dealt with her worth as a sexual being, pathetically asserting her perfection either through possession of an immaculately conceived baby or that of a magically satisfying phallus. In either case, she felt safe from any subjective sense of helplessness.

Once again, however, the functional explanation, although it is cogent, does not suffice to illuminate the *choice* of specific symptom. Why should fantasies of preeminence in the phallic sphere produce orgasm, either with or without prior sexual excitement? Even more important: why did this person need continually to reassert her grandeur in these *phallic* modes? We begin to approximate an answer to these questions when we add the developmental viewpoint to our framework. You will recall that the patient's experience during the original phallic phase of development was characterized by a series of traumatic episodes, induced mostly through terror and sexual excitement. In all likelihood, therefore, she learned to regard being the sexual aggressor or the possessor of the phallus as the guarantee of human psychological integrity—and the converse of her former helplessness and lapses into confusion. Phallic aims in general, and phallic-narcissistic ones in particular, therefore assumed the role of defining this girl as an autonomous person with a coherent hierarchy of personal goals. States of mounting tension, without the possibility of surcease or relief, constituted the danger she needed to ward off by avoiding situations in which she was passive; both self-induced vomiting and spontaneous orgasm signified mastery of such dreaded states of helplessness. As long as she could produce a pseudocyesis or use another person in the guise of an infantile fetish, she felt intact, whole, and fully human—however odd her human needs may have appeared.

Under the impact of her mother's drastic misfortune, the child's guilt-driven need to conform to parental expectations led to severe conflict about this perverse solution to problems of self-esteem. Her effort to dispense with this adaptive option sacrificed her autonomy in the service of a goal which had previously had lower priority, that of gratifying the mother's symbiotic demands. As a symbiotic partner, however, the mother was no longer capable of providing the child with reliable external guidance as she had before her illness, so that this regression produced considerable disorganization. Thus a new source of potential traumatization had emerged; instead of being overstimulated by her father's harassment, the patient was now subject to unbearable tension states because of her own mismanagement. As we have seen, these conditions produced her food addiction as a last-ditch measure against trauma. It should also be noted that in pursuing one subset of goals, that of making reparation to mother by seeming to remain her helpless little girl, the child had to abandon a series of other personal aims, although these were neither disavowed nor repressed. For example, her need to assert phallic perfection was still consciously expressed, albeit only in secret activities, such as her masturbatory fantasies or the incestuous games with her brother. To state this in another way, her overall behavior had disintegrated into at least two uncoordinated fragments. Elsewhere (Gedo and Goldberg, 1973, Chapter 5) I have referred to such unintegrated programs of action as "nuclei of the self."

At any rate, the emergence of alimentary orgasm in adolescence marked the successful synthesis of the disparate aims represented by the addictive and the perverse behaviors of latency into a unified program of potentials for action. The crucial prerequisite for this change was mastery of the patient's chronic dread of overstimulation, particularly that of traumatization by way of sexual excitement. This threat lost much of its menace sometime after menarche because of the secure knowledge that she had acquired the capacity for orgastic gratification. Thus it now became possible to regulate her tensions without external assistance and, through the very same actions, simultaneously to assert her phallic integrity and keep her mother appeased. As Hamlet put it, "Thrift, thrift, Horatio. The funeral bak'd meats did coldly furnish forth the marriage tables."

In summary, this review of the genesis of one person's alimentary orgasms suggests that the efforts at adaptation designated as "symptoms" are chosen and maintained in a manner that will subserve as many functions as possible. In addition to these functional considerations, however, the origin of these patterns of behavior must be sought within the matrix of the specific childhood psychological circumstances in which they emerged, i.e., in terms of hierarchies of highly specific subjective meanings. The great difficulty of unraveling the significance of particular symptom choices therefore stems from the impossibility for the observer accurately to estimate the infantile psychological world of another —a task that can only be accomplished through the analysand's own introspective efforts (see Chapter 6 and Gardner, in preparation).

CHAPTER THIRTEEN

On Some Antecedents of Developmental Arrest

The evolution of nosological schemata in psychoanalysis has proceeded from the application of the genetic point of view within a structural and economic framework (Hartmann, 1950) toward a more explicitly developmental orientation (A. Freud, 1965; Gedo and Goldberg, 1973). As I have tried to demonstrate in Chapter 12, this subtle shift of emphasis has turned the focus of attention from typical patterns of intrapsychic conflict, such as distinctions between syndromes caused by oedipal vicissitudes and those derived from pregenital problems, to the overall organization of the personality as it unfolds throughout the life cycle. It has facilitated the differentiation of age-appropriate maturational vicissitudes from syndromes which constitute sequelae of the solutions of earlier developmental tasks.

An early version of this chapter was presented to the Chicago Psychoanalytic Society in October, 1967, and a summary of that meeting was published in the *Bulletin of the Philadelphia Association for Psychoanalysis,* 18(1968):148–152.

If we conceptualize the increasing complexity of the adaptive repertory as a hierarchy of adaptive possibilities, as I have done for the past decade, it becomes possible in addition to make a second cardinal distinction among the infinite variety of personality disorders: we can differentiate syndromes in which this hierarchy of modes of functional organization is restricted to the more primitive portion of the spectrum from other syndromes in which the hierarchy comprises a full range of possibilities, including areas of optimal adaptation. The first of these nosological groupings has been called that of "arrests in development" (Nagera, 1964, 1966); the second corresponds to those disorders of character in which maladaptation results from functional regressions in the face of conflict or truama in later phases of development.

At the present state of our knowledge, we may still have difficulty in making these clinical distinctions reliably, although I have found systematic use of the hierarchical schema (Gedo and Goldberg, 1973) to diagram the shifts in an individual's modes of psychic functioning throughout his analysis to be very helpful in this regard.

In this chapter, I shall attempt to illustrate the distinctions between arrests in development and other character problems through clinical examples. I have chosen not only to highlight the differences in adult mental functioning between the two syndromes but, more particularly, to try to reconstruct the paths of early psychological development in each.

Case 17

A young woman sought analysis because she had produced and had given away two illegitimate children but felt unable to accept her lover's offer of marriage. She described herself, accurately, as a confused and desperate person, excessively dependent on her mother and older sister. She continued to idolize her father, a man of dubious reliability who had died when the patient was six. The patient's self-image was still that of "an abominable child," and she was immersed in the type of pietistic Christianity which anthropomorphizes its pantheon in the most concrete manner. All this was in startling contrast to her superior intelligence and surface sophistication.

In the first year of the analysis she made direct demands on me to help her to control her impulses, much as a young child might do with the adults available for this purpose. Indeed, she was in need of such help, as she was unable to stop herself from repeatedly incurring the risk of another illegitimate pregnancy. The meaning of this behavior was discovered to be an angry denial that she needed anyone whose love she could not command and a frantic attempt to fill a sense of inner emptiness and depression. After about a year of analytic work, she began to acknowledge her wishes to receive paternal love, and in this context her disavowal of the reality of the loss of her father broke down. She now experienced full-scale mourning for her father for the first time.

Following this dramatic and lengthy phase, she demonstrated the first manifestations of transference in the analysis. Throughout the second year of the analysis and well into the third, an oedipal transference neurosis was elaborated and interpreted in its manifold aspects, without effecting any major changes in the patient's day-to-day functioning. Nevertheless, toward the end of the third year of our work there appeared groping attempts to give up her dependence on analysis, ushering in a lengthy termination phase. A clinging, archaic mother transference now emerged which at long last clarified the reasons for the peculiarly primitive, symbiotic quality of the oedipal ties to the father which she had reexperienced in the transference neurosis. She was now able to recover memories of a major traumatic separation from mother during the second year of life. She had apparently reacted to this misfortune by turning away from mother and attaching herself to father as a symbiotic partner. Ever since that time, she had demanded complete possession of and control over her intimates; the impossibility of possessing father during the oedipal struggle, rather than his death per se, had determined her turning away from people, with the exception of her children—as long as they were literally within her. The last year of the analysis was spent in working through this symbiotic conflict, with apparent success.

In contrast to the expectable course of development, the infantile neurosis in this instance had never led into a latency phase. Not only was there fixation of sexual aims at phallic-oedipal levels, but also regression to the utilization of an array of primitive defenses (most prominently that of disavowal) and archaic behaviors: belief in the omnipotence of thoughts and magical gestures, faulty reality testing, object relations at a symbiotic level, etc. Inability to progress beyond the Oedipus complex was also evident in her failure to consolidate the superego; only archaic controlling devices (erected by enlisting external supervision) and primitive ideals were available. Her self-image was therefore that of a child. All of this added up to arrestation of development at the phase attained at the time of the loss of her father. It was also evident, however, that the clinical picture presented by this patient was in many respects very different from the mental life of a six-year-old whose development is age-appropriate. At age six, *this* child was already highly atypical—her oedipal attachments were not primarily erotic but included the symbiotic needs of a severely traumatized toddler.

The etiological determinants for arrestation of personality development may best be viewed as forming a complementary series, always comprising factors both from the external environment and from the internal milieu. Overwhelming trauma and/or object deprivation (as illustrated by this case example) are the outstanding examples of environmental failure which may contribute to interruption of development; the contribution of the internal (i.e., intrapsychic) world might be conceptualized as structural weakness. A second clinical illustration may help to clarify the role of insufficient structuralization in leading to an eventual arrest of development.

Case 18

A man in his mid-thirties sought analysis for his ineffectiveness in work and sex and a feeling that he was fraudulent in everything. Although he was married to a suitable woman, had two fine children, had obtained a doctorate in his field, and was employed by a reputable university, he felt anxious, inadequate, and undeserving. He was the fourth of five children, but the first son in a fundamentalist family of rural background. His father was a successful merchant of unswerving rectitude and fairness who had expected his elder son to succeed him in the business by working his way up from the bottom; when the patient had decided on other career goals, however, he had supported his son generously. His mother had been warmer and more flexible, especially after the death of her own mother, and she had awakened the patient's interest in the humanities. Since the early death of his next older sister, however, he had felt estranged from both parents. He was initially unable to date this sister's death, except for the certainty that it had preceded the birth of his younger brother when he was six.

He had always resented the parents' alleged preference for this brother and for the sister who had died. In fact, he remembered his childhood as an unending series of provocative struggles with them, which he usually won through passive resistance. In adolescence he had been seriously delinquent, stealing money at home as stakes for gambling and covering his tracks with clever lies. His intellectual brilliance gained him admission to a famous university, where he initiated an active sexual life with disreputable women and stray homosexuals. He felt no conflict about these adventures; in contrast, he was very uneasy about his sadistic masturbatory fantasies. Some years later, while living a bohemian life in New York, pretending to be an avant-garde poet but producing no poetry, he formed a liaison with a woman who had a fatal illness. Subsequently, he believed himself responsible for her death and felt "smashed"; he literally could not believe in the reality of his loss for a long time. After this period of confusion, he undertook graduate training and began a casual affair with his future wife. When she became ill, he once again felt responsible for her condition; he then suddenly married her and permanently gave up his homosexual activities. Although sexually impotent, he managed to lead a better organized and outwardly more productive life under her guidance. She had finally sought therapeutic assistance for her part of the sexual problem, and it had been her improvement that had led him to decide on analysis for himself.

Although I was careful to let him make his own decision about analysis, it took several months to get beyond the patient's efforts to maneuver me into urging him to stay with it. He was aware of behaving fraudulently, i.e., not in accord with his real feelings, but in ways that would create a false impression. He repeated with me his childhood war to wrest a special position from either parent, expressed in the present as a demand for endless, cost-free analytic care. He punished me for frustrating him by refusing to associate; alternatively, he could turn the sessions into clever travesties of psychoanalysis. It became clear that he did not wish to change; his unconscious goal in seeking help was to absorb my fantasied omnipotence.

After about a year, the specifically maternal aspects of the transference came into focus. He experienced the freedom of the analytic situation as the repetition of the covert urinary and fecal games with his mother in which she had been in unconscious collusion with him. He was (and had been) afraid only of the possibility that he would be held responsible for such "unseemliness." It emerged that he had even gained his mother's tacit approval for his stealing; he was now repeating this behavior by trying to involve me in a fraudulent insurance scheme. He was panicky about the possibility of being seen as a helpless baby rather than the giant he wanted to be. His efforts to wreck my analytic work (like his impotence with his wife) were understood as vengeful attempts to drag me down with him. Consistent interpretations that the hollow triumphs of a spoiler were necessitated by his inner feelings of helplessness finally minimized his destructive activities within the treatment during the second year of our work.

With the establishment of this equilibrium, sexual feelings began to emerge in the transference, with great anxiety about the possibility of his being ridiculed as inadequate. A variety of childhood erotic fantasies related to a phallic mother emerged, with fears of abandonment in retaliation for his aggressiveness and his intense anger about my failure to accept him unconditionally. His masochistic compromises turned out to be maneuvers intended to compel such acceptance. In fantasy, father was excluded from the oedipal arena through active disavowal of the man's part in procreation. When the onset of this defense in reaction to the birth of his brother was understood, the patient began to experience jealousy in the transference setting. He began to make efforts—unprecedented in his life experience—to try to please me in order to gain assurance that he could continue in analysis indefinitely.

My vacation brought into focus conflicts on a much more primitive level. I was now experienced as a cruel and neglectful mother who left him parched with thirst, full of vague fantasies of violence. He literally did not believe that I could end his analysis if we reached a stalemate—just as he had been unable to believe in the death of his mistress years before. Through these issues, we clarified his inability to tolerate evidence that people he cared about were separate beings. His symbiotic adaptation was apparently set during the period of his mother's absorption in her grief after the death of her daughter; these events were set in motion when he was about 15 months old. Profound affects of anger and grief were now relived in the analysis, with separation anxiety of particular intensity at bedtime, the time of maximal distance from mother in early childhood. He tried to ward off his murderous rage through fantasies that I shared his misery. In the context of the failure of this defense, his idealization of his mother broke down, and he recovered memories of her outbursts of rage whenever he displeased her.

At the end of the second year of analysis, the use of his passive and oral wishes as a screen for his phallic ones was interpreted. Through such regression he was able to preserve his grandiose self-image. When this defense became untenable, he experienced profound narcissistic mortification about the frustration of his wishes at all levels. He felt desolate and betrayed when he realized that he would have to *work* to get limited satisfactions, and that the analysis would eventually really have to reach an end-point. However, he began to feel genuine for the first time—and like a small, unhappy, lost child. He felt devastated by his awareness of the transience of man but as a result of this insight he began to submit his poetry for publication. After this acknowledgment of his limitations he wanted to topple me and to outdo me, not to *climb* but to *be on top,* a bohemian genius, a Verlaine. He wanted to steal my power and my penis. Genetic interpretations of the childhood oedipal rivalry led to real improvements in his sexual performance, and he became anxious about the possibility that the analysis was moving toward success. As a consequence, he became aware of his dependence on me as a powerful and unattainable mother who had the magical capacity of procreation. His attempts to identify with such a figure led to pregnancy fantasies, and his regressions were now understood as murderous attacks on my creativity, i.e., my children. His childhood depression about not getting everything from mother unconditionally and exclusively now returned in the transference setting, and he could no longer pretend that such feelings were fraudulent or unnecessary because he was in omnipotent control. He tried frantically to prove that I was asexual, as he had felt his parents had been. Yet he felt broken and feeble—no realistic accomplishment could undo his feeling of inadequacy. As the vacation during the third year of analysis approached, however, he began to talk of his infantile wishes as unsatisfiable though permanent, and he began to hope that he could now deal with them by renunciation rather than by denial.

Toward the end of the third year of our work, he began to make efforts to differentiate himself from me (e.g., by raising reasonable questions about my interpretations rather than making irrational sneak attacks on them). He regained memories of his mother nursing his younger brother, and he began to experience his own wishes for tenderness without the omnipotent attitudes that had previously contaminated them. His jealousy now focused on people who might receive pregenital gratifications, and he felt that he would be able to leave if he could insure that nobody else would obtain pregenital gratifications from me either. In fact, it now emerged that he was actively seeking a better job for the following fall in another area of the country, so that he had actually made his own decision to give up the analysis by then. In the meantime, he dreamt of holding me prisoner, and he was filled with rage at the realization that I might receive satisfactions in my marriage of which he was incapable of providing me.

The fourth year of analysis thus led to the breakdown of his disavowal of awareness of his parents' sexual life, and he was forced to acknowledge that he had been unable to arouse his mother, as he was currently unable to arouse me. He realized that he had always wanted the impossible, and he began to feel hopeful about his future. His poetry now focused on the theme of resignation to death. He understood that his regressed, passive behavior had been the price he had to pay to receive continuing opportunities of contact with mother. He recovered childhood fantasies of being a fecal lump, molded and shaped by mother, and he was able to face the realities of his mother's domineering character and his father's passivity. He could now take himself, other people, even literature *seriously*, and he experienced his feelings of love and hate as fully his own for the first time.

In the termination phase he forgot the very fact that his dead sister had existed, but dreamt of *himself* as a ghost at a family reunion. This led to recall of his childhood fears of being taken over by his sister's ghost. At Easter, his identification with Christ emerged, and he recalled his mother's fanatical devotion to Him, Whose eternal bride she hoped to become. He was able to experience his feelings of despair with seriousness now, and he was able to feel genuine sympathy for the grief of others. He felt awful—defeated because I did not need him or want him. He wanted to bite me and smash me because our imminent separation did not make me suffer as he was suffering, but he ended the analysis with the feeling of being his own person and an artist, rather than a seeker after worldly success.

Let me attempt a synopsis of this case report: it seems clear that the patient demonstrated in his adult neurosis not merely a fixation at the oedipal phase of psychosexual development, but also a failure to progress in ego and superego differentiation beyond levels expectable in early childhood. His mode of functioning was, in fact, so primitive that a traditional diagnosis of psychopathy was warranted. The most striking evidence for this arrestation consisted of the nature of this man's object relations, i.e., the all but overt delusion of symbiotic fusion with his objects. Severe distortions of reality testing occurred episodically, and the illusion of omnipotence was persistent, though covert. A pall of depersonalization was the main defense against this unacceptable content. The analysis revealed that this state of affairs had been established during the early phallic phase; the Oedipus complex had remained unresolved—frozen in a strange variation—because of the disavowal of separateness from the mother.

In contrast to conditions in Case 17, here the interruption of development had not occurred as a result of circumstances during the phase in which the patient became arrested; on the contrary, there was so little frustration at that time that this man could have echoed Hamlet's punning complaint about being "too much in the Sun." He had been incapable, however, of making use of the relationship his parents offered because of severe preexisting impairment of his own capacity for tolerating the autonomy of others. As we have seen, this impairment had developed because of circumstances in the second year of life which had overwhelmed him. It may not be superfluous to repeat that the initial trauma had not been the *loss* of mother as an object, but only premature demands on the child to relinquish the sense of reasonable mastery over his universe. This strain led to regression to the pretraumatic symbiosis with mother. Every subsequent attempt to reverse this trend had miscarried at the first sign of narcissistic injury—either by another regressive retreat or through escape into unrealistic identifications with omnipotent figures (e.g., the ghost of the sister, Christ, etc.).

Because this patient had utilized his own mother as the object with whom he lived out a regressed, primitive, "transitional" relationship in the post-traumatic era of his childhood, it is difficult to differentiate this pathological mode of functioning from a more age-appropriate relationship to mother. These developmental vicissitudes rendered this person unable to respond to the people in his environment by accepting what they could offer. Hence arrest in development had not come about in the manner of a deficiency disease; it had *led* to a malabsorption syndrome. In these circumstances, then, the child could not rise to the challenging demands of progressive developmental stages; most crucially, the stress of oedipal frustrations could only be dealt with by renewed regression into symbiosis.

In order to highlight the difference between syndromes of arrested development and character disturbances embedded within personalities which have otherwise matured to expectable adult levels, another brief clinical illustration will prove helpful. This case is in no way remarkable; I have selected it precisely because the patient developed only a "routine" neurosis, in spite of vicissitudes in the oedipal period and later childhood at least as severe as those encountered by the individuals I have described above.

Case 19

This young woman sought analysis because she experienced severe ambivalence about her marriage. She was unable to consider separation because this prospect aroused so much guilt in her; on the other hand, she could not reconcile herself to life with her dull, earnest, compulsive, and pious husband. Her ideals called for broader horizons than he offered; she wished to put her considerable artistic talents to use and to participate in cultural and social life at the level of the intellectual elite to which her husband clearly and correctly felt himself to be unequal. She attempted to solve this dilemma through affairs with men of some accomplishment, but this, too, filled her with guilt.

The patient was the oldest child of an upper-class family from one of the Western states. She had a brother, born when she was four, who had been a sickly child. Her sister was born when the patient was 11, at a time when their mother's ultimately fatal brain tumor had already been discovered. Her mother died within two years, and the patient was sent to live with relatives, while the other children were cared for at home. Her father remarried within a year, so that she was allowed to come home. She subsequently became a source of constant friction in the household. The stepmother aggravated tension between the patient and her father, a strict, bigoted, frugal, and controlling man. The patient's mother, who had been a generous and popular person, had been able to moderate the friction between father and daughter. Her loss had left the patient feeling alone and crushed. She resented both the fact that she had been exiled from home and that her father actively interfered with her social life in high school. In college, she seized the opportunity presented by the dogged courtship of her future husband to escape from her father's orbit. Although marriage to a half-educated cowboy might have seemed like a misalliance in her social milieu, her husband was in fact enthusiastically welcomed by her family, who expected him to keep her out of mischief.

In the analysis, a paternal transference soon made itself manifest, and she relived the sorrow and anger she had felt when her father had sent her away after her mother's death. My first vacation aroused the vengeful misbehavior through which she had tried to punish her father, i.e., a bout of sexual promiscuity. Gradually, the erotic side of the paternal transference began to emerge, with great anxiety about wishes to be the most admirable and beloved of women and strong feelings of humiliation about the frustration of these wishes in the analysis. In this way, the negative aspects of the Oedipus complex came into the open toward the end of the first year of analysis, and their connection to the disappointment of her love for her father was clarified. Guilt about oedipal hostility toward her mother was reexperienced in the transference neurosis, and she became aware of her need to turn the tables by making other people jealous over her.

Well into the second year of our work, the grief and loneliness screened by the erotic and spiteful aspects of her behavior became overt, and a maternal transference made its appearance. She began to relive her exclusive love for mother in the era before her brother's birth, when her father had been serving overseas during the war. She experienced anxiety about separation, and she now tried to forestall the trauma (of being cut off from mother by the birth of a sibling) by "accidentally" getting pregnant herself. In spite of this maneuver she now relived in the transference neurosis her childhood depression and anger at the faithless mother who had other loves.

She took great pleasure in the birth of a son, an event which also helped her to gain insight into her feelings about the birth of her brother. Interpretation of her irrational guilt about such reactions now permitted her to enjoy motherhood and to experience sexual pleasure consistently for the first time. Unfortunately, this put further strain on the marriage, because her husband could not tolerate her femininity. His righteous tirades against her impelled her to justify him by her own misbehavior. It now became clear that she had also misbehaved as a way of justifying her father's accusations that she was a bad person. She recalled that she had felt that her mother's death was punishment for this badness, particularly for her defiance of father's prohibitions about associating with certain children. In this context, she began to be able to pursue some individual interests of which her husband did not approve. In particular, she resumed artistic activities and began new friendships with people who were not interested in him.

The third year of the analysis also brought about mastery of her penis envy and her castrative vengefulness toward men, and her competitiveness developed more and more along feminine lines. In the transference neurosis she began to experience the fear that I would be unable to tolerate direct erotic feelings on her part, just as her father had been unable to do—i.e., that I would send her away as he had done when her mother's presence as a chaperone was lost.

As the analysis entered its fourth year, primal scene material began to appear, and she recovered memories of a man visiting her mother while father was away in the war. She remembered her fear and fascination about the possibility that mother was engaged in sexual activities. Simultaneously, she was able to correct her distortions about her father's lengthy absence—it became apparent that he had been hospitalized for a considerable period of time on his return from overseas because he was overtly paranoid. His delusions were centered on certain people with whom the patient was forbidden to associate;

he had also accused the patient of responsibility for making him ill by washing the dishes inadequately. Everything her father said had been accepted at face value by the whole family. She was now repeating this masochistic surrender in her marriage. Just as father's irrational rages had led him to beat her severely and without warning, with no protest from mother or from the patient, so in the present she dared not oppose her husband to his face. Gradually, however, she gained courage, began to assert herself at home, and as this course led to increasing estrangement, she was able to ask her husband for a divorce. Late in the fourth year of analysis, termination material became ever more prominent. The pregenital tie to mother was relived in the transference neurosis in its most positive aspects, and there was active anticipatory mourning about relinquishing the therapeutic relationship. She was able to bring the analysis to an end just four years after it had begun.

To recapitulate, in spite of the malign influence of a psychotic father, this patient's infantile neurosis was resolved via the tomboyishness often characteristic of latency. The grave illness and death of the mother when the patient was preadolescent was a profound trauma but did not lead to arrestation of development. Mourning for the mother was adequate, and adolescence supervened in the usual manner. Superego functions developed to expectable adult levels and object relations did likewise; there was seldom any evidence of persisting symbiotic needs. The psychopathology in adult life consisted of a sadomasochistic character disturbance which had been formed in early latency as a consequence of oedipal vicissitudes. Fixation to phallic-oedipal sexual aims and the deformation of character implicit in her passive-submissive behavior (in identification with her mother) were the only areas in which personality development had become distorted. In analysis, the transference neurosis developed and was resolved without complication.

Discussion

In 1924, Freud wrote that the personality (what he then called the "ego") in its

> conflicts with its various ruling agencies . . . [can] avoid a rupture in any direction by deforming itself, by submitting to encroachments on its own unity and even perhaps by effecting a cleavage or division in itself. In this way the inconsistencies, eccentricities and follies of men would appear in a similar light to their sexual perversions through the acceptance of which they spare themselves repressions [pp. 152–153].

In other words, psychoanalytic characterology has from its beginnings explained character disturbances as autoplastic changes which are permanently structuralized; i.e., they constitute a fixation which prevents further development of particular personality attributes. Similarly, Freud viewed every transference neurosis as based on a fixation at an immature level. Yet neither the fixation of "ego structure" in character disorders nor the "libidinal" fixation in transference neuroses is complete, and these partial failures of maturation cannot be fruitfully described as arrests of development, since the overall progress of personality differentiation is not halted in these cases. Nagera (1964) has pointed out that fixation at a given phase of development implies "fixation to a given component instinct, to a phase of libidinal and aggressive development, to a type of object choice, to a type of object relationship, and to a traumatic experience" (p. 223). I agree with his definition of arrestation as "fixation to a given phase, because there seems to be a more extended type of disturbance related to the phase as a whole."

To translate this idea into the vocabulary of *Models of the Mind* (Gedo and Goldberg, 1973), development in childhood was interrupted in the course of a given phase: in Case 17, for example, this interruption occurred at the time of the father's death, when the child had barely begun to pass through the nodal point in development from Phase III to Phase IV; i.e., she had just started to acquire an internalized morality. For all intents and purposes, when this woman entered treatment, she was still in Phase III and restricted in her range of functioning to Modes I through III. In Case 18, the same conditions prevailed because of an ongoing symbiotic mode of adaptation, encouraged in childhood by the mother and always restored in subtle ways by the patient as an adult.

In contrast, the analysand in Case 19 had successfully made the transition from Phase III to Phase IV; i.e., she had formed an effective superego and developed the intrapsychic conflicts typical of the oedipal child. Moreover, she went on to cross the next nodal point of development, that resulting in the establishment of a repression barrier. Thus she reached the level of functioning we expect to find in reasonably well-adapted adults. In other words, the pathogenic conflicts that brought this woman into treatment (especially the oedipal attachment to her mother) were entirely unconscious; they manifested themselves in her adult behavior only as characterological attributes—masculine aims and struggles for dominance in personal relationships. I conceptualize such problems as partial, functional regressions into Mode IV in a personality with the overall organization characteristic of Phase V.

CHAPTER FOURTEEN

The Oedipus Complex in Contemporary Perspective

If we accept the lessons of psychoanalytic experience with persons who develop archaic transferences, such as the patient I described in Case 15 in Chapter 7, we are forced to confront the inadequacy of a view of the Oedipus complex that has received much recent support (e.g., T. Shapiro, 1977). This hypothesis holds that the oedipal crisis represents an opportunity to resolve troublesome issues the child brings to it as a result of earlier vicissitudes. My clinical conclusions have, on the contrary, led me to believe that such archaic problems are likely to become part of the individual's character, whatever the specific outcome of the Oedipus complex may turn out to be. Although the contention of Kohut (1977) about the separateness of oedipal and "narcissistic" pathologies is also contradicted by the evidence of such cases—the data point to a unitary conception of personality—such a unitary view of self-organization does not imply that every phase of development presents a repetition of former psychological configurations in their entirety. In other words, the conflicts of the infantile neurosis do not present suitable circumstances for overcoming narcissistic vulnerabilities, deficiencies in the capacity to regulate tension, or confusion regarding goals and values. It is surprising that clinicians who have learned that adult patients are seldom capable of profiting from "corrective" emotional experiences in treatment should ever believe that children could master problems created by earlier transactions by going through further life crises.

We have, of course, had general consensus about the converse of this proposition, namely, that earlier developmental vicissitudes exert a profound influence on the configuration and outcome of the Oedipus complex. Moreover, it is now widely recognized that individuals who seek analytic assistance are seldom troubled by uncomplicated neurotic conflicts alone; almost invariably, their disturbances of character transcend the realm of the derivatives of an infantile neurosis (cf. Gedo, 1979a, Chapter 3). My own clinical practice has not turned up any exceptions to this belief, and I am inclined to suspect that reports about oedipal neuroses found in pure culture, so to speak, oversimplify the actual data. The follow-up studies of Firestein (1978), which I reviewed at some length in Chapter 5, reveal the wide spectrum of archaic disturbances left unaltered by analyses that focus too narrowly on derivatives of an infantile neurosis.

In this work, I have presented a variety of clinical vignettes in order to illustrate various theses, and this body of material (as well as the three lengthier case reports found in *Beyond Interpretation* [1979a]) should suffice to document the importance of elucidating the consequences of unresolved problems at any and all developmental levels. Partly as a corrective to the emphases that typify the intellectual history of psychoanalysis (specifically, the emphasis throughout its evolution, until the most recent past, on the Oedipus complex as the nuclear issue in neurosogenesis), I have concentrated on the need to include more primitive issues in our clinical conceptualizations and our treatment plans. I should, perhaps, correct the misleading impression I may have created through this artifact of presentation by articulating my position on the actual importance of the oedipal phase for the organization of personality.

I should like to attempt this reconsideration by reviewing a dozen cases included elsewhere in this volume in which analyses were carried forward sufficiently to permit assessments of overall personality organization that I believe to be valid. Because these examples were introduced in other contexts, in order to buttress other arguments, for *this* purpose they may well serve as an unselected sample representative of an analytic practice established on the basis of the loosest criteria of analyzability. I might add that, if we add to these examples the three reports included in *Beyond Interpretation* that conform to the conclusions I am about to spell out here, the 15 cases provide an account of my work of the recent past which is as close to being complete as considerations of confidentiality will permit. I should like to supplement this survey by repeating, in a maximally condensed format, the reconstruction we were able to achieve in each instance about the principal transactions of the oedipal period based on the unfolding of the analytic transference. The order of presentation shall roughly approximate the relative importance of oedipal issues in the genesis of the personality disorder (see Appendix).

Perhaps this material will be easiest to comprehend if we approach it from a general perspective. If we assume that the range of patients represented by this sample is reasonably representative of persons who wish to enter analysis, these formulations suggest that uncomplicated neuroses do *not* impel people to undertake such major enterprises.[1] Although significant oedipal configurations determined part of the psychopathology in every instance, in most cases the crucial problems seemed to involve more archaic aspects of the personality. These ranged from the delusional convictions of the patients with whom I failed (Cases 7 and 9), through the severe difficulties in "separation-individuation" of persons with bizarre and intrusive caretakers (Cases 3, 10, 12, 13, and 17), or those who suffered major, traumatic vicissitudes in the second year of life (Cases 11 and 18), to profound problems of disillusionment and grandiosity brought about by pregenital vicissitudes (Cases 15 and 16). In

[1] My experience with analyzing psychoanalytic candidates—and that of colleagues who have informally shared their experiences with me—has yielded results essentially no different from the analyses I have reported here. I am therefore inclined to believe that the concept of a neurosis as a simple clinical entity is only a theoretical fiction.

one instance (Case 19), the archaic aspects of the personality were acquired as a result of a traumatic regression in the oedipal phase. I trust that I have provided sufficient clinical evidence throughout this volume to substantiate the foregoing assertions. Here, it may be useful to spell out once again the specific manner in which these problems stemming from earlier developmental phases influenced the *nature* of the oedipal situation.

The patient in Case 19 did not know her father for the first five years of her life; it was the fact that her mother was her sole parent until then that skewed her development in the direction of the "negative" form of the oedipal constellation. In Case 15, a masochistic oedipal attachment to the mother was largely determined by the child's inability to share a more reliable nursemaid with his brother, probably because of the effects of the disruption of his infantile milieu by the death of his grandmother. At any rate, this child entered the arena of infantile sexuality with grandiose illusions about his worth and a pseudoidealization of his mother. The patient in Case 16 was even more severely traumatized by a series of disruptive changes preceding the phallic phase. The sole island of stability in his experience had been his grandfather, and the women in his environment seemed to be arbitrary, harsh, and unpredictable. Hence the principal love object of his oedipal period turned out to be a kindly stepfather. Three female patients (Cases 10, 12, and 13) were unable to escape symbiotic enmeshment in the psychological world of their disturbed mothers. Alternative relationships were both proscribed and uninviting, so that these girls were forced to make do with the homoerotic components of the Oedipus complex. In Case 3, I have already indicated that only the child's capacity to keep apart her experiences with her parents and grandparents (probably a function of her precocious intellectual development) permitted her to form an Oedipus complex involving the latter, while she was able to see the parents, realistically, as noxious and undesirable. A severe, traumatic disruption of her infantile matrix in the second year of life fixated the patient in Case 17 in a symbiotic adaptation which was directly continued in her oedipal attachment to her father. In Case 18, a very similar catastrophe led to analogous results; in this male patient, the Oedipus complex therefore took a predominantly feminine form. The early childhood background was equally unsatisfactory for the patient in Case 11, except for the nurturant attitude of his father; this also led directly into a passive, homoerotic oedipal configuration. But the frustrations of such a relationship led both of these boys to regress into the grandiose illusions fostered by their mothers. Finally, the patients with delusional thinking (Cases 7 and 9) were able to form oedipal attachments only insofar as these served to confirm their megalomania.

To restate these findings in summary form, the more disrupted and chaotic the first two years of a child's life have been (and/or the more symbiotic the adaptation, for whatever reasons, at the time the child moves into the oedipal phase), the less likely it is that he or she will have the autonomous resources to cope with the maturational challenge posed by the erotic wishes, frustrations, and resulting hostilities that accompany the emergence of oedipal issues. One common consequence of such handicaps is the child's failure to form a loving bond with one of the parents, and all too often, it is the parent of the opposite sex who does not sufficiently arouse the child's affectionate interest (cf. Cases 10, 11, 12, 13, 16, 18, 19). And where the oedipal configuration does predominantly take the expectable "positive" course (e.g., Cases 15 and 17), the relationship is imbued with primitive elements that also prevent successful resolution of the infantile neurosis. The only exception in my sample (Case 3) was a person whose outstanding intellectual gifts matured precociously: the child was able to differentiate her unsatisfactory early transactions with her parents from new experiences (with grandparents and others) around which she was able to organize an Oedipus complex *relatively* free of the legacy of the past. In this instance, it proved to be essential to analyze both sets of unresolved problems, and the connections between them were found to be rather sparse.

If the people who are impelled to enter psychoanalysis by adaptive difficulties seldom if ever turn out to be free of decisive pregenital problems, are we justified in looking upon their oedipal conflicts as epiphenomena, as Kohut (1977, p. 225; 1979) would have us do, at least in those cases that he classifies as disorders of the self?[2] (See

[2] This question can be understood in more than one sense. From the perspective of general clinical theory, it is clearly possible to subsume the

also van der Leeuw [1979].) In my judgment, the decision to frame the question in these terms is the unproductive legacy of Freud's initial conception (1914) of narcissism as a form of libido that develops in antithesis to its alternative, "object love." Within that framework, behaviors usually characteristic of the Oedipus complex have to be viewed with skepticism, for they might represent the discharge of narcissistic libido in the guise of desiring others. Kohut's earliest work (1966) concerning these matters was an effort to overcome the reductionism inherent in this "U tube" hypothesis about the motivating forces of human behavior. His proposal to separate conceptually the issues of "narcissism" (presumably crucial in the pregenital era) from those of "object love" (which take center stage in the oedipal period) proved to be ill-conceived, however, because it conceptualized narcissism and object love from the standpoint of the traditional Freudian drive theory of motivation, and in his work of the past several years Kohut has quietly abandoned that theory. (I have discussed this further in Chapter 8.) It is therefore something of a paradox that, in his approach to psychopathology, Kohut has continued to maintain the old dichotomy in the guise of "self

concept of the infantile neurosis under *any* overall schema, be it the traditional one, the schema of Kohut's "self psychology," or, for that matter, the model I put forward in *Beyond Interpretation* (1979a). But putting the idea into any of the "languages" available to us (cf. Schafer, 1976) does not change our substantive position; an infantile neurosis described in terms of its "narcissistic" implications remains the same entity it has always been (see Kohut, 1977, Chapter 5). It is Kohut's view that certain "oedipal" phenomena (what he calls "pseudotransference neuroses") are essentially devoid of genuine oedipal implications that deserve more careful scrutiny here.

psychology" versus the traditional view of the infantile neurosis, of Tragic Man versus Guilty Man, etc.

As I tried to demonstrate in Chapter 7, the principal issues of human psychology seem to persist throughout the course of development; in the epigenetic framework, various phases are distinguished from each other only in terms of the differing adaptive solutions they make available for the same problems in accord with the child's maturing perceptual-cognitive equipment. From this perspective, the oedipal child differs from one who is still "preoedipal" not in his drive organization, i.e., not by a transformation of narcissism into object love, as Freud (1914) originally postulated, nor by the transmutation of narcissism into a set of virtues, as Kohut (1966) later proposed. Love and hate, sexual excitement, and satisfaction with life (what we have generally called "narcissistic equilibrium") are experiential qualities discernible from the cradle to the grave. The acquisition of a capacity for symbolization in the course of the second year of life makes it possible to connect these experiences with specific entities, i.e., mental representations, such as those of one's own person or of individual caretakers.[3] In other words, in the "early phallic phase" the child can begin to appreciate himself and to desire others—to develop, if you will, both narcissism and object love. The intellectual maturation that enables these passion-

[3] In the hierarchical model (Gedo and Goldberg, 1973; Gedo, 1979a) this nodal point in development marks the transition into Phase III and into the third mode of mental organization, in which behavior can be regulated by the pleasure principle instead of being governed exclusively by automatic repetitions.

ate little creatures to learn certain values from their parents inaugurates the phase of intrapsychic conflicts and, somewhat later perhaps, of behavior regulation in terms of the reality principle, i.e., the taming of self-love and of hatred for rivals and frustrators that characterizes the optimal resolution of the Oedipus complex.

Viewed in these broadened terms, all children have to struggle with the same issues during the oedipal period, and an "Oedipus complex" characterized by megalomanic self-love is just as genuine as one principally focused on the sexual aims Freud discerned in the 1890s (I shall return to this expansion of the oedipal concept below, pp. 361–365). To be sure, the prior dispositions that determine the nature of these specific oedipal configurations will also have the most important bearing, along with the particulars of life experience in the oedipal phase itself, on the *outcome* of the struggle over these universal issues. Thus, a child with grandiose illusions will not form an infantile neurosis, the constellation of personal goals typical of youngsters with a more realistic appreciation of their own limitations. Similarly, one who has failed to differentiate his personal aims from those of his primary caretaker will be unable fully to experience the complexities of the oedipal triangle.

If we conceive of the Oedipus complex in the broad terms implied by the foregoing considerations, we can reject the possibility put forward by Kohut (1977) that certain manifestly oedipal behaviors might merely serve as defensive screens for narcissistic pathology. The issue raised by Kohut is not altogether negligible, however, because it *is* conceivable for people arrested in their development in a preoedipal mode, such as the patients van der Leeuw (1979) has recently written about, to develop shallow identifications of various kinds, including those that eventuate in more or less enduring enactments of "oedipal" dramas.[4] In the prototypical case Kohut (1979) described in his most recent paper, such enactments were not the sources of the patient's oedipal strivings, nor have I actually encountered a situation of that kind in my own clinical experience.

It may be useful at this point to return to the case material (as summarized in the Appendix) for a partial review of the findings from this specific point of view. I believe that even the patients who showed the least pathogenic effect on the basis of their preoedipal vicissitudes (Cases 15 and 19) experienced the inevitable frustrations of their oedipal ambitions as repetitions of the most crucial and traumatic situations of helplessness they had lived through in previous developmental phases. The more significant archaic issues proved to be in the overall configuration of the personality, the clearer it was that various aspects of the Oedipus complex echoed earlier pathogenic vicissitudes. But this generalization may legitimately be restated in another way: children invariably invest the complex transactions Freud (1900) chose to compare to Sophocles' Theban tragedy with those specific meanings that have gained significance for them on the basis of their preceding life experiences. If the pride/

[4] I am referring, of course, to certain primitive personalities of the kind Helene Deutsch (1942) called "as if" characters.

humiliation axis has taken on unusual importance in the first two or three years of life, the primary meaning of sexual rivalries will turn out to be exhibitionistic triumph and narcissistic mortification (e.g., Cases 10, 12, and 16). And if the maintenance of autonomous volition itself is in continuous question when the child enters the oedipal arena, his understanding of the responses of sexual objects will be skewed in the direction of threats of entrapment (e.g., Cases 11 and 18).

I shall rest content with these two demonstrations of the variable meanings of oedipal encounters, instead of attempting an exhaustive discussion of my whole sample. I believe this restraint is justified because the actual number of possible patterns of repetition is very much greater than a series of 15 cases could possibly document. Rather than multiply random illustrations, therefore, I would prefer to stress that the issues I have thus far singled out may well strike me as important elements within the infinitely complex web of my clinical observations because I have grown accustomed to the traditional emphasis on the significance of narcissistic and symbiotic problems in the pregenital era. In other words, it is by no means certain that these were the most important issues from the patients' point of view; they merely happened to be the ones I was capable of discerning at the time these analyses were performed.

In *Beyond Interpretation* (1979a) I suggested that the structured personality—what I prefer to call the "self-organization"—is, in fact, composed of a hierarchy of personal goals and values that we should be able to study from a more detailed and, at the same time, from a more abstract point of view than that of the traditional drive theory (or, for that matter, of the more recent object relations theories) of psychoanalysis. I put forward the hypothesis that such a hierarchy of aims is developed cumulatively, that adaptive success depends on the capacity to assimilate earlier goals into the complex web of the more differentiated, later hierarchy, and that the latter includes not only ambitions and ideals (i.e., the components of human subjectivity that Kohut [1977] regards as the nuclear self) but also certain "biological" aims and patterns which codetermine the configuration of subjective wishes.[5]

This theoretical framework should permit us to approach the question of the relationship between the particular form of the Oedipus complex and the nature of certain landmarks in pregenital development in a novel manner that may resolve some of the puzzling aspects of the problem. To be more specific, we should be able to discern certain goals that form common denominators between the various phase-specific wishes (and/or needs) that motivate the same individual at different stages of development. As a relatively transparent illustration, let us go back to the case of the woman who had illegitimate

[5] In calling these motivations "biological"—to contrast them with the subjective realm which is unequivocally "psychic"—I set up a distinction that is admittedly arbitrary. It is, in fact, impossible to draw a sharp differentiation between what is psychological and what does not yet have "mental" representation. In the hierarchical schema the latter realm is called Phase I, the former Phase III, and the transition is defined as Phase II (Gedo, 1979a, p. 186).

children (Case 17). This complex enactment in adult life had simultaneous meanings referable to oedipal and pregenital strivings. It expressed the fulfillment of childhood fantasies of receiving babies from father (thereby also magically undoing his death). At the same time, it involved the actualization of a more archaic fantasy of incorporating the object, with a clear reversal of roles between child and caretaker. The common denominator between these unconscious wishes is the aim of achieving absolute control over the more significant aspects of the environment.

In other words, this child placed the ambition of controlling the milieu very high within her hierarchy of aims quite early in life, and this ambition came to dominate her oedipal behavior too. It became repressed, along with most other aspects of her archaic psychological strivings, early in latency. Behind these concrete ambitions, we may choose to discern more abstract configurations: the same issues might be characterized in terms of goals such as the achievement of autonomy or that of omnipotence. In any case, these aims remained uppermost in this person's motivational system at every stage of her life, both in her well-adapted behaviors and in her more "pathological" ones. For example, her profession required her to arrange schedules and modes of transportation for large groups of people, and she turned out to be a virtuoso in this activity. And her behavior in the analytic setting was controlling and controlled to an extreme degree: it was not unusual for her to spend large portions of her sessions focused on her consciousness as a subjective experience per se—feeling drowsy, "fighting" her propensity to fall asleep, exerting a quasi-hypnotic effect on the observer, etc.

A second example characterized by a different set of aims is that of the medical student whose mother was so extraordinarily seductive (Case 15). This man behaved in adult life as if a display of his excellence, modeled on his mother's body narcissism, should suffice to satisfy others and to give his own existence its core of meaning. This pattern of behavior turned out to be an extension of oedipal experiences which gave him an illusion of triumphant adequacy through his exhibitionism. At the same time, it repeated an earlier transaction in which he might (or might not) have achieved mutual contentment in the presence of his nursemaid by undoing her depression (and, in the process, giving *her* life meaning) through his very needfulness. In this instance, the common denominator for these overlapping activities is the primacy of one goal, that of pleasing others (cf. Gedo, 1979a, p. 13).

I do not wish to elaborate these illustrations in further detail; suffice it to say that both examples I have used support the thesis that human behavior throughout the life cycle is at bottom characterized by lasting motivations—provided we choose to conceptualize these motivations in terms of basic categories sufficiently distant from the details of specific mental content. In this sense, a hierarchy of "abstract" goals (as opposed to more "concrete" subjective wishes) can serve to organize psychoanalytic data in a manner analogous to the function of the periodic table in chemistry. To extend the metaphor, I see my theoretical proposal as a change of focus in the study of motivations from the molecular to the atomic level. In other words, we can begin to see the Oedipus complex not only as a phase-specific constellation, in some essential respects discontinuous with preceding behaviors, but also as a new variation on the familiar thematic elements that constitute the child's self-organization before he develops the cognitive capacity to conceive of a web of relationships involving at least three individuals.

In this view, then, the Oedipus complex as a universal developmental experience is characterized by the rearrangement of the preexisting set of motivations under the impact of the child's expanding understanding of his universe. Since Freud conceptualized the structural theory, superego formation, or, if you will, the acquisition of a set of moral values from the caretakers, has been regarded as the most significant milestone marking this developmental achievement.[6] However, it is not the only important expansion of the psychological repertory during the oedipal period. The gradual relinquishment of illusions, both about the caretakers and the child's own person, perhaps possesses equal significance. To cite only one of the consequences of the acceptance of a realistic

[6] To be sure, Freud's hypothesis about the *manner* in which the superego is formed has implications very different from certain ideas I have advocated during the past decade (see Gedo and Goldberg, 1973, pp. 143–144; Gedo, 1979a, pp. 222–223). Nonetheless, there has been no serious controversy in psychoanalysis about the subsequent *role* of the morality "internalized" through this process, however the internalization takes place.

assessment of human capacities, this renunciation of illusory perfection is a prerequisite for the age-appropriate experience of competitiveness, failure, jealousy, etc.

It would seem, then, that the innate biological maturation setting the Oedipus complex in motion is perceptual-cognitive, but that its sequelae will pervade the child's whole existence. Yet the fabric of his response is bound to consist of the very same stuff that has constituted his potentials for action all along. I have discussed the kind of aims and patterns we have to take into consideration in this regard in some detail in *Beyond Interpretation* (especially in Chapters 1 and 11), and I shall not repeat that list here.

I shall conclude this chapter by returning once again to the problem of psychoanalytic technique. If the Oedipus complex as a developmental process consists of the rearrangement of an existing set of elements, like the shift of constituents in a kaleidoscope, what is its proper role in the analytic treatment of various personality disorders? In order to suggest an answer, I must reiterate the major argument with which I concluded *Beyond Interpretation.* The therapeutic action of psychoanalysis depends on its success in bringing about another kaleidoscopic shift in the analysand's perceptions of his experience. Insofar as his understanding of his oedipal past plays a determining part in the unfortunate conceptions that have brought him to seek assistance, alteration of that faulty self-knowledge is an essential prerequisite for change. The precise degree of influence of this set of memories (as opposed to those of other developmental phases) in the organization of any given personality is an empirical question that must be approached without theoretical preconceptions.

EPILOGUE

The Art of Psychoanalysis

The culture of science emerged from the intellectual traditions of the West in the course of the seventeenth century. The brilliant results obtained in the natural sciences through the application of the postulates of materialism and empiricism encouraged the simultaneous avoidance of problems that did not lend themselves to investigation through objective means. Hence science generally appeared to neglect issues that concerned meaning rather than causality, and the only value it recognized explicitly was that of searching for truth. Subjectivity—the personality of the investigator—was therefore viewed as an obstacle in the path of knowledge. As David Rapaport (1974) has shown, in the study of mental life associations were seen in the early seventeenth century only as interferents with rational thought. The self was relegated to a domain foreign to science, that of religion and of the arts, i.e., that of a humanistic culture that was falsely regarded as antithetical to science.

During the Renaissance, prior to the age of Descartes, the intellectual world was not divided in this manner and, in the recent past, the increasing divergence of the "two cultures," now an historical commonplace, has come to be decried. And with the passage of more than three centuries, it may once more be possible to articulate the universe of science with that of the humanities, the realm of reason and causality with that of values and meanings, through the medium of a scientifically valid introspective psychology (see Gedo and Pollock, 1976; Gedo, 1977b). In this light, the prominence of Freud in twentieth-century thought is justified by his success in facing forthrightly the fact that scientific endeavor, especially in psychology, is of necessity partly subjective. Freud's work has eventuated in placing the subject squarely in the center of scientific focus; hence depth psychology promises to heal the split in the Western world view created by the untenable dichotomy erected by Descartes between mind and matter—*res cogitans* and *res extensa* (see also Polanyi, 1974).

Freud's discoveries have led us to see more clearly that "reality" can only be perceived through the prism of the observer's self-organization. The psychic structure that is part of a particular self-organization, in turn, has been molded in crucial ways by the perception of reality—culture, biology, and psychology—achieved by the previous generation. Freud's single most enduring accomplishment, the discovery of the psychoanalytic observational method, has served to minimize the idiosyncratic distortions introduced by the observer into the analytic work—distortions particularly prone to occur with regard to observations of human behavior, because in the process of collecting such data we are unavoidably compelled to use certain subjective tools, such as introspection and empathy.

As a body of knowledge, psychoanalysis is based on these specific methods of data collection and on the canons of inference common to all sciences. Although its hypotheses must provisionally stem from the investigator's subjective universe, including his system of personal beliefs, we would prefer to subject these propositions to the usual tests of validation prescribed by the scientific method. This requirement can hardly be met with regard to specific interpretations within a particular clinical situation and is therefore exceedingly difficult as well for the scientific generalizations of the discipline as a whole. Nonetheless, the elevation of any psychoanalytic statement into a dogmatic proposition traduces the real nature of the field. In fact, the scientific world view denies the possibility of attaining valid knowledge through means other than empirical investigation. In contrast to the adherence of psychoanalysis to the scientific view, many psychological systems (notably that of C. G. Jung [see Gedo, 1979b]) take a transcendentalist and gnostic position. Because it is a scientific enterprise, the primary purpose of psychoanalysis is the acquisition of knowledge. Even in the treatment setting, to subordinate this purpose to any other goal is tendentious and counterproductive; only the analysand may appropriately wish to improve his lot. The analyst can, within proper bounds, only aim to assist in a quest for self-knowledge—in the belief, to be sure, that beyond its intrinsic value, this pursuit often has useful pragmatic consequences.

As a psychology, psychoanalysis is probably unique as well in its insistence on focusing on the *meanings* of human intentionality. Its central subject matter is not overt behavior as such but the emotion-laden network of subjective wishes embodied in man's symbolic thinking. Many influential voices (e.g., Lacan, 1966; Ricoeur, 1970; Schafer, 1976) have advocated that we confine ourselves to this realm exclusively, in contrast to Freud's broader and more ambitious program. The latter insisted that we must also consider those circumstances in which man is of necessity passive in relation to his external environment or his biological *milieu intérieur.* These are the psychological events for which Freud (1892) devised the term "trauma," based on the analogy of insults to the integrity of the body. Freud ultimately concluded that traumatic events acquire subjective meanings only as a secondary development; their primary significance lies in the biological realm. Freud (1895b) designated certain consequences stemming from psychoeconomic shifts as "actual neuroses," to contrast them with the psychoneuroses that possess symbolic meanings. In studying traumatic phenomena (and analogous archaic experiences), the psychoanalyst must perforce revert to the role of a natural scientist.

This point deserves special emphasis in the contemporary context because in the past decade we have witnessed a major reassessment of Freud's metapsychology—a desirable shift from the physicalistic assumptions of late nineteenth-century epistemology, but one that threatens a swing of the pendulum to the opposite extreme. To cite one of the most thoughtful and sober of the contributors to this evolution: Psychoanalysis is a "misfit among the physical and biological sciences with which [it] long sought to ally itself and whose rules and methods it sought to follow" (Basch, 1976, p. 420). I have no objection, of course, to proper emphasis on man's disposition for patterned behavior, an enterprise principally dependent on the understanding of values and meanings. In this light, Freud's discovery of the key for translating the presentational symbolism of the unconscious into the discursive mode of everyday speech has justly been likened in its significance for the study of behavior to the discovery of calculus for the natural sciences (Basch, 1976). On the other hand, as I tried to demonstrate in *Beyond Interpretation* (1979a), man's goals and values are not determined by subjectivity alone; they are also expressions of objective psychobiological needs. The latter are the human universals analysts can, it is hoped, grasp through the generally preconscious perceptual-cognitive processes we designate as "empathy."

Whenever we attempt to apply the insights of psychoanalytic psychology outside of the clinical arena and the treatment setting, we are entirely dependent on our subjective tools to match the nonclinical material under scrutiny with the patterns that typify our clinical psychoanalytic "knowledge." In applied analysis, in other words, we are deprived of the most important avenue for validating psychological hypotheses, that of the introspective efforts of the analysand. Actually, the ideal model of an analytic treatment without complications—one obviously never achieved in reality—is that of the analyst lending himself as a reliable witness to the organized introspection of the patient. From this perspective, the analyst's principal role is to assist the analysand in the task of free association (aside from serving as a screen for transferences). The analyst's interpretive efforts are therefore concentrated primarily on the detection of obstacles to the effective performance of the associative responsibility, obstacles that Freud originally called "resistances." As Goldberg and I have argued elsewhere (1973, Chapter 11), in actual practice these activities invariably have to be supplemented by additional interventions. In many instances, departures from a purely catalytic role are necessitated by the analysand's inability to attribute any meaning to the introspective data he has produced; in others, they are required because, for various personal reasons, the analysand may be reluctant (or truly unable) to carry so much of the responsibility for his own analysis.

By the same token, analysts may find it excessively burdensome to confine themselves for lengthy periods to the modest tasks entailed in this "ideal" model of treatment. Yet, our propensity to take on the mantle of the Biblical Joseph, interpreter of dreams, probably adds to the difficulty of analysands reaching self-sufficiency in the introspective effort. The analyst must determine empathically how much assistance the patient really needs to grasp the meanings of his associations at any given moment; he must steer his course between the Scylla of inappropriate intrusiveness and the Charybdis of unhelpfulness of traumatic proportions.

To put this in a different way, much of the analyst's work in the clinical setting has to be devoted to self-analytic vigilance to guard against potential responses to the patient that would be inappropriate—activities that would divert the focus of analytic attention from the analysand's subjective world per se to aspects of the actual transaction between the participants essentially unrelated to the patient's current state but introduced as a function of that of the analyst. It bears repetition that the analyst's necessary interventions of an interpretive nature are, for the most part, prostheses that compensate for the cognitive deficits of the patient (Basch, 1978): interpretations make up for the inability of analysands to put the results of their introspective efforts into the language of rational thought.

In order to assess the significant meanings of another person's communications, the analyst cannot rely on objective criteria; on the contrary, he is forced to screen this material through his own hierarchy of goals and values. Hence the core of the analytic enterprise consists of the analyst's ongoing self-inquiry (cf. Gardner, in preparation). Through his unprecedented, lifelong self-analysis, Sigmund Freud succeeded in reintegrating the introspective tradition of humanism into Western science (Gedo and Pollock, 1976; Gedo, 1977b). And by confronting the relative weakness of reason and the severe limits of any observer's objectivity, psychoanalysis has made a major contribution to the overthrow of the positivist and materialist postulates of nineteenth-century thought. Perhaps as a consequence of their personal schooling in the medical tradition, psychoanalysts —including Freud himself—have generally been reluctant to accept the epistemological conclusions that follow from the nature of their clinical experiences. The unjustified application of physicalistic assumptions to the study of human behavior was long perpetuated through the metapsychological scaffolding Freud provided to organize these data at the turn of the century. As more and more analytic theoreticians have abandoned the postulate of psychic energy (Freud, 1892), we have begun to function within a climate of thought in which we are able to tolerate less and less certainty about our presumed "knowledge" of man's psychology. In *Beyond Interpretation* (1979a), I concluded my argument for a revision of clinical theory by asserting that the analyst's clinical interpretations about the analysand's subjective wishes, whatever their therapeutic consequences may be, are in principle impossible to validate with regard to their truth value: we are obliged to rest content with assessing the extent to which they can assist the individual in assigning new meanings to his past experience.

The implications of this viewpoint for the theory of psychoanalytic technique are far-reaching. The hope of devising "correct" interpretations that lead to insight, in contrast to inexact ones that yield functional alterations by means of suggestion (cf. Glover, 1931) will have to be abandoned. A more fruitful differentiation will have to be made between interventions that reorganize the analysand's hierarchy of personal aims more or less effectively, depending on a variety of factors we have not even begun to classify. In this sense, then, the performance of clinical psychoanalysis is an art that enjoins its practitioners to improvise, unassisted by existing guidelines, in at least two distinct manners. By attempting to conceptualize a series of therapeutic modalities applicable to the full range of various modes of functioning encountered in analytic practice, I have tried to provide a tentative framework to reduce uncertainty in one of these—the choice of noninterpretive interventions wherever necessary. The second area in which analytic skill has been left to the intuition of the clinician concerns the optimal manner in which interpretations should be articulated. Cogent ideas are necessary but not sufficient: *c'est le ton qui fait la musique.* Using a theory of knowledge untainted by the discredited certainties of our past, we can face the second century of psychoanalytic activity with the inspiring challenge of these vast uncharted territories beckoning us.

APPENDIX

Oedipal Content of Case Material

(a) *Case 19* (see Chapter 13): The young woman whose mother died when she was 13, leaving her to cope unaided with her father's paranoid delusions about her, managed to experience the heterosexual aspects of the Oedipus complex in age-appropriate fashion, although her father's savage response impelled her to regress into masculine identification. This retreat was also facilitated by the exclusive attachment to her excellent mother she had formed during the years of her father's absence from the home and by her sexual rivalry with men for her mother's preference.

(b) *Case 15* (see Chapter 7): The medical student who aspired to become an analyst formed a strong erotic bond with his seductive mother, one in which she was decidedly the aggressor and the patient a willing victim. He felt himself her ally in her chronic conflict with his father, a role for which he did not have to fear retaliation from the latter. His castration complex was focused on the maternal grandfather; this led to a water phobia which also stood for the dread of phallic inadequacy vis-à-vis the adult woman. Ultimately, the boy's preference for his biological mother, in spite of her exploitativeness, was determined by the hopelessness of mitigating his nursemaid's chronic depression, a cherished goal that overwhelmed the child with a sense of helplessness.

(c) *Case 16* (see Chapter 11): The man whose mother was the beautiful pianist had a similar erotic attachment to her, but this expectable developmental achievement was weakly sustained in the context of a relationship to a stepfather who, because of his identification with the fatherless boy, was less of a rival than an alter ego. Castration anxiety or phobic manifestations did not appear; instead, a masochistic perversion, based principally on preoedipal vicissitudes, came to include among its meanings and functions the fear and hatred of the irresistible female. The oedipal stage was more stably represented, however, by a homosexual bond to the stepfather.

(d) *Case 12* (see Chapter 12): The young woman who developed alimentary orgasms as an adolescent was arrested in an early oedipal love relationship with her mother, competing with men for the latter's favor. She was terrified by her father's sadistic behavior which she experienced, in part, as retaliation for her phallic competitiveness. The repetitive enactment of traumatizing confrontations probably rendered the production of additional symptoms superfluous. It also led to an identification with the aggressor that included a need to turn passive erotic stimulation into seductive activity. When the child succeeded in forming an incestuous relationship with a younger brother, that heterosexual bond approximated progression into a later phase of the female Oedipus complex—but, in fantasy, this aggressive transaction made her the possessor of a phallus and opened the path to her perverse adaptation by means of a series of fetishes.

(e) *Case 10* (see Chapter 4): A similar arrest in an early stage of the Oedipus complex characterized the social worker who came to view analysis as a set of golden tools. In contrast to the patient in Case 12, this woman came out of the competitive struggle for her mother's preference not as a victim but as a guilt-ridden aggressor with a need to atone for the disastrous consequences of her destructive wishes. These circumstances led to an identification with her eccentric mother, including the latter's hatred and contempt for men. Thus several factors conspired to block the child's capacity to make use of her father. She did establish a bond with him in secret, but only as an emergency substitute for the mother in the latter's absence. Her relationship with men in later life had the same fetishistic quality as the preceding patient's misuse of her brother.

(f) *Case 13* (see Chapter 4): The woman who dreamt about analysis as an enormous airplane taking her on amazing journeys was, in one sense, giving expression to the same wish to possess a magical phallus. Her identification with an anhedonic mother created intense conflict about these infantile sexual wishes, however, so that she could not resort to perverse adaptation. Instead, her phallic competitiveness led to the formation of a number of childhood phobias. But the need to merge with a man in fantasy was also part of the identification with the mother—the parents led an overtly symbiotic existence. The father's extraordinary servility in the role of his wife's phallus prevented the child from establishing even minimal contact with him as an alternative to her mother. The latter remained the principal oedipal object, unattainable except for certain regressive transactions in which the child was able to satisfy the mother's narcissistic requirements better than anyone else. This circumstance led to the anal degradation of sexuality and lent a more archaic flavor to the patient's personality than her actual attainment of the oedipal stage might have led one to expect.

(g) *Case 3* (see Chapter 1): The patient whose analysis

followed several attempts to treat her depressive episodes psychotherapeutically was so severely disillusioned by both parents before the age of three that she had to avoid them, lest she be flooded with hatred. Archaic transactions at preoedipal levels turned out to be the primary issues in her analysis, in spite of the fact that she also developed a transference neurosis. These parallel modes of functioning occurred simultaneously, and the contradictions between them remained unresolved and disavowed. This "split" reflected the childhood need to erect an island of healthy functioning in the relationship to her (maternal) grandparents. Her Oedipus complex involved these grandparents and confirmed her sense of worthlessness and overwhelming guilt because of their successive deaths when she was four and eight, respectively. In spite of the resultant inhibition about establishing loving relationships, the patient's femininity was unimpaired, and sexuality constituted the haven of normalcy in her adulthood.

(h) *Case 17* (see Chapter 13): The patient who had given up two illegitimate children had been arrested in her development in the course of an intense oedipal attachment to her father when the latter suddenly died. This relationship had many primitive qualities because it had replaced a symbiotic bond to the mother which, in turn, had been disrupted by a lengthy, traumatic separation late in the second year of life.

(i) *Case 18* (see Chapter 13): The psychopathic college professor of fundamentalist background lived in a regressive world of omnipotent illusions in which he was emotionally isolated from everyone. Among other narcissistic injuries, he was therefore immune to the frustrations of his erotic attachments and to the overwhelming hostility and guilt evoked by situations in which he had to compete for anyone's preference. His symbiotic adaptation stemmed from the second year of life, when his relationship to his mother was disrupted by the latter's mourning after the death of a (younger) child, but it had not prevented the development of oedipal strivings, especially in the form of feminine procreative wishes.

(j) *Case 11* (see Chapter 4): The would-be prophet and operatic singer who repetitively enacted mutually frustrating, hopeless transactions in the analytic transference had fallen into an attitude of chronic negativism toward his intrusive and unpredictable mother early in childhood. He also tried to seek refuge from her with his indulgent father (and, to a lesser extent, with some of his older brothers). His feminine identification—or incomplete differentiation from his mother—and the calming and organizing influence of the relationship to the father, led to the formation of a negative oedipal constellation. But the child's narcissistic vulnerability rendered him incapable of tolerating the disappointment of his wishes in this context without regressing into grandiose illusions.

(k) *Case 7* (see Chapter 3): The student with a masochistic perversion who was unconsciously identified with the Infant Jesus had reacted to the marriage of his older sister, his primary caretaker after the first year of life, by forming an erotized relationship with her husband. His psychological development was arrested in this state, which simultaneously constituted a grandiose fantasy and a passive homosexual variant of the Oedipus complex.

(l) *Case 9* (see Chapter 3): The actor with a nihilistic delusion never differentiated himself from his mother, an overtly psychotic character. His homosexual longings for a paternal figure were, however, quite unacceptable to him as a result of the attitudes he learned from both parents; they were consequently warded off through the use of projections, particularly projections directed onto his wife.

References

Abraham, K. (1924), A short study of the development of the libido, viewed in the light of mental disorders. In: *Selected Papers on Psycho-Analysis*. London: Hogarth Press, 1942, pp. 418–419.

Aichhorn, A. (1951), *Wayward Youth*. London: Imago.

Alexander, F. (1925), Dreams in pairs and series. *Internat. J. Psycho-Anal.*, 6:446–450.

______ (1956), *Psychoanalysis and Psychotherapy*. New York: Norton.

______ & French, T. (1946), *Psychoanalytic Therapy*. New York: Ronald Press.

Arlow, J. (1979), The genesis of interpretation. *J. Amer. Psychoanal. Assn.*, 27(Suppl.): 193–206.

______ & Brenner, C. (1964), *Psychoanalytic Concepts and the Structural Theory*. New York: International Universities Press.

Bak, R. (1974), Distortions of the concept of fetishism. *The Psychoanalytic Study of the Child*, 29:191–214. New Haven: Yale University Press.

Basch, M. F. (1976), Psychoanalysis and communication science. *The Annual of Psychoanalysis*, 4:385–422. New York: International Universities Press.

______ (1978), Psychoanalysis and cognitive psychology. Unpublished manuscript.

Bibring, E. (1954), Psychoanalysis and the dynamic psychotherapies. *J. Amer. Psychoanal. Assn.*, 2:745–770.

Boesky, D. (1980), Introduction to symposium on object relations. *Psychoanal. Quart.*, 49:48–55.

Breuer, J., & Freud, S. (1893), On the psychical mechanism of hysterical phenomena: Preliminary communication. *Standard Edition*, 2:3–17.

Dahl, H. (1978), A new psychoanalytic model of motivation: The emotions as appetites and signals. *Psychoanal. Contemp. Thought*, 1:373–408.

Deutsch, F. (1949), *Applied Psychoanalysis.* New York: Grune & Stratton.

Deutsch, H. (1942), Some forms of emotional disturbances and their relationship to schizophrenia. *Psychoanal. Quart.,* 11:301–321.

Eissler, K. (1953), The effect of the structure of the ego on psychoanalytic technique. *J. Amer. Psychoanal. Assn.,* 1:104–143.

——— (1968), The relation of explaining and understanding in psychoanalysis: Demonstrated by one aspect of Freud's approach to literature. *The Psychoanalytic Study of the Child,* 23:141–155. New York: International Universities Press.

Erikson, E. H. (1959), *Identity and the Life Cycle* [*Psychol. Issues,* Monogr. 1]. New York: International Universities Press.

Erle, J. (1979), An approach to the study of analyzability and analyses: The course of forty consecutive cases selected for supervised analysis. *Psychoanal. Quart.,* 48:198–228.

Fairbairn, W. R. D. (1954), *An Object-Relations Theory of the Personality.* New York: Basic Books.

Ferenczi, S. (1912), Transitory symptom-constructions during the analysis. In: *Sex in Psychoanalysis.* New York: Basic Books, 1950, pp. 193–212.

——— (1933), Confusion of tongues between adults and children. In: *Final Contributions to the Problems and Methods of Psychoanalysis.* New York: Basic Books, 1955, pp. 156–167.

Firestein, S. (1978), *Termination in Psychoanalysis.* New York: International Universities Press.

Freud, A. (1965), *Normality and Pathology in Childhood.* New York: International Universities Press.

Freud, E., Ed. (1960), *Letters of Sigmund Freud.* New York: Basic Books.

Freud, S. (1886–1940), *The Standard Edition of the Complete Psychological Works of Sigmund Freud,* ed. J. Strachey. London: Hogarth Press, 1953–1974.

——— (1892), Sketches for the 'preliminary communication' of 1893. *Standard Edition,* 1:147–154.

——— (1895a), The psychotherapy of hysteria. *Standard Edition,* 2:255–305.

——— (1895b), A reply to criticisms of my paper on anxiety neurosis. *Standard Edition,* 3:123–139.

——— (1899), Screen memories. *Standard Edition,* 3:303–322.

——— (1900), The interpretation of dreams. *Standard Edition,* 4 & 5.

——— (1905a), Fragment of an analysis of a case of hysteria. *Standard Edition,* 7:7–122.

——— (1905b), Three essays on the theory of sexuality. *Standard Edition,* 7:130–243.

______ (1908), Character and anal erotism. *Standard Edition,* 9:167–175.
______ (1909), Notes upon a case of obsessional neurosis. *Standard Edition,* 10:155–249.
______ (1911–1915), Papers on technique. *Standard Edition,* 12:89–171.
______ (1912), Recommendations to physicians practicising psychoanalysis. *Standard Edition,* 12:111–120.
______ (1914), On narcissism: An introduction. *Standard Edition,* 14:73–102.
______ (1916), Some character-types met with in psycho-analytic work. *Standard Edition,* 14:311–333.
______ (1918), From the history of an infantile neurosis. *Standard Edition,* 17:7–122.
______ (1919), Lines of advance in psycho-analytic therapy. *Standard Edition,* 17:159–168.
______ (1920), Beyond the pleasure principle. *Standard Edition,* 18:7–64.
______ (1921), Group psychology and the analysis of the ego. *Standard Edition,* 18:69–143.
______ (1923), The ego and the id. *Standard Edition,* 19:12–66.
______ (1924), Neurosis and psychosis. *Standard Edition,* 19:149–143.
______ (1925), Preface to Aichhorn's *Wayward Youth. Standard Edition,* 19: 273–275.
______ (1926), Inhibitions, symptoms and anxiety. *Standard Edition,* 20: 87–172.
______ (1937), Analysis terminable and interminable. *Standard Edition,* 23:216–253.
Fromm-Reichmann, F. (1950), *Principles of Intensive Psychotherapy.* Chicago: University of Chicago Press.
Gardner, R. (in preparation), Untitled monograph.
Gedo, J. E. (1964), Concepts for a classification of the psychotherapies. *Internat. J. Psycho-Anal.,* 45:530–539.
______ (1966), The psychotherapy of developmental arrest. *Brit. J. Med. Psychol.,* 39:25–33.
______ (1967), On critical periods for corrective experience in the therapy of arrested development. *Brit. J. Med. Psychol.,* 40:79–83.
______ (1968), The wise baby reconsidered. In: *Freud: The Fusion of Science and Humanism* [*Psychol. Issues,* Monogr. 34/35], ed. J. Gedo & G. Pollock. New York: International Universities Press, 1976, pp. 357–378.
______ (1975a), Forms of idealization in the analytic transference. *J. Amer. Psychoanal. Assn.,* 23:485–505.
______ (1975b), To Heinz Kohut: On his 60th birthday. *The Annual of Psychoanalysis,* 3:313–322. New York: International Universities Press.

——— (1977a), Notes on the psychoanalytic management of archaic transferences. *J. Amer. Psychoanal. Assn.*, 25:787–803.

——— (1977b), Sigmund Freud and the Socratic tradition. *Dialogue,* 1:2–15.

——— (1979a), *Beyond Interpretation: Toward a Revised Theory for Psychoanalysis.* New York: International Universities Press.

——— (1979b), Magna est vis veritatis tuae, et praevalebit! *The Annual of Psychoanalysis,* 7:53–82. New York: International Universities Press.

——— (1979c), A psychoanalyst reports at mid-career. *Amer. J. Psychiat.*, 136:646–649.

——— & Goldberg, A. (1973), *Models of the Mind: A Psychoanalytic Theory.* Chicago: University of Chicago Press.

——— & Pollock, G. H., Eds. (1976), *Freud: The Fusion of Science and Humanism* [*Psychol. Issues,* Monogr. 34/35]. New York: International Universities Press.

Gitelson, M. (1948), Character synthesis: The psychotherapeutic problem of adolescence. *Amer. J. Orthopsychiat.*, 18:422–431.

Glover, E. (1931), The therapeutic effect of inexact interpretations: A contribution to the theory of suggestion. In: *The Technique of Psycho-Analysis.* New York: International Universities Press, 1955, pp. 353–366.

——— (1960), Psychoanalysis and psychotherapy. *Brit. J. Med. Psychol.*, 33:73–82, 225–230.

Goldberg, A., Ed. (1978), *The Psychology of the Self: A Casebook.* New York: International Universities Press.

Greenacre, P. (1969), The fetish and the transitional object. In: *Emotional Growth.* New York: International Universities Press, 1971, pp. 315–334.

Greenson, R. R. (1967), *The Technique and Practice of Psychoanalysis,* Vol. 1. New York: International Universities Press.

Grinker, R., et al. (1961), *Psychiatric Social Work.* New York: Basic Books.

Grotjahn, M. (1979), New insight into the life and work of Sigmund Freud: An overview of the literature since 1975. *J. Amer. Acad. Psychoanal.*, 2:299–313.

Habermas, J. (1968), *Knowledge and Human Interest.* Boston: Beacon Press, 1971.

Hannett, F. (1964), The haunting lyric: The personal and social significance of American popular songs. *Psychoanal. Quart.*, 33:226–269.

Hartmann, H. (1927), Understanding and explanation. In: *Essays on Ego Psychology.* New York: International Universities Press, 1964, pp. 369–403.

——— (1939), *Ego Psychology and the Problem of Adaptation.* New York:

International Universities Press, 1958.
______ (1948), Comments on the psychoanalytic theory of instinctual drives. In: *Essays on Ego Psychology.* New York: International Universities Press, 1964, pp. 69–89.
______ (1950), Psychoanalysis and developmental psychology. In: *Essays on Ego Psychology.* New York: International Universities Press, 1964, pp. 99–112.
______ & Loewenstein, R. M. (1962), Notes on the superego. In: *Papers on Psychoanalytic Psychology* [*Psychol. Issues,* Monogr. 14], by H. Hartmann, E. Kris, & R. M. Loewenstein. New York: International Universities Press, pp. 144–181.
______ (1964), *Essays on Ego Psychology.* New York: International Universities Press.
______ Kris, E., & Loewenstein, R. M. (1964), *Papers on Psychoanalytic Psychology* [*Psychol. Issues,* Monogr. 14]. New York: International Universities Press.
Horowitz, M. (1977), The quantitative line of approach in psychoanalysis: A clinical assessment of its current status. *J. Amer. Psychoanal. Assn.,* 25:559–580.
Isakower, O. (1938), A contribution to the patho-psychology of phenomena associated with falling asleep. *Internat. J. Psycho-Anal.,* 19:331–345.
Jacobson, E. (1964), *The Self and the Object World.* New York: International Universities Press.
Kernberg, O. F. (1974), Further contributions to the treatment of narcissistic personalities. *J. Amer. Psychoanal. Assn.,* 19:595–635.
______ (1975), *Borderline Conditions and Pathological Narcissism.* New York: Aronson.
______ (1976), Technical considerations in the treatment of borderline personality organization. *J. Amer. Psychoanal. Assn.,* 24:795–830.
______ (1979), Some implications of object relations theory for psychoanalytic technique. *J. Amer. Psychoanal. Assn.,* 27(Suppl.):207–240.
Klein, G. (1968), The ego in psychoanalysis: A concept in search of identity. In: *Psychoanalytic Theory: An Exploration of Essentials.* New York: International Universities Press, 1976, pp. 121–160.
______ (1976), *Psychoanalytic Theory: An Exploration of Essentials.* New York: International Universities Press.
Kohut, H. (1959), Introspection, empathy, and psychoanalysis. *J. Amer. Psychoanal. Assn.,* 7:459–483. Also in Kohut (1978).
______ (1966), Forms and transformations of narcissism. *J. Amer. Psychoanal. Assn.,* 14:243–272. Also in Kohut (1978).
______ (1968), The psychoanalytic treatment of narcissistic personality disorders. *The Psychoanalytic Study of the Child,* 23:86–113. New York: International Universities Press. Also in Kohut (1978).
______ (1970), Discussion of "The self: A contribution to its place in

theory and technique," by Douglas C. Levin. *Internat. J. Psycho-Anal.*, 51:176–181. Also in Kohut (1978).

——— (1971), *The Analysis of the Self.* New York: International Universities Press.

——— (1972), Thoughts on narcissism and narcissistic rage. *The Psychoanalytic Study of the Child,* 27:360–400. New York: Quadrangle. Also in Kohut (1978).

——— (1975a), The future of psychoanalysis. *The Annual of Psychoanalysis,* 3:325–340. New York: International Universities Press. Also in Kohut (1978).

——— (1975b), The psychoanalyst in the community of scholars. *The Annual of Psychoanalysis,* 3:341–370. New York: International Universities Press. Also in Kohut (1978).

——— (1977), *The Restoration of the Self.* New York: International Universities Press.

——— (1978), *The Search for the Self,* 2 vols., ed. P. Ornstein. New York: International Universities Press.

——— (1979), The two analyses of Mr. Z. *Internat. J. Psycho-Anal.*, 60: 3–28.

——— & Wolf, E. (1978), The disorders of the self and their treatment: An outline. *Internat. J. Psycho-Anal.*, 59:413–426.

Kris, E. (1956), The personal myth: A problem in psychoanalytic technique. In: *Selected Papers.* New Haven: Yale University Press, 1975, pp. 272–300.

Lacan, J. (1966), *Ecrits.* Paris: Editions du Seuil.

Lewin, B. (1946), Sleep, the mouth, and the dream screen. *Psychoanal. Quart.*, 15:419–434.

Lichtenstein, H. (1961), Identity and sexuality: A study of their interrelationship in man. *J. Amer. Psychoanal. Assn.*, 9:179–260.

Loewald, H. (1960), On the therapeutic action of psycho-analysis. *Internat. J. Psycho-Anal.*, 41:16–33.

——— (1971), On motivation and instinct theory. *The Psychoanalytic Study of the Child,* 26:91–128. New York: Quadrangle.

Luborsky, L., et al. (1958), Treatment variables: Second report of psychotherapy research project of the Menninger Foundation. *Bull. Menninger Clinic,* 22:126–147.

Ludowyk-Gyomroi, E. (1963), The analysis of a young concentration camp victim. *The Psychoanalytic Study of the Child,* 18:484–510. New York: International Universities Press.

Mahler, M. S., Pine, F., & Bergman, A. (1975), *The Psychological Birth of the Human Infant: Symbiosis and Individuation.* New York: Basic Books.

Meissner, W. W. (1978), Theoretical assumptions of concepts of the bor-

derline personality. *J. Amer. Psychoanal. Assn.*, 26:559–598.
Modell, A. (1965), On having the right to a life: An aspect of the superego's development. *Internat. J. Psycho-Anal.*, 46:323–331.
______ (1968), *Object Love and Reality.* New York: International Universities Press.
______ (1976), "The holding environment" and the therapeutic action of psychoanalysis. *J. Amer. Psychoanal. Assn.*, 24:285–308.
______ (1978), Affects and the complementarity of biologic and historical meaning. *The Annual of Psychoanalysis,* 6:167–180. New York: International Universities Press.
Moore, B. (1975), Toward a clarification of the concept of narcissism. *The Psychoanalytic Study of the Child,* 30:243–278. New Haven: Yale University Press.
Moraitis, G. (1981), The psychoanalyst's response to the limitations of his science. *Psychoanal. Inquiry,* 1:57–79.
Nagera, H. (1964), On arrest in development, fixation, and regression. *The Psychoanalytic Study of the Child,* 19:222–239. New York: International Universities Press.
______ (1966), *Early Childhood Disturbances, the Infantile Neurosis, and the Adult Disturbances.* New York: International Universities Press.
Nunberg, H. (1930), The synthetic function of the ego. In: *The Practice and Theory of Psychoanalysis,* Vol. 1. New York: International Universities Press, 1955, pp. 120–136.
Ornstein, P. (1974), Discussion of paper by Otto F. Kernberg. *Internat. J. Psycho-Anal.*, 55:241–248.
Panel (1954), Psychoanalysis and dynamic psychotherapy: Similarities and differences. L. Rangell, reporter. *J. Amer. Psychoanal. Assn.*, 2:152–166.
Panel (1973), Technique and prognosis in narcissistic personality disorders. L. Schwartz, reporter. *J. Amer. Psychoanal. Assn.*, 21:617–632.
Panel (1976), New horizons in metapsychology. W. W. Meissner, reporter. *J. Amer. Psychoanal. Assn.*, 24:161–180.
Panel (1977), Varieties of oedipal distortions in severe character pathologies. W. S. Robbins, reporter. *J. Amer. Psychoanal. Assn.*, 25:201–218.
Polanyi, M. (1974), *Scientific Thought and Social Reality* [*Psychol. Issues,* Monogr. 32]. New York: International Universities Press.
______ & Prosch, H. (1975), *Meaning.* Chicago: University of Chicago Press.
Rapaport, D. (1959), *The Structure of Psychoanalytic Theory* [*Psychol. Issues,* Monogr. 6]. New York: International Universities Press, 1960.
______ (1974), *The History of the Concept of Association of Ideas.* New York: International Universities Press.

Rappaport, E. (1960), Preparation for analysis. *Internat. J. Psycho-Anal.*, 41:626–632.

Ricoeur, P. (1970), *Freud and Philosophy.* New Haven: Yale University Press.

Rieff, P. (1966), *The Triumph of the Therapeutic.* New York: Harper & Row.

Sadow, L. (1979), Discussion of paper by H. Kohut and M. Tolpin. Presented to Chicago Psychoanalytic Society, May.

——— ,Gedo, J., Miller, J., Pollock, G., Sabshin, M., & Schlessinger, N. (1968), The process of hypothesis change in three early psychoanalytic concepts. *J. Amer. Psychoanal. Assn.*, 16:245–273.

Sandler, J., & Rosenblatt, B. (1962), The concept of the representational world. *The Psychoanalytic Study of the Child,* 17:128–145. New York: International Universities Press.

——— & Sandler, A. M. (1978), On the development of object relationships and affects. *Internat. J. Psycho-Anal.*, 59:285–296.

Schafer, R. (1976), *A New Language for Psychoanalysis.* New Haven: Yale University Press.

Segal, H. (1974), *Introduction to the Work of Melanie Klein,* 2nd. Ed. New York: Basic Books.

——— & Britton, R. (1981), Review of J. Gedo, *Beyond Interpretation. Psychoanal. Inquiry* (in press).

Settlage, C. (1977), The psychoanalytic understanding of narcissistic and borderline personality disorders: Advances in developmental theory. *J. Amer. Psychoanal. Assn.*, 25:805–833.

Shapiro, E. (1978), The psychodynamics and developmental psychology of the borderline patient: A review of the literature. *Amer. J. Psychiat.*, 135:1305–1315.

Shapiro, T. (1977), Oedipal distortions in severe character pathologies: Developmental and theoretical considerations. *Psychoanal. Quart.*, 46:559–579.

Stolorow, R. (1975), Toward a functional definition of narcissism. *Internat. J. Psycho-Anal.*, 45:179–186.

Stone, L. (1961), *The Psychoanalytic Situation.* New York: International Universities Press.

Swanson, D. (1977), A critique of psychic energy as an explanatory concept. *J. Amer. Psychoanal. Assn.*, 25:603–633.

Tarachow, S. (1962), Interpretation and reality in psychotherapy. *Internat. J. Psycho-Anal.*, 43:377–387.

——— (1963), *An Introduction to Psychotherapy.* New York: International Universities Press.

Thomä, H., & Kächele, H. (1975), Problems of metascience and methodology in clinical psychoanalytic research. *The Annual of Psychoanalysis,*

3:49–122. New York: International Universities Press.

Tolpin, M. (1971), On the beginnings of a cohesive self. *The Psychoanalytic Study of the Child,* 26:316–352. New York: Quadrangle.

Tolpin, P. (1971), Some psychic determinants of orgastic dysfunction. In: *Adolescent Psychiatry,* ed. S. Feinstein, P. Giovacchini, & A. Miller. New York: Basic Books.

Toulmin, S. (1978), Psychoanalysis, physics, and the mind-body problem. *The Annual of Psychoanalysis,* 6:315–336. New York: International Universities Press.

Van der Leeuw, P. (1979), Some additional remarks on problems of transference. *J. Amer. Psychoanal. Assn.,* 27(Suppl.):315–326.

Waelder, R. (1962), Psychoanalysis, scientific method, and philosophy. *J. Amer. Psychoanal. Assn.,* 10:617–637.

Winnicott, D. W. (1954), Metapsychological and clinical aspects of regression within the psychoanalytical set-up. In: *Collected Papers.* New York: Basic Books, 1958, pp. 278–294.

______ (1958), *Collected Papers.* New York: Basic Books.

______ (1960), The theory of the parent-infant relationship. In: *The Maturational Processes and the Facilitating Environment.* New York: International Universities Press, 1965, pp. 37–55.

______ (1965), A clinical study of the effect of a failure of average expectable environment on a child's mental functioning. *Internat. J. Psycho-Anal.,* 46:81–87.

Wolf, E. (1976), Ambience and abstinence. *The Annual of Psychoanalysis,* 4:101–115. New York: International Universities Press.

______ , Gedo, J., & Terman, D. (1972), On the adolescent process as a transformation of the self. *J. Youth Adoles.,* 1:257–272.

Zavitzianos, G. (1967), Problems of technique in the analysis of a juvenile delinquent. *Internat. J. Psycho-Anal.,* 48:439–447.

______ (1971), Fetishism and exhibitionism in the female and their relationship to psychopathy and kleptomania. *Internat. J. Psycho-Anal.,* 52:297–305.

______ (1977), The object in fetishism, homeovestism, and transvestism. *Internat. J. Psycho-Anal.,* 58:487–495.

Name Index

Subject Index